APPLETON'S POPULAR LIBRARY

OF THE BEST AUTHORS.

ESSAYS FROM THE LONDON TIMES.

ESSAYS

FROM

THE LONDON TIMES:

A COLLECTION OF

PERSONAL AND HISTORICAL SKETCHES.

NEW-YORK:
D. APPLETON & COMPANY, 200 BROADWAY.
M.DCCC.LII.

PUBLISHER'S ADVERTISEMENT.

It is generally acknowledged that the London "Times" is among the most accomplished intellectual products of England. Its leaders influence opinion throughout the world; not less by the force of conviction or prejudice than by the charms of a full, varied, commanding style. The reader of the following pages will perceive an equally high order of ability in a series of papers which have, from time to time, appeared in its columns, illustrating topics of a permanent biographical and historical interest. These papers, under the form of reviews, are really brilliant original Essays, frequently displaying the neat humour of a Sydney Smith, or the glowing narrative sweep of a Macaulay.

The Essays in this volume exhibit a variety of treatment, and are models of their class. The sketch of the French Revolution of 1848, and the paper on the Amours of Dean Swift are masterpieces in their different ways; the one as a forcibly painted, picturesque panorama of startling events, the other as a subtle investigation of character. The story of Lord Nelson's Lady Hamilton is an example of pathos where the interest grows out of a clear firmly presented statement. The paper on Egypt is an admirable resumé of the results of Antiquarian study, in a style at once learned and popular.

This selection is, with the exception of two articles, for which three others of a less dependent form and of a more general interest have been substituted, the same with that recently published by Mr. Murray in London.

New-York, March, 1852.

CONTENTS.

PERSONAL AND HISTORICAL

SKETCHES.

LORD NELSON AND LADY HAMILTON.

ANOTHER *Life of Nelson* is not necessarily another contribution to the country's waste-paper basket. Much as we have heard of the nation's darling hero, there still remains something to be told. Southey, in his short but perfect biography, satisfied our patriotism and did homage to a people's love. Sir Harris Nicolas, in his more voluminous collection of the despatches and letters, made due provision for the graver requirements of posterity; but neither the one nor the other possessed the key that could carry us very far into the recesses of Nelson's history —hidden retreats, possessing to many minds attractions not to be found in the more open and dazzling field of his glorious public career. For every one who prefers a visit to the state apartments of Windsor Castle, there are a thousand who would willingly desert the magnificient halls to linger for a moment in the quietier rooms daily inhabited by a Queen. That which is nearest to us touches us most, and hence it is something more than vulgar curiosity that renders us so eager to ascertain the domestic movements of the great. Humanity loses sight of itself in soaring to the contemplation of a demigod. It meets itself again, and is contented and instructed when tracking the deity upon the earth, and watching his impulses upon the path of passion common to all.

According to our notions, Nelson realized the ideal of a hero as completely as any worshipped at any time in any land. His piety was of the simplest; his love of country was fervent and self-subjugating; his gentleness was equalled only by his valour; and his energy, which has perhaps never been rivalled, corresponded with the genius that inspired it. Delicate in body, and insignificant in appearance, he electrified all within his atmosphere, and secured love and devotion that could accomplish any thing, because in his presence they could recognise no difficulty or check. But Nelson was not a complete man. Dazzling as was his moral nature, the bright sun had still its disfiguring spot. Humility, the essential lesson in our passage through time to eternity, is never so effectually taught as when the most illustrious present themselves to the most abject stained and degraded by pitiable sin. It is the blotted page of Nelson's history to which our attention is now chiefly called. We must take courage and survey it.

Romance has been beaten in its own domain by the surpassingly romantic history of Lady Hamilton. Before no other woman, perhaps, could Nelson have so completely fallen; upon no other woman of her time were fascinations of every kind so lavishly bestowed. Her life reads like a fable. She was the daughter of Henry Lyon, or Lyons, a labouring man, living at Preston, in Lancashire. He dying whilst she was still a child, the mother removed to Hawarden, in Flintshire, and there supported herself as best she could. As to bestowing education upon her offspring, to talk of it is absurd. The family belonged to the dragged-up class of the community, and when, by dint of instruction, perseverance, and uncommon tact in later years, Lady Hamilton contrived to correspond with the most notable people of her day, the difficulty with which she managed to spell correctly testified to the meagreness of her earliest acquisitions. It is presumed she was born in the year 1764, and the first years of her life after quitting home were spent in ordinary servitude. Her first engagement was as nursery-maid in the family of Mr. Thomas, of Hawarden, the brother-in law of Mr. Alderman Boydell; but she afterwards went to London and held the same situation in the house of Dr. Budd, who then resided in Chatham-place, Blackfriars, and was one of the physicians of St. Bartholomew's Hospital. Her fellow-servant here —the housemaid—singularly enough, became Mrs. Powell, the celebrated actress of Drury-lane Theatre. Years afterwards, when Lady Hamilton was in the meridian of her glory, and had won renown by her archievmements and beauty, she visited Drury-lane Theatre with her husband, and Mrs. Powell performed upon the occasion. The admiration of the house was divided between the accomplished actress and the still more famous visitor. You may search the history of domestic servitude in vain for a parallel coincidence.

Leaving the service of Dr. Budd, Emma Lyon descended a step or two, and became the servant of a dealer in St. James's-market. Here her appearance and manners attracted the attention of a lady of quality, and she was invited to what, for want of a better expression, we may call a "higher sphere." With much leisure in the house of a fashionable lady, with an ardent temperament, an extraordinary capacity, and a strong will, she took up such books as fell in her way, and grew into a desperate novel reader. It is but fair to the memory of Lady Hamilton, who will have but little of the reader's sympathy after the next dozen lines are read, to state her difficulties and temptations at the outset of her career, and to show how far circumstances and society itself were guilty of her many offences. The trash of a circulating library was not the only poison that crept into her soul. She was already a lovely woman, full of energy and animation, endowed with great powers of mimicry, an exquisite ear, and an incomparable voice. Without education, and surrounded by flattery and vice, we must not wonder if the servant yielded to solicitations against which the well-born and the well-informed are not always proof.

We are told that she first became the mistress of Captain, afterwards Rear-Admiral John Willett Payne, but that she soon deserted this gentleman for the protection of Sir Harry Featherstonhaugh, Bart., of Up Park, Sussex. The baronet was fond of field-sports; Emma Lyon, who excelled in whatever she attempted, took to riding in consequence, and rendered herself one of the most most remarkable horse-women of the period. Up Park, Sussex, however, under the influence of its new mistress, became a scene of headlong dissipation; the protector was soon ruined, and the "protected" thrown upon the world, into which she went dishonoured. Friendless and without a home, it was perhaps creditable to the discarded woman to earn her livelihood by any honest means that offered. One Dr. Graham was delivering lectures at the time in the Adelphi, upon health and beauty, and Emma Lyon engaged herself to the quack as an illustration. Whatever may have been the merit of the lectures, there could be no doubt respecting the form that threw life and light upon them. Romney, the Royal Academician, pronounced it perfect, and took it for the subject of his most celebrated pictures. Hayley, the friend of Cowper, in his *Life of Romney* tells us that the talents which nature bestowed upon this person, led her to delight "in the two kindred arts of music and painting; in the first she acquired great practical ability; for the second she had exquisite taste, and such expressive powers as could furnish to an historical painter an inspiring model for the various characters, either delicate or sublime, that he might have occasion to represent;" from which statement we may conclude that the intellectual ability, as well as physical beauty of the model, was appreciated and admired by Romney. The poet was as bewitched as the painter; both drew inspiration from the subject, and we have sonnets as well as portraits extant to perpetuate the loveliness that drove both mad.

We have said above that the existence of Lady Hamilton reads like a fable. Every step we take leads us further from what we are accustomed to regard as real life, and deeper into the realms of fiction. We have seen the labourer's daughter, a poor servant girl, a rich man's mistress, the painter's hired model. We pursue her history. Whilst acting in the last named capacity she became acquainted with Mr. Charles Francis Greville. Mr. Greville was the nephew of Sir William Hamilton, and famous in his generation "for his taste in objects of art and *vertu*." He offered a home to Emma Lyon, and the girl accepted it. But he did more! He attempted to cultivate the wild luxuriance of an undoubted genius, and to a certain extent with signal success. Could he have sharpened her moral perceptions as happily as he improved her mental endowments, he might have lost a mistress, but he would have spared the world much shame, and the woman he professed to love infinite degradation, and long and unavailing sorrow. She had masters for everything. Her knowledge of music was intuitive. Receiving instruction in the art, she soon sang to perfection. An anecdote told of the lady at this period is too characteristic to be omitted. Mr. Greville took her one night to Ranelagh, the Vauxhall of our fathers. Excited by the scene, and carried away by the admiration of those who surrounded her, she insisted upon a public exhibition of her vocal powers. She sang and met with rapturous applause. Upon returning home Mr. Greville, alarmed, remonstrated with the performer upon the impropriety of her act. He knew not the consummate powers of the actress with whom he had to deal. The rebuked penitent retired to her room, discarded the finery in which she was dressed, reappeared in a humble garment, and begged to be dismissed. Reader, imagine the *tableau*, and form your own conclusion.

Be sure the sorceress was *not* dismissed; she remained with her protector, and became the mother of three children, who called her aunt. Her own name had been changed from Lyon to Harte; for what reason we are not informed.

We are anxious as we proceed to let what glimmering of light we can upon this dark and melancholy picture. We need all the relief the subject affords, and cannot spare one sunny ray; the shadows fall deep and thick enough anon. In the midst of her renewed splendour the unfortunate woman remembered her mother and her home. Through life she continued attentive and affectionate in her conduct towards that mother, and so far vindicated humanity from the all but unredeemed disgrace her conduct otherwise threatened to inflict upon it. Mrs. Lyon, converted into Mrs. Cadogan in order to fit the poor woman for her equivocal elevation, came to her daughter whilst the latter enjoyed the protection of Mr. Greville, and partook of her child's good fortune.

Such good fortune, however, seldom abides. The affairs of Mr. Greville, like those of Sir Harry Featherstonhaugh, fell into disorder; though, in the case of the former, the French Revolution, and not the mistress, is chargeable with the disaster. In 1789 Mr. Greville reduced his establishment, called his creditors together, and parted with his mistress. We are loth to go on.

We have stated that Mr. Greville was famous "for his taste in objects of art and *vertu*." He had an uncle, already named, Sir William Hamilton, who was famous in that way too. Sir William Hamilton was a native of Scotland, born in 1730, and minister at Naples for the long period of thirty-six years. He was a distinguished antiquary, remarkable for his taste in and appreciation of the fine arts. He possessed also scientific acquirements, and had some knowledge of mineralogy. He was a trustee of the British Museum, a Fellow of the Royal Society, and a Vice-President of the Society of Antiquaries. He was also a distinguished member of the Dilettanti Club, and appears among the portraits in their room of meeting at the Thatched-house Tavern. A portrait of him, by Sir Joshua Reynolds, one of his intimate friends, may be seen in the National Gallery. He is known as an author by his works. With the King of Naples he was a great favourite, and largely shared with him the enjoyment of the chase and other sports, to which the sovereign is well known to have been egregiously addicted.

Now, after such a catalogue of unquestionable virtues, one may fairly be prepared to treat the possessor of them with unqualified respect. How easy it is, however, in this degenerate world of ours, to be scientific, to be the member of every society of the land, and to have your portrait painted, with a title to nothing but the loathing of your fellows, may be seen in the history of this very man. Mr. Greville, for a large consideration, parted with his mistress to his uncle, the Right Hon. Sir William Hamilton, K. B.: and the representative of his majesty, having completed his bargain with his nephew, set out for Naples, accompanied by Anne Harte and her mother.

Italy was a scene fit for the development of this extraordinary woman's powers. Upon this sunny and dissolute soil she was at home and revelled. The external graces, that are not slow to adapt themselves to the dullest genius beneath a soft and southern sky, gave voluptuousness to a form already perfect, and made still more exuberant a spirit richto overflowing in its passionate character and marvellous resources. All that could heighten loveliness of form and give intensity to intellectual strength came at the syren's bidding. In the midst of luxury and wealth, she had but to command in order to possess. The improvement that took place in the mind and person of this unscrupulous beauty under the tutelage, guidance, and instruction of Sir William, is said to have been extraordinary. Her singing, we learn, rivalled the performances of the great musical celebrities of her time, and when she acted, Siddons could not surpass the grandeur of her style, or O'Neil be more melting in the utterance of deep pathos.

With a common piece of stuff, it has been stated—

"She could so arrange and clothe herself, as to offer the most appropriate representations of a Jewess, a Roman matron, a Helen, Penelope, or Aspasia. No character seemed foreign to her, and the grace she was in the habit of displaying under such representations, excited the admiration of all who were fortunate enough to have been present on such occasions. The celebrated shawl dance owes its origin to her invention: but it is admitted to have been executed by her with a grace and elegance far surpassing that with which it has ever been rendered on the stage of any of our theatres."

Prudent and calculating for a moment, the adventuress resolved to turn the great gifts of nature to account. The ambassador and his mistress went back to England in 1791, and upon the 6th day of September in that year, the two were married in St. George's Church, the ambassador being sixty years of age, his wife just twenty-seven. The world, after all, is not particular. Society welcomed the bride with open arms, and adulation followed her steps. There was but one drawback to a perfect triumph, but it was serious enough in its way. The fastidious court of Queen Charlotte refused to receive the renowned courtezan, though she came endorsed with the name of the king's representative. The happy couple returned to Naples with the lamentations of fashionable life, which we are informed, "was greatly relieved by Lady Hamilton's displays as a singer and an actress," but with a rebuke in bestowing which it is to be regretted that society as well as royalty did not have a share.

Upon the re-appearance of Sir William Hamilton at the court of Naples, it became a question how far the queen of that country could condescend towards an English lady who had been refused by her own sovereign; but Maria Caroline of Naples was far too shrewd a woman, and much too daring in the use of her instruments, to suffer a small matter of etiquette to stand between her and the friendship of a rare ally. Lady Hamilton was not only received at the court of the Queen of Naples, but to all intents and purposes became the prime councillor and chief adviser of the queen, who having a fool for a husband, herself usurped all the authority of an independent sovereign. It is not too much to say that these two women, the sister of the unhappy Marie Antoinette, and the nursery-maid of Dr. Budd, for years wielded the destinies of Naples, and seriously affected the character of the wars that ended with the peace of Europe in 1815, when both were dead. No account of celebrated women can be perfect which shall omit the history of this pair. Both were endowed with powers of mind far beyond the average of their sex; both exhibited energy and understanding that inspired them to bold and decisive, if not always laudable, deeds; both were as remarkable for their personal beauty as for their self-reliance, their knowledge of men, and their determination to make the most of their information. To say that Maria Caroline loved Lady Hamilton is to misstate a fact; there was no love in the royal composition; but her ungovernable and undying hatred of the French inclined her, no doubt, in the first instance towards the wife of the English ambassador, and the subsequent devotion of the favourite secured an attachment that is confessed and reiterated through whole pages of a vehement and overstrained correspondence.

In the year 1793, two years after the marriage of Lady Hamilton, Nelson being then thirty-five years old, was appointed to the Agamemnon. He had himself married in 1787, and from that time until 1793 had resided, with his wife, chiefly at Burnham Thorpe, the place of his birth. In June, 1793, he sailed in the Agamemnon for the Mediterranean, under Lord Hood. It will be remembered that when Lord Hood reached the Mediterranean at this juncture of affairs he took his station off Toulon, and opened a negotiation with the French for the surrender of the town, arsenal, forts, &c., to the British forces acting on behalf of Louis XVIII. Toulon surrendering, Nelson was ordered to carry the despatches to the minister at Turin, and afterwards to proceed to Naples with despatches for Sir William Hamilton. He was, moreover, urged to press Sir William to hasten the Neapolitan troops to Toulon as much as possible, in order to guard the works surrounding that place, Lord Hood having great anxiety upon the subject. Before we introduce Captain Nelson to Lady Hamilton, and give him over to the perils of that seductive presence, it is worth while noting his personal appearance. The late king thus described the hero as he had seen him in 1783, and ten years of labor and sickness had not improved the picture,—

"I was a midshipman," said his majesty, "on board the Barfleur, lying in the Narrows, off Staten Island, and had the watch on deck, when Captain Nelson, of the Albemarle, came in his barge alongside, and appeared to be the merest boy of a captain I ever beheld; his dress was worthy of attention; he had on a full laced uniform: his lank unpowdered hair was tied in a stiff Hessian tail of an extraordinary length: the old-fashioned flaps of his waistcoat added to the general quaintness of his figure, and produced an appearance which particularly attracted my notice, for I had never seen anything like it before, nor could I imagine who he was nor what he came about. My doubts were, however, removed when Lord Hood introduced me to him. There was something irresistibly pleasing in his address and conversation, and an enthusiasm when speaking on professional subjects that showed he was no common being."

In due time Nelson reached Naples, and delivered his despatches to Sir William Hamilton. The deepest tragedies have often the quietest possible beginnings. The soldier on guard at Elsinore is the humble prologue to the dire catastrophe of the family of the Prince of Denmark.

"The King and the court," says one of Nelson's biographers, "were lavish in their praises of the English—'the saviours of Italy,' as they were called. The King paid Nelson the most marked attention, and entrusted to him 'the handsomest letter that can be penned, in his own hand,' to Lord Hood, and offered 6,000 troops to assist in the preservation of Toulon."

An account, written under Lady Hamilton's eye, of Sir William's first interview with Nelson, furnishes the following statement:—

"Sir William, on returning home, after his first interview with Nelson, told Lady Hamilton that he was about to introduce to her a little man who could not boast of being very handsome, but who would become the greatest man that England ever produced. 'I know it from the very few words of conversation I have already had with him. I pronounce that he will one day astonish the world.'"

Nelson was introduced accordingly. His first impression of the beauty is briefly stated in a letter to his wife.

"Lady Hamilton," he writes, "has been wonderfully kind and good to Josiah (Mrs. Nelson's son by a former marriage). She is a young woman of amiable manners, and who does honor to the station to which she is raised."

In another day or two Nelson was on his way to rejoin the fleet, little dreaming of the toils into which he had already entered, and in the simplicity of his grand and noble nature never suspecting the possibility of falling into crime that should leave an ineffaceable blot upon a character which it was the ambition and glory of his life to render worthy of his country.

We have beheld Lady Hamilton under many aspects. From the date of her introduction to Nelson she presents herself in a new and striking character. In Naples, in the midst of politics, surrounded by her countrymen who were fighting on the seas for the glory of their native land and for the peace of the world, Lady Hamilton was no longer ambitious to be renowned for accomplishments which she shared with the opera-dancer, and for qualities which, however dazzling they might be in fashionable saloons, could add nothing to the power of a queen's adviser and the chosen friend of mighty chiefs. The woman was never below the occasion. It was evidently a matter of indifference to her whether she was placed in circumstances to dance "the shawl dance," or to contribute to the successful issue of a great battle. In either case, her part was performed to perfection. Her talents were prodigious; her vanity and self-confidence quite as unbounded.

The character assumed by the ambassador's wife, at the period to which we refer, was one that could not fail to call forth the admiration of Nelson, and to win his regard. His magnificent egotism was flattered by her devotion to his country's flag, and by the impassioned earnestness with which she undertook any service conducive to its influence. As we have seen, it was only necessary for Lady Hamilton to attire herself in a "common piece of stuff," in order to furnish an appropriate representation of a Jewess or a Roman matron, a Penelope or an Aspasia. Her garment now is that of Britannia ruling the seas. Miss Stewart, in effigy upon our pennypieces, with a branch in one hand and a trident in the other, does not more emphatically picture the genius of our sea-girt island, than did Lady Hamilton represent the tutelary angel of all British sailors commissioned to bring down the pride of France, and to uphold the honour of England. There was no misunderstanding as to the relation. The sailors write to the lady upon matters of business, just as Romney wrote of her, when he informed his friend that the "greatest part of the summer" he would be engaged "in painting pictures from the divine lady," to whom he could give no other epithet, "for I think her superior to all womankind." The letters of bluff admirals and weather-beaten captains addressed to the divinity reveal an appreciation of her merits about which there can be no mistake. "I cannot," writes Captain Ball, "let slip this occasion to address a few lines to the best friend and patroness of the navy, and to assure you and Sir William Hamilton, that I shall ever retain the most lively sense of your attention. I have brought upon myself a great deal of envy by showing the official order I received from you." Sir Thomas Troubridge, "a pattern of professional excellence, of undaunted valour, and of patriotic worth," on one occasion tells Lady Hamilton that "he begins to think she will spoil them all, and that we shall not be able to stay out for eight or nine months cruising after all this attention." The great St. Vincent himself sends "ten thousand most grateful thanks to her ladyship for restoring the health of our valuable friend;" is sure "that Lady St. Vincent will be transported with your attention to her," and has immediately "obeyed her ladyship's commands respecting Tom Bowen, who is now Captain of L'Aguillon," and, "should her ladyship have any other *protegés*," Earl St. Vincent implores that he may not be spared. Mr. Disraeli has it that the secret of all success consists in being master of your subject. If ever woman was mistress of the art of bringing all men to her feet, Lady Hamilton is she. The valiant old tars who swept the seas that England might sail empress of them all were helpless children in her hands.

Five years elapsed between the first and second meeting of Nelson and Lady Hamilton; but the former had passed a whole life in the interim. We saw him quitting Naples in 1793, after having delivered his despatches to Sir William Hamilton, plain Captain Nelson of the Agamemnon. He returned to the Neapolitan shores in 1798, with a title to the peerage, a famous commander, a proud conqueror, and followed in his course by loud and grateful acclamations. At Calvi, in 1794, he had conducted the siege, and lost an eye. In 1797, crying to his men, whom he led to as desperate an assault as ever tempted bravery to the jaws of death, "*Westminster Abbey or glorious victory!*" he captured, as it were, with his own hand, the San Josef and San Nicholas at the immortal battle of St. Vincent. Two months afterwards he parted with his right arm at Teneriffe, and within a twelvemonth again he received a wound in the head almost at the moment of achieving the splendid and decisive victory of the Nile. At this crisis of his career, we say, overflowing with honours, worshipped by his fellow-countrymen, laden with presents conferred upon him by every potentate interested in the peace of Europe, from the Russian Emperor to the Grand Signor, Nelson for the second time set foot in Naples, and saw his future mistress. His reception was a triumph. King and Queen gave way to him, and the people received him as they are apt to receive those whom their rulers deem worthy of enthusiastic welcome.

Lady Hamilton in the meanwhile had not been idle. In her peculiar sphere she had laboured, so to speak, hand-in-hand with the hero, and contributed not a little to the success of his movements, and the consequent splendour of his renown. From the moment she undertook the cause of the British Navy, she gave her whole soul to the work. Her nature did not permit her to leave one stone unturned in order to reach her end, and what her will suggested she had art enough to compass. She had been but a short time at Naples before it was asserted that she had contrived to "de-Bourbonise the whole Royal family, and to make them all English." This was but clearing the field for subsequent operations. A single instance of her unremitting zeal and daring patriotism speaks for a thousand. One morning Lady Hamilton received intelligence that a courier had brought to the King of Naples a private letter from the King of Spain. What were its contents? Lady Hamilton could not guess, but she was resolved to ascertain. By the aid of the Queen the document was stolen from the King, transcribed by the ambassador's wife, and then quietly deposited again in the King's cabinet or waistcoat-pocket. The letter had been worth the stealing. It announced the King of Spain's determination "to withdraw from the coalition into which he had entered," and to join the French against England. The vigilant woman lost not a moment. Sir William Hamilton lay dangerously ill; but, taking counsel of herself, she at once despatched a copy of the declaration to Lord Grenville, the Minister in England, and, from her own private purse, paid 400*l*., in order to insure the delivery of the letter into his lordship's hands.

In June, 1798, Nelson, as all acquainted with the history of those times will vividly remember, was in search of the French fleet. How he discovered it at Alexandria towards the end of July, and what havoc in the course of twelve hours he played with it on the 1st of August, no Englishman is ever likely to forget. But there are incidents connected with this wonderful pursuit, and this noble victory, with which our readers are perhaps not so familiar. They belong rather to the history of Lady Hamilton than to that of Nelson, yet how potently do they affect the character and fate of both!

Sir William and Lady Hamilton were aroused from their slumbers one morning in the aforesaid June by the arrival of Captain Troubridge, with letters from Sir Horatio Nelson, "requesting that the ambassador would procure him permission to enter with his fleet into Naples, or any of the Sicilian ports, to provision, water, &c., as otherwise he must run for Gibraltar, being in urgent want, and that consequently he would be obliged to give over all further pursuit of the French fleet, which he had missed at Egypt, on account of their having put into Malta." It was much easier for Sir Horatio to make the request than for the ambassador to comply with it. At that very time Naples was at peace with France, a French ambassador was resident in the Neapolitan capital, and Ferdinand had stipulated with France, that *no more than two English ships of war should enter into any of the Neapolitan or Sicilian ports.* What was to be done? Sir William Hamilton did the best he could. He jumped out of bed, hastened to Sir John Acton, Ferdinand's prime minister, who convened a council immediately, at which the King himself was present. The council sat down to consider Sir Horatio's demand at half-past six o'clock, and took one hour and a half exactly to come to a determination, for they did not rise until eight. Captain Troubridge accompanied Sir William Hamilton to his residence after the council had broken up, but Lady Hamilton had already gathered from the countenances of the King and Sir John Acton the dismal confession that Naples could not break with France—that the fleet of Nelson could receive no help. We are reaching a point in the narrative at which the craft of the penman fails him, and the superiority of the painter becomes strikingly manifest. Imagine the vexation of the disappointed ambassador, picture to yourself the bitter regret and downcast looks of the faithful Troubridge, and then behold, close to them both, a form lovely as an angel's, a face beaming with the animation of triumph, and the ecstacy of an irrepressible delight,—observe her hand trembling with the consciousness of the precious treasure it grasps, and then see her waving high up exultingly in the air the order which the council had refused, and the King himself could not obtain. Dr. Budd's nurserymaid had positively in her possession the permission for which

Nelson had petitioned in vain, and without which it was impossible satisfactorily to carry on the war. Oh, how the sorceress must have chuckled when she saw King, ministers, and councillors, all issuing from their solemn consultation with their lugubrious visages indicating helplessness, inability, and unutterable disgust!

We have had occasion to observe that the King of Naples was a fool, and his Queen very much the reverse. This was unfortunate enough for his Majesty; but, what was worse still, his loving people were cognizant of the fact. The King certainly commanded in his dominions; but his wife was obeyed. Who knew this better than Lady Hamilton? That very clever lady suffered Sir William to wake up Sir John Acton, to get the King out of his bed, to cause the council to be summoned, and when all was done, and the wise men were fully engaged in discussion, she herself quietly slipped into the Queen's bedchamber, and got up a little council of her own. The reader bears in mind the consummate ability of this actress. He has been told that Siddons could not be more tragic, O'Neil not more pathetic; and he has seen how exquisitely she performed in the presence of her *quondam* protector, when that gentleman found fault with her imprudence, and she in suitable costume humbly begged leave to be dismissed from his roof. Domestic drama in the apartment of majesty gave place to classic tragedy. Not a moment was to be lost, and Lady Hamilton came at once to the catastrophe. In the most passionate manner she threw herself upon her knees, and told the Queen that the fate of the Two Sicilies now depended upon her resolution; the council were sitting; let them decide upon negative or half measures, and the family of Ferdinand was doomed. The great French force must be followed; it could not be pursued unless the English fleet found refreshment in the Sicilian ports; and if allowed to go free, the peril, not to England, but to Naples, could not be overrated. The terrified Queen became alive to the danger of the situation, but she had faith in the King then sitting in council, and was sure he would provide for the emergency. He might, replied the petitioner, or he might not; and, if not, who could reflect with patience upon the fate that threatened Naples and the royal family? Her Majesty, with a stroke of the pen, could be her own deliverer. Why hesitate? Her sign-manual was respected throughout the king's dominions; a line, and her country, her husband, and his crown, were rescued from destruction. No doubt the word was suited to the action, and the action to the word; pen, ink, and paper were in the room; Lady Hamilton dictated, and the Queen with her own right hand directed "all governors of the Two Sicilies to receive with hospitality the British fleet, to water, victual, and aid them." Lady Hamilton inclosed that order to Nelson, and bade him commit the Queen no further than the glory and service of England required. Nelson answered that if he gained a battle it should be called hers and the Queen's, for to them alone would his country be indebted for the victory. He did gain a battle, and it was that of the memorable Nile; had his fleet not been furnished with the necessaries of life at Syracuse, the battle would not have been fought. It was for the country to remember that fact. Against the faults of Lady Hamilton moralists cannot too strongly inveigh; society for its own protection cannot too emphatically protest; but, had Lady Hamilton been the most degraded of her kind, England was bound not to forget this great and unparalleled service. How she did forget it we shall presently blush to read.

Broken in health and wounded in body, Nelson reached Naples on the 20th of September. He was taken into the British minister's house, and there personally tended by her whose sympathies had been so awakened, and by whose attentions he was, after a time, restored to health. It is difficult to repress a smile as we read Nelson's account of his reception, in a letter addressed from Naples, shortly after this period, to his wife. The marvellous simplicity of the hero, and the histrionic excellence of the heroine, are too instructive to be overlooked:—

"I must endeavour," says Nelson, "to convey to you something of what passed; but if it were so affecting to those who were only united to me by bonds of friendship, what must it be to my dearest wife—my friend—my everything which is most dear to me in this world? Sir William and Lady Hamilton came out to sea, attended by numerous boats with emblems, &c. They, my most respectable friends, had nearly been laid up and seriously ill, first from anxiety and then from joy. It was imprudently told Lady Hamilton in a moment, and the effect was like a shot; she fell, apparently dead, and is not yet perfectly recovered from severe bruises. Alongside came my honoured friends: the scene in the boat was terribly affecting; up flew her ladyship, and exclaiming, 'O God! is it possible?' she fell into my arm more dead than alive. Tears, however, soon set matters to rights; when alongside came the King. . . . . . I hope, some day, to have the pleasure of introducing you to Lady Hamilton. She is one of the very best women in this world; she is an honour to her sex. Her kindness, with Sir William's, to me, is more than I can express. I am in their house, and I may now tell you, it required all the kindness of my friends to set me up. Lady Hamilton intends writing to you. May God Almighty bless you, and give us in due time a happy meeting."

Lady Hamilton did write to Lady Nelson accordingly.

As may be supposed, the French ambassador at Naples was not slow to remonstrate against the Neapolitan breach of faith. Lady Hamilton took advantage of the remonstrance to break off that connexion altogether. So plausibly did she argue with the Queen upon the advantages to be gained from an open rupture with France, that the said ambassador and his suite were requested to go home at twenty-four hours' notice. The step was not without its evil consequences. A Neapolitan army was raised to defend the Two Sicilies from French aggression, but the general in command did not understand his business, and the soldiers were either traitors, or cowards, or both. In the month of December, 1798, the French were marching on the capital, and the King and Queen were obliged to decamp. But for Lady Hamilton there is no doubt that the stupid Ferdinand would have fallen a victim to popular fury, and Maria Caroline might have shared the fate of her sister, Marie Antoinette. The conduct of Lady Hamilton at this emergency is above all praise.

The royal family, their property, their immediate friends, were to be conveyed from the palace to British ships waiting to receive them, and not a score of the King's subjects could be asked to help in the undertaking. The labour was performed by Lady Hamilton alone; her genius designed the plan of escape; her activity rendered the plan successful. "Lady Hamilton," says Southey, "like a heroine of romance, explored, with no little danger, a subterraneous passage, leading from the palace to the sea-side; through this passage the royal treasures, the choicest pieces of painting and sculpture, and other property, to the amount of two millions and a half, were conveyed to the shore, and stowed safely on board the English ships." During the whole proceeding the movements of Lady Hamilton, as well as those of her husband, were closely watched, but ineffectually. Lady Hamilton seemed, in the words of Nelson, "to be an angel dropped from heaven," for the preservation of the royal family, and she performed an angel's part in conducting them from the ruin that awaited them amongst their own people to the protection and security of British ships. The loss to Sir William Hamilton and his wife by the service was great. In order to lull suspicion and prevent discovery, the ambassador was obliged to abandon his house, and to leave behind him, belonging to himself, property amounting to £30,000, and movables to the value of £9,000, the property of his wife. Nelson received the King and Queen, Sir William and Lady Hamilton, on board the Vanguard, and conducted them all in safety to Palermo.

It is not necessary to discuss the nature of the sentiments which incited the mistress of Sir William Hamilton's nephew to disgrace still further Sir William Hamilton's wife. The reader may be safely left to his own conclusions upon the subject. As to Nelson himself, as little doubt can be entertained that he was the slave of an overpowering infatuation. Without worldly knowledge, simple as a child, with a spirit as gentle as it was unsuspecting, he doated upon this woman with a passionate ardour that concealed from his own upright mind the culpable character of his love, and rendered him regardless of all its consequences, if not insensible to them. His marriage had not been very fortunate. We do not find that Lady Nelson sympathized very heartily with her husband's career, or, indeed, took much pains to secure his domestic comfort, whether afloat or ashore.

"My dear Fanny," begins a letter from Spithead, in 1798, "at half-past five I arrived here, and, what you will be surprised to hear, with great difficulty found one pair of raw silk stockings. I suppose in some place or other I shall find my linen, for there is scarcely any in this trunk."

The letter is valuable as an indication of the wife's regard. Again, Nelson had been absent three years from England. During that time he had won for himself imperishable fame, and had made his wife a peeress. He landed at Yarmouth amidst the enthusiasm of his fellow-countrymen, but no Lady Nelson was there to wish him joy upon his glorious and safe return. Such was the wife. Upon the other side all was temptation and witchery, incessant kindness, unlimited devotion. For his country Nelson was at any moment prepared to lay down his life. Lady Hamilton, if it would redound to his honor, was ready to share the same fate. The exertions of the ambassador's wife on behalf of her king were the subject of universal applause; but Nelson would have been blind had he not perceived that not for the ambassador, and not for the king, but to place laurels on his own brow, all the energy was called forth and every triumph won. "Pray," writes Earl St. Vincent to Lady Hamilton, "do not let your fascinating Neapolitan dames approach too near our hero." There was no necessity for the advice, but it sufficiently betrayed the susceptible temperament of the man upon whom his own wife had not even cared to make an impression.

We content ourselves with this statement. No impartial reader of the whole case will fail to conclude that Lady Hamilton employed the rare gifts that nature and education had conferred upon her to bring one of the greatest of his time to her feet, and to complete the history of her conquests by linking her name and life with those of a man who will never be forgotten whilst the history of his country endures. As difficult will it be for the same reader to recognize any but the most enthusiastic, the most unselfish, the most devoted affection, in the hero thus sorely tempted and overcome. Nelson guilty never believed himself an offender. His language in his private journals and in his letters all testifies to the equanimity with which he regarded his *liaison* with Sir William Hamilton's wife. Of all the anomalies that reveal themselves in humanity, none is more singular than that of an individual in the act of committing crime calling upon Heaven to look down approvingly upon the exhibition of virtue. We repeat, we content ourselves with announcing Lord Nelson's fall. We shall not insult the reader by requesting him to pursue the history of the connection. Let it be sufficient to say that Lord Nelson, after separating from his wife, lived openly with Lady Hamilton, as her protector, her husband not being dead. Nelson perished at Trafalgar in 1805. Sir William Hamilton died in 1808. On the 30th of January, 1801, Lady Hamilton gave birth to a daughter, in London. Her name was Horatia; her father was Lord Nelson.

If this were all we had to say, we should have little excuse for thrusting the painful history upon public notice. The last act of the tragedy is, as usual, the most melancholy and instructive. The career of Lady Hamilton ends fitly for mankind, woefully and dreadfully for her.

Upon the return of Sir William Hamilton and his wife to England, after their heavy losses in Naples, the former petitioned Government for compensation, and the latter parted with her jewels to support both until such compensation should be granted. Before it came Sir William died. Dying, he commissioned his nephew, the Hon. Mr. Greville, to pray to his Majesty for a continuation of his pension to his wife after his decease, in consideration of her zeal and services. The zeal and services, however, were never recognised.

On the 21st day of October, 1805, and on board the Victory, "then in sight of the combined fleets of France and Spain, distant about ten miles," Lord Nelson retired to his cabin and made a codicil to his will. He recorded the services performed by Lady

Hamilton (the reader is acquainted with them), and then wrote as follows :—

"Could I have rewarded those services, I would not *now* call upon my country; but as that has not been in my power, I leave Emma Lady Hamilton, therefore, a legacy to my King and country, that they will give her an ample provision to maintain her rank in life.

"I also leave to the beneficence of my country my adopted daughter, Horatia Nelson Thompson; and I desire she will use in future the name of Nelson only. These are the only favours I ask of my King and country at this moment when I am going to fight their battle.

"May God bless my King and country, and all those who I loved dear. My relations it is needless to mention; they will, of course, be amply provided for."

Within a few hours of his signing the document Nelson lay upon a bed, stripped of his clothes, and covered with a sheet. A shot from the mizentop of the *Redoubtable* had done its work. As the men placed the wounded hero on his back, he looked round for Dr. Scott. "Doctor," he said, "I told you so—I am gone." And after a short pause he added, in a low voice, "I have to leave Lady Hamilton and my adopted daughter Horatia as a legacy to my country."

An hour and a quarter afterwards Captain Hardy was at his side.

"I hope," said the dying man, "none of *our* ships have struck, Hardy?" "No, my lord," replied Captain Hardy, "there is no fear of that." Lord

Nelson then said, "I am a dead man, Hardy. I am going fast, it will be all over with me soon. Come nearer to me. Pray let my dear Lady Hamilton have my hair, and all other things belonging to me."

Another hour elapsed, and Hardy was at the bedside again. He told the captain "he felt that in a few minutes he should be no more," and added in a low tone, "Don't throw me overboard, Hardy." The captain answered, "O no, certainly not." "Then," replied Nelson, "you know what to do. *Take care of my dear Lady Hamilton; take care of poor Lady Hamilton!*"

A few minutes more, and Nelson uttered his last words. They were—"Thank God, I have done my duty!" But the words that immediately preceded them were the old plaintive sounds—"Remember, Dr. Scott, that I leave Lady Hamilton and my daughter Horatia as a legacy to my country. Never forget Horatia."

Nelson's codicil proved waste paper. His last imploring accents passed into the air. Lady Hamilton derived no help from either. We do not apologise for the Government that took no heed of the last breath of Nelson; but on behalf of humanity we ask pardon for the treachery of the man who kept back the codicil. Captain Blackwood, faithful to his friend, brought home that document after the battle of Trafalgar, and placed it in the hands of the Rev. William Nelson, the brother of the Admiral, and subsequently Earl of the name. At this period *the rev. gentleman, his wife, and family, were residing with Lady Hamilton, and had partaken of her hospitality for many months. Indeed, for six years his daughter had been consigned exclusively to Lady Hamilton's care.* The rev. gentleman, fearful that the codicil would affect the sum about to be voted by Parliament for Lord Nelson's family, quietly kept it in his pocket until the day when 120,000*l.* were duly voted for their support. On that day he dined with Lady Hamilton in Clarges-street, and with the satisfaction of a man amply provided for, produced the paper, and sarcastically told his hostess to do what she liked with it. Lady Hamilton registered it at Doctors'-Commons the very next day; there it has been ever since, and may be seen any day by the curious reader upon the payment of one shilling.

It is, perhaps, hardly necessary to add, that all the good and great people who flocked round Lady Hamilton during the lifetime of Nelson, became all at once shocked at the improprieties of a lady left destitute. As for the Rev. William Nelson, who tumbled into the title and fortune which Lady Hamilton had helped to earn, that respectable gentleman very properly removed his daughter from her instructress's roof, without even condescending to give the usual quarter's notice. In the year 1801 the Rev. William Nelson, writing to Lady Hamilton, took occasion to observe that—

"Now we have secured the peerage, we have only *one* thing to ask, and that is, my promotion in the Church, handsomely and honorably, such as becomes Lord Nelson's brother and heir-apparent to the title. No put-off with small, beggarly stalls. Mr. Addington must be kept steady to that point. I am sure *Nelson* is doing everything for him. But a word is enough for your good, sensible heart."

In 1805 there was nothing to ask, and the Rev. Mr. Nelson forgot that Lady Hamilton had a heart at all.

Nothing to ask, did we say? Yes, there was bread to ask for a fallen and a starving woman. Not far from the Merton turnpike, and within a few miles of London, there is to be seen a field, upon which once stood the home of Nelson and his mistress. It was left, with its debts and liabilities, to Lady Hamilton. These were large enough, for extravagance accompanied the meridian of her life, as it had characterised the dawn. The Government proving obdurate to the last, the owner of Merton was dismissed from the place. She went to Richmond, and then took temporary lodgings in Bond-street. Hence she was chased by importunate creditors, and for a time hid herself from the world. In 1813 we find her imprisoned in the King's Bench, but charitably liberated therefrom by a city alderman. Threatened again with arrest by a coachman, in sickness of heart the unhappy woman escaped to Calais. Here the English interpreter gave the refugee a small and wretchedly furnished house. What follows completes the romance of Lady Hamilton's life. There is sublimity in the moral.

An English lady in Calais was in the habit of ordering meat daily for a favourite dog. She was met on one occasion at the butcher's shop by the English interpreter. "Ah, madame, madame," said M. de Rheims,

"I know you to be good to the English. There is a lady here that would be glad of the worst bit of meat you provide for your dog." M. de Rheims received permission to supply the poor woman with whatever she needed, but he dared not reveal the sufferer's name, for he had promised secrecy, and she was too proud to see visitors. Through the charitable kindness of the English lady (let her name be recorded for the credit of her countrywomen; she resided in Brighton, and her name was Hunter), wine and food were supplied to the pauper until she became too ill either to eat or drink. M. de Rheims entreated the poor wretch again and again to see the lady who had been so good to her. Finally she said she would, if the lady *were not a woman of title.* Mrs. Hunter came—the poor patient thanked and blessed her—and so Lady Hamilton died: "beautiful," says her humane visitor, "even in death."

Is the lesson told? Not yet. Mrs. Hunter desired to bury the remains according to English custom. She was laughed at for her importunities upon the subject, and Emma Hamilton was placed in a deal box without inscription, her pall being a black silk petticoat stitched on a white curtain. No English Protestant clergyman could be found in Calais, but an Irish half-pay officer was sent for, and he read the burial service. The ground in which the body lies interred is now a timber-yard; it ceased to be a public cemetery in 1816, and Lady Hamilton had found her resting-place in the January of the preceding year.

"The Earl of Nelson" (it is written) "went over to demand Lady Hamilton's property, but found only the duplicates of trinkets, &c., pledged, and which he wished to take away without payment. He declined repaying any expenses that had been incurred."

Fit ending to the poor nursery-maid's history!

August 22, 1849.

RAILWAY NOVELS.

"READ now and then a romance to keep the fancy *under*," was the counsel of a writer who knew something of life and human nature, to a friend ben*t* upon a visit to the Antipodes. The wisdom of the advice is acknowledged by every living man beyond the age of thirty. Novels may concentrate action, excite interest, touch the heart, but they cannot heighten the power of imagination. It is reality that astonishes: fiction dares not, if it would, be half so bold. What if we should tell the reader that—say a century and a half ago—there lived a man in England who in his youth gave himself up to riot, gambling, and debauchery, who, driven at last to desperation by absolute beggary, quarelled with an acquaintance, fought and killed him, who was tried, convicted of murder, and sentenced to death, yet managed to escape unhurt to the Continent; who, in the course of his wretched wanderings, became known and marked at every notorious gambling house in Europe; who was publicly expelled, first from Venice, then from Genoa, and finally from indulgent Paris itself; who, venturing to visit the capital of France, encountered a prince of the blood royal at a public gaming-table, and won his friendship; who, trading upon the necessities of that prince, succeeded in obtaining the highest consideration in France—for his wife, the adulation of women in whose veins poured the richest blood of the land—for his son, the companionship of a king—for himself, the obsequious worship of millions? What if we should go on to say, how, in order to obtain but a moment's interview with this sublime adventurer, a duchess bade her coachman overturn her carriage at the great man's gate, and a marchioness, with the same intent, on the same spot, raised a cry of fire; how, in the course of a very few months, the convicted murderer, the beggared outlaw, the outcast gambler, became the owner of more than one magnificent estate in France, and generously filled the land of his adoption with wealth beyond the power of man to calculate or enjoy; how, in an hour, as if by the breath of an avenging angel, the fabric fell, the bubble burst, and the proud architect himself was fain to sneak in obscure hiding-places, lest they should take his worthless life who but an hour before had knelt to him adoringly as before a god; how, finishing his wild career precisely as he commenced it, he eluded again the hands of justice, again walked up and down and through the world, eating the foul crumbs that might be gathered in the common gambling booth, until he reached, poor as at first, that very city of Venice, which he honoured with his death, as before he had polluted it with his living presence? What, we ask, if we were to narrate this tale, and fill up the sketch with all the incidents necessary to complete the startling history? Who would listen patiently to the ravings of one who, for want of better employment and greater skill, must needs communicate the inspirations of some feverish dream? Dream, forsooth! The life and death of John Law, and the national bankruptcy of France, the result of his daring and splendid imposture, are as real as the life of George Hudson, and the history of railway speculation in England.

And not only are both histories true, but to the observant and inquiring mind both present points of resemblance in their details very remarkable, and in the highest degree instructive. Mr. Hudson, like Mr. Law, emerged from obscurity to dazzle a whole kingdom with his amazing refulgence. He also filled the coffers of men with fictitious wealth, and brought high and low, rich and poor, cringing to his feet. He gambled, too, venturing his credit and good name in a desperate game with fortune; he, too, counted his magnificent estates, and reckoned amongst his common associates the most renowned and the most illustrious of their kind. He, too, had his altar, upon which wealth-worshippers flung their daily incense, and offered up the sacrifice of their mercenary souls; and he awoke from a dream of bliss to a day of reckoning, to find himself hooted by throats already hoarse in singing his praise, smitten by hands erewhile too much honoured in receiving the bare droppings of his disgraceful gains.

A century and a half have carried us high up into the realms of civilization. During the interval, what has science not accomplished for the comfort of man—what have the spread of intelligence, the labour of missionaries—sacred and profane—the intercommunication of thought, the better understanding of nations and classes—not wrought for his happiness? To dwell upon human progress during the last hundred and fifty years is to behold at a glance the spoils of as noble a victory as ever rewarded patient endurance, unflinching energy, and heroic devotion. Yet in some respects we are precisely as we were. In the days of John Law a duchess was required to accompany one of the royal family to Genoa. "Oh, if you want a duchess," said a courtier, "send to Madame Law's; you can have a choice of them; they are all assembled there." Had a lady of fashion been suddenly demanded at court whilst Mrs. Hudson the other day was receiving "friends," the lord in waiting might have addressed his messenger in language similar to that of his French brother. The bait that enticed the whole world to the saloons of Madame Law in 1720, took the whole world again to the saloons of Mrs. Hudson in 1848. Generations had passed away, but the lure remained. In Law's time a vast deal of business was done in la rue Quincampoix—in which stood his bank—upon the hump of a poor deformed fellow, who let out his hunch as a writing-desk at so much the day or hour. Morally speaking, who lives without a hump? Lords and ladies, fashioned like the rest of us, for a consideration let out their's at Albert-gate.

It was a pity. We are an imitative species, and are prone to ape the manners of our betters. When Mr. Law's coachman found his master growing rich by the sale of waste paper, he entered into the same profitable business, and gave his master warning,—it must be admitted like a gentleman. He presented two candidates for the office about to be vacated. "Take your choice, sir," said the coachman, "you have the refusal; one is for you, the other for myself." How many flunkies in England, four years ago, spurred by the example of their patrons, neglected honest employment in order to strut in fine clothes and to eat the bread of vicious laziness! We say it is a pity to reveal the potter's clay so admirably concealed beneath velvet and ermine, under stars, ribbons, and coronets that seem actual regal crowns. It is well that we should look up to the nobly born from our social valleys, and be awe-struck by the mighty interval between us. It is a mournful lesson that we learn when we see a clodhopper filling his capacious pockets with fine dust, and by the very act reducing all men to his level, and below it, precisely as a birdcatcher, filling his fist with crumbs, calls down the sweetest singers of the grove almost from the skies to his feet.

But let it not be imagined that money worship is peculiar to the aristocracy of this or any other country. Marchionesses, it is true, have forgotten their dignity in pursuit of their idol; but the ignorant, the poor, and the ungovernable have waded through blood and unnatural murder in order to reach it. Crime had never gained a higher pitch or assumed a more melancholy aspect than when the speculative spirit created by Mr. Law filled Paris with luxuries, and with enormous wealth to purchase and enjoy them. Household murder for the sake of burial fees would seem to have flourished in England in the days that gave us railway speculations for a creed and Hudson for the chief priest of the mysteries; and between the two extremes—between the elegant *dilettante* desire for gold and the bloody thirst for it that allows no obstacle to stand between it and its draught—what confronts us but another form of the same eternally recurring passion? Heaven knows we are a charitable people. It is a miracle how so much is spared from the requirements of life, to be applied to the wants of the starving, to the healing of the wounds of the sick and the sorrows of the bereaved. The law compels charity, but our newspapers daily testify that there is a higher law of love abidingly at work at the heart of man, teaching him humanity towards his brother man, and the most practical mode of evincing his tenderness. M. Guizot, who has studied the English character with a philosophical and searching spirit, declares that there is nothing in the land that so fills the mind of the stranger at once with amazement at our resources and admiration of our use of them, as the noble free-gift monuments raised on every side for the relief of multiform suffering. The historian might have spoken more boldly, and added that nothing surpasses the Englishman's lavish distribution of his substance save his greedy acquisition of it; and that whilst it is his great virtue to be purse-liberal, it is also his curse to be purse-proud.

There are a hundred anomalies in our social system impossible to account for if we do not admit the fact. You enter a crowded chapel on a Sunday; you listen to eloquence that weekly fills to inconvenience the seats on which you find no resting-place. The preacher who holds forth is very popular. He receives at least a thousand a-year from the owner of the chapel in payment of the power that crams the edifice even to the roof. His name is without reproach. His congregation revere him even whilst he lashes them, and beyond the parish in which he lives, amongst deans and bishops, his usefulness is confessed if not patronised. His standard of doctrine and life is very high. He tells you that to be covetous is to ensure your own certain ruin; he warns you that to desire wealth and the good things of this life, to strive for riches, to be discontented with the competence you have, is to forego your rich inheritance; he cites authority for his denunciations; he submits chapter and verse, and after he has convinced you by his references, he strikes home the pregnant truths by a force of oratory that melt and win you to his argument. You go home, resolved to be a wiser and a better man upon the Monday; but on the Monday you take up a newspaper—a golden lectureship is vacant—four hundred a-year, and a sermon once a-week; one or two poor curates with eighty pounds per annum would give their ears for it; but there are many applicants for the prize, and before them all, stands the name of your popular instructor, notwithstanding his creed, his thousand a-year, and the sermon upon self-denial that almost drew you from the error of your ways.

You are, perhaps, a lord. Parliament being up, you go into the country. Your friend, Lord Birmingham, is "entertaining a select circle of the aristocracy" at his noble country seat. You are asked to join the favoured few. You reach the house just at luncheon time. The guests are all assembled. There is a duke, a marquis, an earl, a viscount, and a baron; you are yourself a younger son, and are *not* surprised to find the baron toadying the duke—as though he were a tailor waiting upon a city knight. Let that pass. There are two other guests (if we may call that poor, silent, pale-faced, uncomfortable-looking, self-immolated young man in the corner, a guest, who looks very like a criminal taking his meals before execution), a youth and a man of forty. Everybody votes the former absent, and nobody can have too much of the latter. The youth is a clergyman's son, tutor to Lord Birmingham's son and heir; he took honours at Cambridge, and means to fight hard in the world by and by. He has gentle blood in his veins, but not a sixpence in his pocket; part of his salary goes home to his family, and as much of his good breeding and learning as the patient will take is transferred to the son and heir. The scholar is good enough to stand *in loco parentis* to his pupil; but his honours, his erudition, and his cultivation buy for him at the table the simple rank of an upper servant. You know the style of the place, and are not surprised to see the youth, after a moderate and silent repast, retreat, ghost-like and unnoticed, from the fine apartment. Well, the aristocracy have a duty to perform; they must sustain their order and respect themselves. You hear a horse-laugh. It is from the gentleman of forty. You never met him before, but you saw somebody very like him as you once passed through Smithfield-market. It is the renowned Snobson; ten years ago he served behind a counter (many a better man has done it). Speculation and something else have made him a man of millions, but nothing more. Vulgarity is enthroned in his heart and is exuberant on his tongue. My lord's butler is a king to him—an emperor—a pope. The humblest occupant of plush is a hero at his side.

You feel it when he talks, moves, eats, or drinks; your flesh creeps in his company; you suspect that the groom of the chambers would think the individual out of his place in the steward's room. You are satisfied that if you could scrape off all the gold that encases that carcase, you would find nothing but the muddiest of mud huts. You have the keenest possible perception of all this; yet Lady Birmingham, who treats her son's tutor as though he were a learned pig, and nothing higher in the animal chain, is absorbed in visible admiration. It is the same with all the ladies; and as for the gentlemen—including the Duke—they are as proud of their acquaintance as they are innocent of his vulgarity and complaisant to his grossness. You know well enough what it all means. The thing is made of money. But then you remember again that the aristocracy have a duty to perform, must sustain their order and respect themselves, and, for the life of you, you cannot conceive how the personal respect is consistent with the degrading adulation.

Illustrations abound. They occur to us all. We pay our highest respect to money, and desiring to be respected, we strain after the possession of that for which we know we shall be admired, courted, and esteemed, though we lack every virtue in the calendar. We see folks—no doubt charming people in their way—endowed with every quality of Adam before he transgressed, neglected because they are poor, and we hate poverty for the cruel penalty it inflicts. Hence the universal treading upon one another's heels, the pulling at the skirts of those above us, the shocks received from the struggling gentry immediately behind us; hence the banishment of all simplicity from our lives; the shame that attaches to the condition of life to which it has pleased God to call us, and the difficulties that surround the station into which we ridiculously call ourselves. Hence domestic miseries, heartrending bankruptcies, gentlewomen left by insolvent fathers to boast in humble servitude of better days, ingenuous youths thrown upon the world to contend with it in the spirit of bitter foes; hence, too, the starvation that glares upon us from the holes and corners of the world, holes in which men, women, and children labour for a crust through the long hours of day and night, that some prosperous, sleek, and "universally respected" tradesman may minister to an inhuman love of cheapness, and fatten upon the flesh and blood of his obscure and helpless fellow-creatures.

Enough! Money-worship, let us not deny it, *is* a national sin, and he deserves well of society who makes it the subject of his written thoughts, whether he speak in prose or verse. One phase of the passion prominently presented itself in the recent history of railway speculation, and we recommended writers of fiction, whose office it is to catch folly as it flies, not to let the opportunity slip unused. The author of one of the two novels now before us—the *Golden Calf*—tells us in his preface, that when our hint came under his observation.

"He had already written at least half the present volumes upon a plan very similar to the one" laid down by ourselves, "but comprehending other objects which certain events that had recently come before the public with a painful prominence had suggested to him. He desired to show not only the pernicious influence on society of the great speculators, but the almost equally injurious influence of the great squanderers."

It would afford us real pleasure to say that the success of the endeavour is equal to its aim. The *Golden Calf* is a meagre sketch by a feeble hand. It takes an inventory of a house, but does not communicate the spirit that pervades it;—the mechanical broker, not the instructed artist, is at work throughout. In the recommendations given in these columns last September, we unhesitatingly affirmed that an author, provided he winnowed his facts well and discharged his self-appointed task in a spirit of conscientiousness and integrity, might deal boldly with names, and be utterly fearless of consequences. And bold enough the author of the *Golden Calf* is in all conscience. Not only have we Mr. Hudson, Mr. Delafield, and the Duke of Buckingham brought upon the stage, but also the Marquis of Londonderry, old Mr. Coutts, Miss Burdett Coutts, and other individuals, whom there is no more reason to disturb and summon, than there is to drag the author's own father before the public for the unnecessary purpose of making a bow. Yet, though we have a great array of public characters, we learn no more concerning them than we have hitherto gathered from the well-known records of their lives. The dull level of narrative is never broken by the pungency of satire; personality is never redeemed by brilliancy or force of expression. We have no insight into the souls of individuals whom we do not care to transfer from actual life to the pages of the novelist, unless it be to see the springs of action hidden from our gaze in the broad daylight of the world. The lover of scandal will be grievously disappointed who looks for "revelations" in the *Golden Calf.* The accomplished and instructed novel-reader will find his appetite pall upon insipidity.

Sir Edward Graham, the second novel, is in one respect the very antithesis of the *Golden Calf.* The object of the latter seems to be a simple clustering together of a few unworthies of the present generation. The intention is declared in the preface. The preface of *Sir Edward Graham* protests against its being imagined for a moment that the authoress had any man or woman in her eye in the prosecution of her labours. Nobody will suspect Miss Sinclair of the unkind intention. Her ladies and gentlemen are all strangers, and so we wish them to continue. Before Miss Sinclair proceeds to the main purpose of her work, she fills many pages with edifying remarks upon the degenerate tendency of our age, which prefers highly-seasoned and piquant dishes to the rigid and unadulterated fare suited to the palates of rational and enlightened beings; and then, by way of illustration to her lecture, she writes as thrilling, as melo-dramatic, and as unnatural a story as ever issued from the Minerva press or delighted hall-porters in Grosvenor-square. There is power in her work, such as we do not find in the companion novel above referred to. The lady has skill in dialogue, and can use a delicate pencil in the development of character, but *Sir Edward Graham* is certainly as admirable an instance of the vice in order to counteract which the book was expressly written, as it is possible to place in the hands of the young.

The moral of "Railway Speculation" has yet to be written; the tale that shall instruct mankind has still to be told. It is no journeyman's hand that is competent to the task. It will be the glory of genius to accomplish with a touch, that which the tedious and often-repeated efforts of mediocrity will never reach. In the very simplicity and obviousness of the theme consists the difficulty of dealing with it as it deserves.

DECEMBER 14, 1849.

LOUIS PHILIPPE AND HIS FAMILY.

CHAPTER THE FIRST.

THE time had passed for history to be serviceable either as guide or counsellor to Louis Philippe, King of the French, when he was paying in exile the penalty of opportunity misused in the day of vast prosperity and power. To the Count de Neuilly, the inhabitant of Claremont, with no future before him save the illimitable, which he must share with the meanest, what availed the upbraiding voice of experience—of what use the tremendous lesson learned too late, and at a sacrifice that beggars calculation!

Events repeat themselves. In the daily walk of every man, scenes, actions and thoughts recur which have already played their part in the mysterious drama of his existence. Amidst the thousand new combinations of life, a well-known series presents itself to startle the actor and to confound his judgment. The public history of the family of Orleans is a continually returning narrative of the same characters, incidents and passions. The first chapter is identical with the last. The most illustrious ancestor exhibits the political features of the least remarkable descendant. Make due allowance for the altered aspect of the age, and the difference between the public career of the crowned representative of the house and that of its founder is comparatively trifling. When Louis XIV. sat upon the throne of France, a Philip of Orleans courted the people, and mocked it with a show of popular concession. When the same monarch lay quietly in his grave, a Philip of Orleans took virtual possession of his seat at the bidding of a parliament, whose supreme voice he worshipped only the more effectually to insult and silence it. An Orleans, voted ruler by the representatives of the people at the close of a protracted reign of tyranny and despotism, a century and a half ago gave to France, in exchange for a government of arbitrary power, a government of still more deadly corruption. What are these but tales of the day in which we have moved? Nearer yet to our time, an Orleans, faithless to his blood, regardless of the ties of family and race, made common cause with the revolution, that he might the more securely ride upon the storm, and yet lived to be the victim of the bloody saturnalia of which he had been the chosen hero. To gratify the mob, the father of Louis Philippe signed the death-warrant of Louis XVI., and then for reward was himself dragged by his patrons to the scaffold. Louis Philippe, profiting by the exile of Charles X., is flung even more ignominiously into banishment than the king whose downfall was the signal of his own sudden rise. Different phases of the same historial picture meet us at every turn. Throughout the series of portraits there is no mistaking the family likeness. An impure stream mingles with the waters from their source. A Nemesis attends and accompanies the stock from the cradle. It is impossible, in the space to which we are necessarily limited, to illustrate these remarks by more than a slight notice of a few of the extraordinary events in connection with the family of Orleans, that crowd themselves into the last two hundred years. Such as we shall use for our purpose have a surpassing interest in themselves, and overflow with instruction.

A son was born to Louis XIII. and Anne of Austria in the September of 1638. Another was born to the same parents on the 21st of the same month in 1640. The first became Louis XIV.; the latter was founder of the house with whose history we are now concerned. The children as they grew up exhibited a marked difference, both in their personal appearance and natural tastes. Louis was tall and well proportioned, with a fair complexion, and a commanding face. Philip, remarkably small, exhibited a long and repulsive countenance, which jet black hair and eyebrows, and fine dark eyes, could not redeem from ugliness. The dauphin loved to play at soldiers as a boy; Monsieur, shy and retiring, spent his time in his mother's apartments, with the ladies of the court. Arrived at manhood, the elder loved the chase, music, and the drama: the younger found his enjoyment in good eating, gambling, and dress. Throughout life the King was jealous and suspicious of the Duke, whose affability to the populace set a never-to-be-forgotten example to his descendants. The Duke disliked, but feared the King, trembling, it is said, in his presence, and never venturing to remonstrate against a royal command, whatever pangs obedience might cost. In 1661 Louis became the husband of the Infanta Maria Theresa, daughter of Philip IV. of

Spain, and immediately afterwards his brother married Henrietta Anne, daughter of our own unfortunate Charles I.

A fascination not wholly unconnected with the sorrows of her birth, and the sadness of her early death, pervades the character of the volatile and light-hearted Henrietta. Her father had never known her. She was born at Exeter during the height of the civil wars, and she was an exile when he perished. Appearing in Paris after her marriage, she took that gay city by surprise, by the force of "her beauty, her wit, and readiness in repartee." And amongst the chief of her admirers was the King himself. A picture of the times is presented by a stroke. Louis XIV., eager to subjugate Holland, was anxious to obtain, not merely the neutrality, but the active support and help of England. Henrietta of Orleans, a favourite sister of Charles II., was commissioned by the King of France to win the co-operation of her brother by the offer of a mistress and a pension. The ambassadress fulfilled her mission to the letter. The money was paid; the mistress was created Duchess of Portsmouth, and Henrietta of Orleans acquired all the honours of a successful and therefore a great negotiator. She returned to France to receive the grateful thanks of the King, and to be poisoned by her husband's friends. On the 29th June, 1670, the Duchess of Orleans rose earlier than usual, and visited her daughter, Maria Louisa, then a lovely child not more than eight years old. Before night she had swallowed the draught that killed her. Eighteen years afterwards that lovely child, who inherited much of the character and beauty, and far too much of the fate of her mother, as Queen of Spain, took from the hands of an attendant a glass of milk, and within a few hourse was a corpse. Trouble and trial commenced their work with this afflicted family at its root.

The Duke of Orleans married again, his second wife being Charlotte Elizabeth of Bavaria. This lady's own description of herself will serve for her portrait. In her memoirs she says, "I must be very ugly: I have no features, small eyes, a snub nose, long and flat lips—poor elements wherewith to compound a physiognomy. I have large pendant cheeks and a broad face. My stature is short, and my person large; both my body and legs are short; altogether I am a fright." There is no reason to doubt the correctness of the drawing. When the Duke of Orleans first saw his wife in Paris, after he had been married to her by proxy, he could not conceal his disappointment and chagrin. "In truth," writes the good-humoured Duchess, "I was not surprised at this, on account of my ugliness. However, I resolved to live on good terms with Monsieur, in order that my attentions might habituate him to me, and that at length he might find me endurable, which was the result in the end." The Duke, surrounded by worthless favourites of either sex, proposed to the Duchess, after the birth of a second child, that for the future they should occupy separate apartments. The Duchess, always compliant, and whose sole desire was that she and her husband might live together on terms of mutual forbearance, had peculiar reasons for acquiescence instantly and cheerfully in the request. "It was very unpleasant, " writes this very sensible and sharp-witted woman, "to sleep with Monsieur. He could not bear that any one should touch him during his slumbers: consequently, I had to sleep at the very edge of the bed, whence I often tumbled out on the ground like a sack. I was therefore enchanted when Monsieur in all friendship, and without a quarrel, proposed that we should have separate rooms."

The two children of Philip and Charlotte Elizabeth were the Duc de Chartres, afterwards the Regent Orleans, and Elizabeth, afterwards Duchess of Lorraine. Blunt and rough spoken as the mother might be, she had a rare pride of birth, much dignity, and a sincere love for her offspring. The great affliction of her life was the marriage of her son with Mademoiselle Blois, the natural daughter of Louis XIV. by Madame de Montespan, and the circumstances preceding the marriage are well worth the relating. From the King downwards, every one dreaded to make known to the proud Bavarian princess the alliance upon which the Grand Monarque was resolutely bent. The consent of the Duke of Orleans was obtained as a matter of course; the Duc de Chartres submitted to his father and the King. When the youth finally ventured to communicate the project to his mother, the enraged lady turned him fairly out of doors. When his father attempted to remonstrate, the demeanour of his injured wife sent him abashed and thoroughly ashamed of himself from her presence.

The intended marriage was to be announced at court that evening. An eye-witness, who saw the Duchess promenading the galleries of the palace, describes her as "walking rapidly, taking large strides, waving the handkerchief she held in her hand, weeping without restraint, speaking loudly, gesticulating violently, and looking for all the world like Ceres, when deprived of Proserpine, seeking her furiously, and demanding her from Jupiter." At the supper-table the Duc de Chartres took his place at his mother's side, the King being present, but the ill-favoured yet high-spirited lady took no notice whatever of King, husband, or child. Her eyes filled with tears until the monarch tenderly offered her of some dish upon the table, when the weeper sternly refused the dainty, with no other effect than that of increasing the attentions of the suppliant monarch. Upon quitting the table, his Majesty made Madame a very low bow, "during which," it is written, "she wheeled round so nicely on her heel, that when the King raised his head he saw nothing but her back advanced one step toward the door." The next morning the King held his usual levee of the council after mass. Madame attended. Her son, according to custom, approached to kiss her hand. In presence of the whole court, and to the confusion and amazement of all the spectators, the Duchess greeted her boy with a slap in the face that was heard in the next apartment. The Duc de Chartres married the King's natural daughter nevertheless.

The Duke, his father, died in 1701. A profligate throughout life, he fell at last a victim to sheer gluttony. He had engaged to dine with the King at Marly. Before dinner, Louis reproached his brother for not prohibiting the infidelities of his son, which had grown into a public scandal. Monsieur replied sarcastically, that fathers who led bad lives had no authority over erring children. The rebuke was felt, and led to loud dispute. Monsieur vowed that not one of the promises had been fulfilled which had induced him to allow his son to marry a bastard. The King retorted; the language of both became disgracefully coarse, and might have grown coarser, had not an attendant ventured to inform the royal squabblers that their reciprocal abuse was overheard in the antechamber.

Dinner was announced. The King was passionless at the meal, as a king should be. The Duke was feverish and flushed, but he ate of everything. After dinner the King went to visit James II. of England, an exile at St. Germains. The Duke accompanied his brother to the gates, and then returned to take his usual supper "with the ladies of St. Cloud." He enjoyed the supper even more than the dinner. But during the third course, whilst pouring out a glass of wine, he was observed to speak thick, and to make strange gestures with his hand. The next moment he fell into the arms of his son, in a fit of apoplexy. At three in the morning the King arrived at St. Cloud, and found his brother speechless and insensible. At twelve o'clock the same day he expired. The intelligence was carried at once to the Duchess, who was in her own room when her husband breathed his last. The poor lady could say nothing but "No convent, no convent! let no one speak to me of a convent!" By her marriage contract, the Duchess of Orleans was bound to choose between a convent and a residence at the castle of Montarges, which was her dower, and before the Duke was cold the lady had taken steps to avoid either alternative. Indeed, the breath was hardly out of his body when Louis XIV. and Madame de Maintenon were seen rehearsing the overture of an opera! Glorious age! Magnificent epoch! Who looks one inch deeper for the origin of bloody revolution and European conflagration? The desperate heartlessness, if there were nothing else, explains it all.

The son of the deceased inherited the faults of his father, and, with virtues peculiar to himself, exhibited vices as rare as they were monstrous. His passion for knowledge was intense; he was an excellent linguist, a sound historian, a good mathematician, and an expert naturalist. Devoted to philosophical pursuits, he excelled in chemistry, and prosecuted the study of that infant branch of science with a zeal that drew upon him suspicions rife enough in all countries at the period. At sixteen the future regent had penetrated fields of information at the bare entrance of which royal youth is seldom found. But if the boy was in advance of his princely contemporaries as a lover of learning, he left the whole world behind him in his practice of profligacy and the grossest sensuality. At sixteen, it is said, he had all the experience in vice of a man of sixty. "My son," wrote his mother, "is like Madame de Longueville, who almost died of *ennui* when with her husband in Normandy. He hates *innocent amusements*." His tutor, who lived to be a cardinal, was an atheist, and lost to virtue in every other respect, but his pupil outstripped his master in his mad career of blasphemy and dissipation.

The war of succession found the Duke of Orleans, then in his thirtieth year, intrusted with the command of the army in Italy. There was no evidence of emasculated energy in his military conduct. He inspired confidence by his courage and undoubted skill, and France, from the king to the peasant, paid homage to his genius. Commanding afterwards in Spain, he gained fresh laurels, and returned to Paris after a victorious campaign, to be fêted for his success, and execrated for his continued and glaring impiety. By Louis XIV. and his family the Duke was execrated shortly afterwards on private and especial grounds. Whilst fighting the battles of his country in Spain, it would appear that the young Duke had carried on negotiations somewhat too exclusively on his own account. To put an end to the war his Royal Highness proposed to the allies that he should be placed upon the Spanish throne, upon conditions favourable to the enemy, and likely to conduce to the peace of Europe. The proposition was under consideration when intelligence of the treachery, and documents that confirmed it, reached the court of France, and threw it into panic and consternation.

Other circumstances tended rapidly to establish and extend the Duke's unpopularity. On the 6th of July, 1710, the daughter of the Duke of Orleans (the infamous offspring of an infamous sire) married the Duc de Berri, son of the dauphin of France. On the 9th of April, 1711, as the dauphin was preparing for the chase at Meudon, he was suddenly seized with a fainting fit, and four days afterwards died of the smallpox. The title of "dauphin" was then transferred to the Duke of Burgundy, the late dauphin's eldest surviving son. Early in 1712 the Duchess of Burgundy was attacked with scarlatina. She fell a victim to the disease on the 12th of February. Six days afterwards the Duke her husband died of the same complaint. On the 8th of March their eldest boy shared his parents' fate. Between the Duke of Orleans and the throne of France there interposed, after the decease of the Duc de Berri, only a sickly child at the breast, the remaining son of the Duke of Burgundy. Henrietta of England, Maria Louisa, Queen of Spain, had fallen by the hand of the poisoner; could the wholesale destruction in the family of the King be the work of chance and nature? The facts were remembered and the question was asked. France by common consent accused the Duke of Orleans of being the murderer of his race, and the wretched man reeled under the terrible and unmerited accusation.

Frowned upon at court, insulted by the mob, the Duke of Orleans sought consolation amidst furnaces and alembics, and in orgies at which the Duchess de Berri presided—herself the incarnation of blasphemy and unrestrained licentiousness. The companions of father and daughter were the most corrupted and hardened of their kind, the title to admission to a hellish feast being simply a readiness to laugh at morality and to insult God. But whilst dividing his time between the study of astrology and magical divination, in which he religiously believed, and the profanation of the laws of his Maker, which he sacrilegiously contemned, the extraordinary man of whom we speak found means to repair the reputation accident had broken, and to indemnify himself for the unjust calumnies of a whole people. Louis XIV. was King, parliament, and all. His magnificent will was supreme law, and France, under his rule, answered to his nod as nature moves at the behest of its Creator. The Duke of Orleans, in his disgrace, suddenly conceived the highest reverence for the decrees of parliament, and a boundless respect for its prerogatives. He was familiar with the constitution of England as it had been remodelled under the house of Orange. His sympathies were with the English Whigs, and it grieved him to the heart to note the vast difference between the masculine representative system of the English people, and the feeble and abject name of a system beneath which France groaned. The Duke, wise in his generation, resolved that political liberality should take the place of charity, and cover all his sins. How needy are the spirits of men of the freedom which is the breath of life: how much is overlooked and cheerfully forgiven in the man who, with the power to make his fellow-creatures walk erect, bids them go forth in independent strength, the incredulous now may learn. The Duke of Orleans was the murderer of the dauphins, so it was believed; he dealt in the forbidden arts of magic and necromancy: he had defied Heaven and raised the devil; accusations with respect to his own daughter too terrible to repeat, were the common theme of the multitude; his daring impiety scared the discreet; his disregard of public decency offended even the unscrupulous;—yet it was bruited abroad, in an age of acute, though splendid tyranny, that a prince near to the throne felt for the wrongs of a people, and sighed to give them liberty of soul and body: and in a moment all was forgotten and washed out. The lesson is tremendous; so is another; but will either ever be thoroughly learnt? The Duke of Orleans received the condonation and support of his clients, and then laughed outright at them for their credulity and pains.

Louis XIV. made a will. His grandson was a child when his own foot was at the grave. Dreading a regency which should give uncontrolled power to his nephew, he desired that the regency might consist of a council, at which the Duke of Orleans should sit as president; the remaining members of the council were the Duke's known enemies. The will was deposited with much state and ceremony in the wall of the Parliament House, and after the King's death the solemn document was read. Concerning the death itself little need be said. The King was seventy-seven years old, and he quitted the world with magnanimity. His power during his long and singular reign is known to every boy. His magnificence has passed into a proverb. No monarch had ever been so flattered in life; few have been so insulted in death. His funeral procession was poor and mean. It was a time of general rejoicing. Everybody, according to a contemporary authority, "was eating and drinking along the whole road to St. Denis;" and whilst the coffin was being deposited in its final resting-place, the writers of lampoons, pamphlets, and satires were hard at work at the poor King's expense.

The royal will, we say, was read, and proved waste paper. During the operation the Duke of Orleans took care that the parliament should be surrounded by soldiers, lest the Assembly might object to his Highness's sole regency: but the parliament, eager to welcome a constitutional chief, needed not the touch of the sword to give the Duke of Orleans unlimited power as

Regent of the kingdom. The worst man in France became the first in virtue of a lie. It was a fatal mistake, and has been repeated.

The morals of the court of Louis XIV. were bad enough, but they were pure in comparison with those of the Regency. There was an affectation of stern piety in the midst of fearful libertinism so long as Louis lived. If offences against society and the laws of man and Heaven were hourly perpetrated, shame was not wholly lost in the transgressors. Ladies escaped from the embraces of their paramours to find immediate absolution in the convent. There was a recognition of the claims of morality even whilst they were set at defiance. Madame de Maintenon was a devotee, and Louis XIV., who blazoned forth his adulteries, and set aside the laws of marriage, when he proclaimed the children of his mistress as legitimate as his lawful issue, could remonstrate like a virtuous patriarch with the daring nephew, whose proceedings after all were shaped according to the model supplied him by his uncle. The King cloaked the delinquencies of his court by a specious etiquette, and the practices he pretended to abhor when they assumed the form of naked vice, passed unreproved in the taking garb of knightly gallantry. Upon the death of Louis XIV. the court threw off the hypocritical mask, and gloried in its unblushing infamy. The Regent had no respect for virtue, and no desire to conceal his great contempt for it. Restraint was weakness. The consequence of the change was soon evident enough. Infidelity and immorality, that blazed at the apex of society, found their way rapidly to its broad and wide extended base. Literature reflected the tone of the palace; generally sparkling and clever, the publications of the day were always intolerably indecent. The bloodiest heroes of the revolution were the sons and grandsons of the men who had been taught by their rulers that there is no God in the universe, and no happiness on earth that is not found in the overthrow of the moral sense and in the anarchy of the passions. The rising of the people against authority at the close of the eighteenth century had been preceded by the rising of authority against the people at the beginning of it. There was as clear a renunciation, upon the part of the Regent Orleans and his government, of all the duties they owed to the state, as there was, in 1792, of all the loyalty and obedience due from subjects to the Crown. Had the Duke of Orleans, the nephew of Louis XIV., kept faith with the parliament, his last memorable descendant in all probability would never have reached his kingly eminence or earned his bitter suffering. He broke that faith, he unloosed the bands that kept society together, and so prepared the way for a catastrophe that filled Europe with horror and amazement, but made no impression upon any member of the House of Orleans.

The minister of the Regent was Dubois, who had been his tutor. The character of that worthy has been already briefly given. In his youth he had been an apothecary's apprentice; in his old age he brought up the whole conclave at Rome to "ensure the election of a Pope pledged to the elevation of Dubois," and was made a cardinal, having previously, on account of his desperate immorality, found some difficulty in receiving common ordination. For a financial coadjutor the Duke of Orleans took to himself the celebrated Mr. John Law, who because he was a Protestant could not legally dupe the Roman Catholic population of Paris, and who was therefore made a Roman Catholic for a present of his own banknotes by a perjured abbé, the brother of Dubois' mistress; the very gentleman, by the way, who carried the bribes to the conclave at Rome, and did, in fact, all the dirty work of his sister's holy and powerful protector. Law's skill as a financier in universally appreciated. The exchequer of the Regent was in a deplorable condition, when Law undertook to revive it by a *coup de main.* The professional gambler manufactured notes by the basketful, distributed them, impressed the Parisians with a notion that they were more valuable than specie, and thus providing, for a time at least, against the possibility of their being converted into coin, poured heaps of wealth into a nation that awoke from a delusion to find itself irretrievably bankrupt. Rotten from beginning to end, the kingdom of France passed from the hands of the Regent to those of Louis XV., ripe for the dissolution that awaited it. In 1723, eight years after he had received a sacred trust from the parliament, the Regent transferred it to the King, his nephew, very much the worse for wear. Parliament had been treated with even greater contumely than during the monarchy; and civil and religious liberty, that had expected so much from the promises of selfishness, had been bound down by chains more galling than any it had ever known. Corruption pervaded every branch of the public service, profanity characterized the upper classes, penury and suffering afflicted the lowest. Between the two extremities a disposition had taken root to question the authority of kings and the abiding providence of God.

An incident that occurred during the regency is too remarkable to be overlooked. Dubois proposed a reconciliation between France and Spain. The condition of the minister was the marriage of Louis XV., then twelve years of age, with the Spanish Infanta, upon her arriving at maturity; and this condition was accompanied by another:—the marriage of the Prince of the Asturias, fourteen years of age, with *Mademoiselle de Montpensier, fourth daughter of the Duke of Orleans*, in her thirteenth year. When the marriages were announced in France, it was whispered that the Regent had selected a child for the king in order to increase the chances of his own family in France and Spain. Fifteen years must elapse before an heir could be born to Louis XV.; and in that interval what might not accident or crime achieve? Events, as we have said, repeat themselves.

Upon the 2nd of December, 1723—the year in which Louis XV. ascended the throne of his fathers—his uncle, the ex-regent, dined with the Duchess of Phalaria, his last mistress. During the morning he had received a visit from his physician, who had for some days recommended abstinence and the loss of blood for ailments with which the Duke was troubled. "Wait until to-morrow, my good doctor," said the Duke, "I will enjoy myself to-day." The doctor ventured to remonstrate, but his patient told him that he had more faith in his cook than in his physician, and so dismissed him. After dinner he retired to the apartment of the Duchess, and sat upon a sofa whilst she took a low stool and placed herself at his feet. As her head reposed upon his knees the Duke bade her relate one of those lively stories which she could so well tell. "Once upon a time," began the Duchess, "there lived a king and a Queen." The words were hardly uttered before the Duke's head sank on his breast, and he fell sideways on her shoulder. The lady went on with her story; she had often before sung her lover to sleep; but his limbs stiffened, and then she sprang to the bell and rang it violently. No one answered. The accident had happened when everybody was either occupied or away. Half an hour elapsed before a doctor could be brought, and he came in time to find the Duke dead. So disappeared the royal philosopher and sensualist. One may charitably conclude that a spark of honest shame still lingered in the land defiled by the wickedness which the deceased had so largely helped to create; for we read that no real mourner presented himself at the cold funeral of the Duke of Orleans, and that the Bishop of Angers, who delivered the last oration at the tomb, declined to bestow any eulogy upon the departed.

CHAPTER THE SECOND.

Louis Philippe of Orleans, son of the Regent, was born August 4, 1703. According to his father's description, the youth, deformed in person and dull in intellect, united in himself the defects of all the other princes of the blood. But, whatsoever the deficiencies of his mind, blame rested with that unworthy father alone: not the slightest attention had been paid to the boy's education. The Palais Royal was his home when that palace was a den of infamy; through its dissipated circles he was allowed to wander at will, and with the eager interest of thoughtless childhood, listened intently to conversation which manhood, if not lost to shame, could not hear without a blush. Fortunately for the youth, a tutor was found at an early age, who contrived to chain his passions down by the most extraordinary revelation concerning the punishments of Hell. Religious asceticism saved the Regent's son possibly from the Regent's fate. The fashion of the day compelled the young Duke to take an opera dancer for his mistress, but such time as he passed with the lady he generally employed in a harmless endeavour to convince her of the truth of the metempsychosis theory, in which he himself devoutly believed. It is difficult to overrate the great benefit conferred upon the Duke by his stern and astute preceptor. Upon one occasion, after the Duke had passed some hours in the Queen's apartment, no one being present but her majesty, the young man suddenly fell upon his knees and spent several minutes in prayer, earnestly supplicating God to pardon the thoughts which, during the interview, had presented themselves to his imagination. The Queen used to relate the incident as one in which perfect gallantry and perfect piety met in combination.

Nothwithstanding the pious tendencies of the Duke, however, he contrived, like the more worldly, to have an eye for business. So long as the Queen of Louis XV. continued childless, he remained at court vigilantly watching the chances that might transfer to him the prize to which his family looked in vain for years, and reached at last only to grasp, and then renounce it; making his game, and preparing foı contingencies. From his sire he had learned to court alliance with England, to advocate peace, and to hate with all his heart the Spanish branch of the house of Bourbon. When, on the 4th of December, 1729, the birth of a Dauphin was announced, the Duke, who had nothing to gain from public life, withdrew within the sphere most congenial to his habits. He applied himself exclusively to the study of theology, and of the languages connected with biblical lilerature. Regarding himself as a divinely appointed missionary, he plunged into polemics, and wrote treatises too learned to be generally appreciated, and, indeed, too metaphysical to be thoroughly understood by any one. He wasted entire days in the convent of St. Geneviève, disputing with the fathers of the monastery upon the punctuation of a verse in the Bible, or concerning the exact locality of the Garden of Eden. No religious procession took place in which he had not a part; and the parochial clergymen, whilst he lived, were never without an assistant in catechising the poorer children. Earnest and harmless occupation gains respect at all times. When piety tinctures the labour, it commands our homage. We may smile for a moment at the proceedings of the deformed son of the Regent Orleans, but the feeling of pity is transient, and gives place to a nobler. He died February 4, 1752, bequeathing all his manuscripts to the Jacobin Fathers; he had already founded a professorship of biblical Hebrew at the Sorbonne, "in order that heretics should not be the only Christians who studied the Holy Scriptures in their original languages."

The devout Duke of Orleans left a son, Louis Philippe of Orleans, who was born at Versailles, May 12, 1725. History has preserved few records of this prince's life, but such as we pick up are characteristic enough of the race, and leave no doubt as to the identity. In selecting a wife for his son, the Duc de Chartres, Louis Philippe's first and sole consideration was to obtain for him the largest dowry that the country could produce; his extravagance had crippled his own splendid resources, and his meanness in pecuniary transactions rendered him unscrupulous in the mode of repairing them. The exquisite cold-bloodedness of this whole affair, the profound indifference of the father for the happiness of his son, the utter disregard exhibited by the calculator for the feelings of the lady chiefly concerned in his negotiation, are all striking points in the otherwise commonplace character now upon our stage. Louis XIV. had heaped treasures upon his natural children. At the time of which we speak, the inheritance of all was about to devolve upon M. de Lamballe and Mademoiselle de Penthièvre, the surviving children of the Duc de Penthièvre, the event waiting only for the death of the Count d'Eu, a bachelor advanced in life, and in indifferent health. When Mademoiselle Penthièvre was first proposed to the Duke of Orleans as a suitable wife for his successor, the Duke is said to have betrayed the strongest indignation. The lady was descended from the bastards, the declared enemies of the house of

Orleans; that was impediment enough, but it might have been removed. Again, her fortune, though large, was not the largest in the kingdom—that obstacle was insuperable. The admirable parent would not listen to the proposition; not then, at least. Afterwards, circumstances occurred to render him more tractable. M. de Lamballe, joint heir with the young lady, was suddenly attacked with a painful disease, and was compelled to submit to a still more painful operation; the doctors pronounced the sufferer in most imminent danger. Should he die, Mademoiselle de Penthièvre would eventually inherit no less a sum than 120,000*l*. per annum. The Duke of Orleans asked for the young lady in marriage for his son immediately.

But M. de Lamballe was not yet dead. As he was oscillating between this world and the next, the Duke of Orleans occupied himself in investigating the family papers. The Duc de Penthièvre, who gave his consent to the match, generously showed the Duke of Orleans his will, besides making known to him his present intentions with regard to his daughter. The generosity was thrown away upon a gentleman who was simply disgusted at the pitiful allowance which the Duke proposed for his child during his own life-time, but he consoled himself, like a prudent man and a good father, with the thought of poor M. de Lambelle's approaching dissolution. M. de Lamballe, however, was not yet dead. On the contrary, to the astonishment of everybody, a change took place for the better. It was enough for Louis Philippe, Duke of Orleans;

by this time Mademoiselle de Penthièvre was over head and ears in love with the Duc de Chartres, but what was that to the purpose? Half the girl's fortune would go should M. de Lamballe recover; he was recovering very fast, and accordingly, the Duke of Orleans broke off the match *instanter*, and once more scouted all idea of union with virtuous indignation. His son should have nothing to say to bastards.

The fiend was very busy with the Duke. The politic gentleman had secured the natural anger of M. de Penthièvre, the fury of the Duc de Choiseul, who had made up the match, and the scorn of all right-hearted men, when M. de Lamballe suddenly suffered a relapse, from which everybody agreed he could not possibly recover, and he did not recover. He died, leaving Mademoiselle de Penthièvre heiress to a fortune which a king need not disdain. As we have seen, the Duke of Orleans had been very far from disdaining it. Yet he had suffered it to slip through his fingers. Not he; his was a happy nature, that suffered him to go forward or to go backward precisely as it suited his convenience, and answered his purpose. Mademoiselle de Penthièvre is described by all the writers of her time as the gentlest and the most timid of her sex, but her devotion to the Duc de Chartres elicited the strong passion that lies slumbering in the feeblest woman's breast. She had already vowed to end her days in the cloister, when the incorrigible Duke once more ventured, and successfully, to trade upon her affection, and to open fresh negotiations for the union.

Would that he had lived to see the full-blown triumph of his scheming! Greater splendour had never been witnessed at a wedding feast than that which adorned the celebration at Versailles in the month of May, 1768. Greater calamity has never been endured by woman than that suffered by Mademoiselle de Penthièvre in consequence of that alliance. No doubt the Duke of Orleans would have sold his soul to obtain the largest dowry in the kingdom for his son; to secure a tolerably good one he, in fact, considerably tarnished that better portion of his nature; yet poor Mademoiselle, sweet-tempered, delicately fashioned, bashful, and modest, lived to see her husband without a shilling to buy a poor man's prayers as he laid his head upon the block, and to know that her children were beggars and outcasts, driven through the world without a name—without a home!

A few words must suffice to dismiss the grandson of the Regent from the scene. We have too much to say of his wretched son, the husband of Mademoiselle de Penthièvre, of his unfortunate grandsons, her children, to admit of lingering on the way. Indeed, his history is soon told. It has been stated he was born in 1725. At the age of thirteen he was appointed to a regiment of infantry. At the affair of Dettingen he served with honour, and he was present at the battles of Fontenoy, Harcourt, and Lawfeld, "besides taking an active part in the sieges which have established the martial reputation of Marshal Saxe." The last of his exploits was in 1757, when he served under Marshal d'Estrés, and contributed largely, according to contemporary accounts, to the great victory obtained by the Marshal over the English at Hastenbeck. At court he was a simple spectator of the political vicissitudes of his age, contenting himself with enacting the parts which Madame de Pompadour assigned to him in the dramatic representations set on foot within the precincts of the Palace for the amusement of the King. The sensual indulgence and abominable selfishness of Louis XV., immersed in the frivolities and hollow etiquette of a corrupt court, contrasted disadvantageously with the simpler life of a prince, who recommended himself to the people by the apparent amiability of his manners, and the kindliness of his disposition. Louis Philippe would not have been an Orleans had he failed quietly to make the most of his favourable position. We learn, during the extravagant and impolitic festivities held in 1770, to celebrate the marriage of the Dauphin with Marie Antoinette, whilst France heaved beneath the miseries of a consuming famine, how a horrible accident occurred at the Place de Louis XV., in which 1,200 lives were sacrificed: how insensible to the sufferings of the poor were the Counts of Provence and Artois (better known afterwards as Louis XVIII., and Charles X.), and how tenderly solicitous for the welfare of the people were the Duke of Orleans and his son. Nothing, it is stated, could exceed the fervour with which father and son personally attended to the distresses and complaints of all comers. They opened the Palais Royal to the houseless and necessitous, and distributed bread, wine, and medicine, with their own hands. No wonder when, in 1785, Louis Philippe, in his sixtieth year, fell a victim to an attack of gout, that the people of the capital playfully called him "King of Paris," by way of distinguishing him from the actual King, who kept himself aloof from his subjects at Versailles; no wonder that the ancient jealousies between the elder and the younger branches of the house of Bourbon were rather keener, and more bitter than they had been a century before.

We approach the history of our own times,—the characters, events, and passions with which we are familiar, either from our own observation, or from the records transmitted by our immediate predecessors. We are within hearing of the mighty din of civil war, and within sight of the melancholy spectacle of European conflagration. The scene changes. The gaudy tinsel, the splendid immorality, the god-like sway of royalty, rotten to its core, passes away, and leaves behind an empty throne for ignorance to outrage, for brutal vengeance to besmear with blood. When the father of the late King of the French became Duke of Orleans, in 1785, debauchery and blasphemy, selfishness and impious neglect in high places, had done their worst. An angel from Heaven interposing might have stayed the oncoming flood; but nothing short of miraculous interposition could have saved France from the legitimate consequences of its own unparalleled infamy. A rapid stride had been made in political knowledge within the briefest possible space of time, but the alphabet of morals, and the social virtues, had yet to be acquired. One stands aghast in presence of the hideous picture. Blame not shivering poverty, taught by its rulers to scoff at Heaven, and to laugh down truth! Vent not your indignation upon wild ignorance raging through the streets, a knife in one hand, and a flaming torch in the other! Pity, if you will, the illustrious victims of their own tremendous folly and unpardonable neglect of duty, but attempt not to entangle the links of cause and effect, or to pronounce an act of suicide a deliberate, cold-blooded, and unauthorised murder.

Louis Philippe Joseph of Orleans was born at the Palace of St. Cloud, April 17, 1747. His father, as already stated, was mourned at his death as "King of Paris." He himself, from his youth upwards, seems to have been morbidly ambitious of the same distinction. His great-grandfather, the Regent, had united in his person the characters of a libertine and a popular leader. The model was not of the best, but it was adopted. Times, it is true, were altered. The orgies of the Palais Royal, presided over by the Duchess de Berri, could not be repeated, and the liberty of the people had acquired a new definition. Still the change was but an alteration of costume. Louis Philippe, or "Egalité," as he afterwards styled himself, could not wear his ancestor's enormous wig and heavy armour as a modern Colonel of Hussars, though the same martial spirit beat within his breast. The Regent delighted in atheism and midnight revelries. Egalité toasted women in wine, patronised horse-racing, and the dependent sciences, and was a modern rake. The gentleman in armour stood up for Parliament, and the principal of popular representation; the Hussar was a Radical, a Chartist, a six-point man, and something more. If plain truth must be spoken, Egalité overdid his part, and so failed. Like Renault, the conspirator, in *Venice*

Preserved, he conspired too much, and betrayed his insincerity by the vehemence of his protestations.

The hospitalities of the Palais Royal during the days of Egalité were universally celebrated. Learning was courted, and patriotism was banqueted in the halls. Buffon was the intimate friend and associate of the Duke, Franklin his constant visitor, and Voltaire, who arrived in Paris in the spring of 1788, to be rejected at court, was not only received at the Palais Royal, but was permitted to stand in the presence of the master of the house. The first visit of the cynic is worth noticing. The Duchess was in bed at the time, but she hurried down, half dressed, to welcome the illustrious guest. Voltaire asked to see the children; they appeared, and the philosopher, taking especial notice of the eldest boy, the late Count de Neuilly, said that he reminded him forcibly of the Regent. In his twenty-fifth year, Egalité, then Duc de Chartres, entered the naval service of his country as *Garde de la Marine*, a rank equivalent to that of English midshipman. In 1778 he was raised to the rank of Lieutenant-General of Marines, and was appointed Inspector-General of the Northern parts of France. The war breaking out with England during that year, the Duc de Chartres joined the French fleet under the Count d'Orvillers, and on the 27th of July took part in the attack upon the English fleet, under Keppel and Palliser, which ended in the trial of Keppel and Palliser by courts-martial in their own country, and in fixing a stigma of cowardice upon the young Duke, which his subsequent career could not efface. Marie Antoinette, the wife of Louis XVI., caused it to be industriously circulated that, during the whole engagement, the valiant Duc de Chartres had quietly waited the issue of events in the hold of his vessel. The Duke traced the report to its source. Her Majesty had committed a fault. Egalité esteemed it a crime, and through life treated the criminal accordingly.

In 1779 the Duc de Chartres finally quitted the navy, and was appointed by the King Colonel-General of the Hussars and light troops, with the command of a regiment. In 1784 he visited England, and became the intimate of George IV., then Prince of Wales, joining in all the dissipation for which the youth of that Prince was remarkable, and taking his place amongst that group of choice spirits who surrounded and took possession of the heir-apparent, with the view of showing him how manly recreation may be made to consist in the prosecution of the lowest pursuits of which the human mind is capable. In 1785 Egalité, as we have noted, succeeded his father, and in 1786 he returned to England with the view of offering the Prince of Wales the loan of a sum of money sufficient to pay his heavy debts. Fortunately for the Prince and for his country, English gentlemen, aware of the negotiation, put a stop to it, and spared the King's son so deep a humiliation. To transplant the pleasures of England to the soil of France was a natural movement. Betting and horse-racing in France acquired an alarming popu larity. The Duke of Orleans placed no limits to h. gambling, and his example spread far and wide. It is related that he gave great offence to the court at this period by the downright republican spirit of all his pleasures and tastes. Once he laid a wager with the Count d'Artois; he backed his horse against the Count's for, we forget how many thousands; the trial came off, a crowd of poor people assembled to witness it: the Duke won, and, on the spot, distributed his winnings to the mob. The trick was worthy of "The King of Paris." But this was not all. The offences of Egalité against the constituted order of things carried consternation to the remotest recesses of the court, and are, indeed, too numerous to mention. He was the first of French gentlemen to discard the use of hair-powder; he banished breeches, and introduced pantaloons; in half-dress he wore boots instead of shoes, with enormous silver buckles; he drove his own phaeton when it was decidedly low for a man of fashion to handle the ribands; he was ready to ride his own horse against any jockey for any sum; and he formed one of the party which made the first successful balloon ascent in Paris on the 17th day of June, 1784. There was no limit to his plebeian propensities. "Our cousin," the great people used to say, "comes very seldom to court since he has turned shopkeeper." The sneer had reference to the galleries and arches of shops built by the Duke under his own rooms in the Palais Royal, with the unprincely, but still very sensible design, of adding to a considerably damaged income.

In the spring of 1787 matters looked ominous enough in France. We have already dwelt upon the accumulated wrongs of generations remorselessly heaped up, as though there were no retribution either on earth or in heaven. At the time to which we refer, public attention was directed especially to one of many grievances—the first to excite the unappeasable anger of the oppressed, the last from which mediocrity is able to devise escape;—the finances of the country were in inextricable confusion. The system of taxation, intolerable in itself, failed to supply the wants of the Exchequer. Two-thirds of France belonged to the privileged classes, who, in virtue of their privileges, were exempt altogether from taxation; the unprivileged suffered, of course, in proportion to the immunity enjoyed by their fellows. There is no need to recapitulate the hardships borne by the peasantry of France upon the eve of the revolution —to repeat the deplorable recital found in every historian of the period. Suffice it to say that the crisis of the time was a monetary one. The deficit since 1776 amounted to 66,000,000*l.* sterling, and was increasing at the rate of 6,000,000*l.* per annum. On the 19th of November, 1787, the King, accompanied by his ministers, went down to parliament and presented a project for a gradual loan. It was received with dissatisfaction, and his Majesty was implored to convoke the States-General for the purpose of obtaining measures that would save the country from utter ruin. The votes were about to be taken, when ministers, perceiving that they would be left in a minority, declared that no vote could be received in the presence of the King. The law being thus interpreted, two edicts were read, one establishing the gradual loan, the other convening the States-General in five years. The keeper of the Seals was about to complete the enrolment when the Duke of Orleans, amidst the profound silence of the assembly, rose, and in the presence of the King protested against the act as illegal. His Royal Highness was joined by others in the remonstrance, and on the following day was banished by royal ordinance to his estates at Villers Cotterets, his brother-offenders being dispatched to the Hières Islands. The Duke's misfortune was a triumph. The world flocked to him in his disgrace, the King received a petition for his recall which had nothing of humility about it but its title. On the 17th of April, 1788, the exile was suffered to return, and the States-General were ordered to be convoked forthwith."

The winter of 1788-9 was unusually severe. The Duke of Orleans kept open house for the famishing poor. Driving one day through the Faubourg de St. Germain, he was so affected by the misery he there beheld, that he stopped, hired spacious apartments on the spot, and converted the rooms into a public kitchen, from which, at his own expense, he distributed a daily supply of food to all who chose to apply for it. Was not this a "King of Paris" indeed? About the same time the Duke published "a circular of instructions to the constituencies in electing deputies," a document containing the writer's confession of political faith, and pronouncing his own severance from the King and the court. "The effect of these instructions," says a modern writer, "was unparalleled. Whenever the Duke appeared in public, the very air rang with shouts of applause. Never did the presence of Titus,—never did that of Henri Quatre, excite higher or more rapturous transports." Did he visit the theatre the performances were suspended that actors and audience might join in one tumultuous welcome of the hero. Was he met in the public walks, the enthusiasm of idolatry knew no bounds. Did he present himself to the people, surrounded by his family, the people threw themselves at the feet of their benefactor, and loaded him with blessings. A "King of Paris" truly!

The elections to the States-General took place throughout France between the 10th and 16th of March, 1789. The Duke of Orleans was returned by the *noblesse* for Paris and by the *bailliages* of Villers Cotterets and Crespy-en-Valois. He made his selection for Crespy, and presented himself as a deputy of the *Tiers Etat.* As he passed in the procession, which preceded the opening of the States-General, he was vociferously cheered by the populace, who suffered the Royal Family to pass on in silence. On the 3d of May, 1789, the States-General met at Versailles, under the auspices of the King himself. The three orders having taken their places, Louis XVI. looked amongst the princes of the blood for the Duke of Orleans. The ostentatious democrat had taken his place amongst the deputies of his baillage. When summoned to his proper seat the duke declined to occupy it. "Sire," said the Prince, "my birth gives me *always* the *right* to be near your Majesty; my duty at this moment bids me take the rank assigned me by the baillage that has deputed me." The monarch made no answer; the popular deputies were exultant.

The next day the three orders assembled. An important question arose, which placed the nobility and clergy at issue with the *Tiers Etat.* A fierce struggle ensued; a large section of the clergy soon made common cause with the commons, but the nobles were obdurate. The Duke of Orleans proposed that the nobles should give way, and when the latter refused, and addressed the King, complaining of the exorbitant claims advanced by the commons, the Duke boldly took part with the representatives of the people, and protested against the address forwarded by the nobles to the King. The protest had a remarkable result. On the 25th of May, the Duke of Orleans, with some eight-and-forty peers, seceded in a body and joined the commons; the majority of the clergy had already preceded them, and the united faction arrogated to itself the title of "the National Assembly." Of this National Assembly the Duke of Orleans was elected first President by 533 out of 660 votes. His time was not yet come, and Egalité declined the proffered distinction.

Events now thickened, and, after a short struggle between the weak King and the National Assembly, the peasants rose throughout France against their feudal lords. France awoke from a dream, but the daylight came too suddenly. It blinded men, and made them mad. Whilst the peasants, looking upon a rich man's house as a bastile, attacked and pillaged it, leaving marks of blood at every hearth, the National Assembly, affrighted, made concessions to the people in the spirit of frenzy. A few years before, the people were unworthy of any rights whatever; now nobody but themselves had any rights to be respected. Such was the desperate movement of terror hurried to folly by a consciousness of deep injustice. On the night of the 5th of August, the Assembly passed sweeping resolutions in favour of the populace, which the King was fain to accept, together with the altogether unmerited title of "Restorer of French Liberty." In the moment of accepting them he secretly resolved never to abide by them. So revolutions advance.

The Duke of Orleans, throughout the whole of these proceedings, had continued a passive spectator of the storm, although his friends had been busy enough, suggesting the necessity of dethroning Louis XVI., and of proclaiming the Duke Lieutenant-General of the kingdom. In the midst of their intrigues, the King, by a master-stroke of policy, appointed the Duke of Orleans Ambassador-Extraordinary to England. The National Assembly protested against his departure—the citizens of Boulogne would have prevented his embarkation. The Duke, however, set out. The step was a false one; but Egalité, with all his egregious vanity and love of popular applause, had neither strength of purpose to sustain, nor lofty principle to guide him. His desertion of the King and his flattery of the people had their origin in one and the same high sentiment—intense devotion to himself.

On the 4th of February, 1790, Louis XVI. took an oath of fidelity to the new constitution prepared for France, and to this constitution the Duke of Orleans sent in his adhesion on the 13th of the same month. On the 14th of July, the anniversary of the storming of the Bastile, a national solemnity took place, at which the King and the authorities assembled round "the altar of the country," and ratified the pledge given in the preceding February. A universal amnesty was proclaimed, and peace and the promise of liberty for a moment glimmered upon the soil of France. How that promise faded almost as soon as it appeared the world too well knows. Upon the 10th of August, 1792. Louis XVI. ceased to be king of France. Popular fury was that day at its height; an accident led to a collision between the guards and the mob, and, whilst blood flowed in the streets, the Assembly, at the instigation of the Clubs, decreed the suspension of the constitutional powers of the King, and the speedy convocation of a National Convention, elected by all classes of citizens, and charged to decide finally upon the destinies of the country.

The fate of France was in the balance—so was that of the Duke of Orleans. By a singular concatenation of events, the popularity of the unfortunate Egalité had tumbled down from boiling point to zero. His admirably arranged contrivances had left him without a party, almost without a friend in the world. His adherence to the popular cause had robbed him of the sympathies of the court, and the agitation of the clubs at the time of the revolution deposited him miles in the rear of public opinion. Democratic leaders of the people wanted no princely rivals. A man who had played false to his own family could hardly be trusted by strangers. And, if he might, what had royal blood to do with a convention elected by all classes of the people, and rendered necessary by royal treachery and oppression? The clubs of Paris were grateful to the Duke of Orleans for having helped democracy so far on its journey. Democracy could find its further way alone, and begged respectfully to part company. Nor was this the only blow. The Duke was a ruined man in his fortunes. He had lived unhappily with his wife, and that much-injured lady, scandalized by his open adultery with Madame de Genlis, to whom he transferred the care and education of his children, after repeated attempts to reconcile herself to the shame of her position, finally quitted her husband's roof on the twenty-first anniversary of her marriage, and retired to the Chateau d'Eu, the residence of her father. The family of the Duchess at once commenced a lawsuit for the recovery of her dowry. It was plain to the Duke that such a lawsuit could have but one termination. Bankruptcy in every shape stared him in the face. Gamester as he was in feeling and in conduct, at the last hour of his life he staked every thing upon the hazard of a die.

A decree against all emigrants was hurriedly adopted by the Executive Council, who did the King's work until the Convention should assemble. The Duke of Orleans entreated that his daughter, who had gone to England with Madame de Genlis for the benefit of her health, might not be included in the list. He was desired to draw up a formal requisition; he did so, and presented it to the Procureur Syndic at the Hotel de Ville. A petition signed by a Bourbon could not be received. What was to be done? The statues of Liberty and Equality adorned the apartment of the Hotel de Ville in which the Duke found himself. The Procureur Syndic seriously proposed one of the statues as a sponsor for the Duke in the baptism which had now become inevitable. His royal highness submitted. He signed his petition as "Philip Egalité," and by that name was thenceforth known.

Philip Egalité became a candidate for the National Convention in the city of Paris, and was returned, but he was one of a society who had no sympathies in common with him. The clubs of Paris, and not the people of France, were represented in that dreadful Assembly. On the 5th of December, the first year of the republic, the Municipality of Paris commanded that Madame de Genlis and the Princess (who had previously returned from England) should quit Paris in twenty-four hours, and France within forty-eight. They were conducted beyond the frontier by the eldest son of Egalité, the Duc de Chartres, the Louis Philippe of our own day, who left his sister at Tournai, and returned to Paris, in the hope of being able to persuade his luckless father to quit a scene of too evident danger. Egalité, bent upon his destruction, obstinately refused to move; like a lunatic he smiled upon the advancing waters that were about to embrace and drown him.

Two questions were put to the National Convention on the 15th of January, 1793. The first was, "Is Louis XVI. guilty of conspiracy against the liberty of the nation, and of treason against the safety of the state?" Of course he was, or the question would never have been put. The second was answered differently. —"Shall the judgment of the National Convention against Louis XVI. be submitted to the ratification of the people?" 286 voices said "Yes;" 424 answered "No;" five votes were given conditionally. A third question was put on the following day. It was a solemn one, and was addressed individually by the President to every deputy,—"What punishment shall be inflicted on Louis?" Philip Egalité was a deputy, and in due order the momentous question came to him. Let the subsequent punishment of the man plead for him whilst we register his reply:—"Solely occupied by my duties, and convinced that those who have conspired, or may conspire, against the sovereignty of the people, merit death, *I vote for death!*" A thrill of horror pervaded that dread assembly, filled with men in whom the sense of humanity was all but extinct. When will posterity cease to shudder at an act for which the vocabulary of crime supplies no fitting name?

The avenger was at the heels of the murderer. His crime left him desolate in the world. His wife and children stood aloof from his guilt. His boys upon their knees, and sobbing as children sob, had entreated him to take no part in the unauthorized murder, and they quitted his side when protestations and entreaties proved in vain. As for the Jacobin crew, to please whom he had stamped the name of Orleans with eternal blackness, they learned nothing from his republicanism but a still stronger hatred for the Bourbon blood, that, in spite of his new baptism, still flowed in Philip Egaité's veins. There needs no offence to be committed by the man whose death is already decided by those who have power to put their will into execution. The National Convention suddenly discovered that "it had always been intended to comprehend Louis Philippe Joseph Egalité in the decree which ordained the arrest of the Bourbons," and Philip Egalité was accordingly arrested. The wretched prisoner, with his young son the Count de Beaujolais, was sent to Marseilles, where the father wes doomed to find in captivity, another son, the Duc de Montpensier, whom he believed to be then serving in the army of Italy as Adjutant-General. One morning, during the captivity of the family at Marseilles, the Duc de Montpensier was awoke by his father, who entered his dungeon accompanied by strangers. "I come, my child," said the Duke of Orleans," to bid you adieu. I am just setting off." The youth, unable to speak, pressed his father to his bosom and wept. "I meant," continued the afflicted parent. "to have gone without saying farewell, for such moments are always painful. But I could not resist the desire of seeing you once more before my departure. Adieu, my child, console yourself, console your brother, and think how happy we shall be when next we meet." So father and child separated, but never to meet again.

The trial of Philip Egalité took place in Paris on the 6th of November following. In truth, there was no accusation against him, and no evidence was adduced. He was interrogated, and his replies were all that his judges had before them to guide them to their verdict. Philip Egalité was pronounced guilty, and guilty Heaven and his own conscience knew him to be, but not against the republic, which he had only too eagerly served; not against the people, whose willing slave he had been, even to his destruction and lasting infamy. The Duke knew from experience what the verdict meant. He said nothing, he asked nothing, but to be led to death that moment.

Philip Egalité quitted the world with a finer spirit than he had engaged in its anxious and unthankful pursuits. When brought back to his prison a delegate waited upon him for his confession. The Duke answered, he had none to make; he bore no animosity against his tribunal; he wished to die forgiving all men. A fellow-prisoner, the Abbé Lothringer, administered to him the last rites of the Church, and at half-past three o'clock he took his place, with a resigned and calm demeanour, in the cart which was to conduct him to the scaffold. "I am bound to say," writes a royalist, himself a prisoner at the time, and an observer of his movements at this moment, "that, from his proud and steady march, and his truly noble air, he might have been taken for a general commanding his troops rather than a victim led to execution." On his road to the place of punishment he passed the Palais Royal. The words "National Property" were inscribed upon his home. The victim gave way and wept. His confessor whispered consolation, but obtained no answer. Death could not inflict so sharp a pang as had been already felt. Reaching the scaffold, however, the Prince forgot the scene he had passed, and resumed his first serenity. He embraced his confessor and delivered himself to the executioner, bidding him make haste. The stroke was given, and the body was buried without ceremony in the cemetery of the Madeleine.

So perished the father of Louis Philippe, but yesterday King of the French!—sacrificed by Jacobins, himself a Jacobin, the victim of a republic which he had largely helped to constitute and fashion. Had the kings of his race been faithful to their mission, France would have known no republic, and the exigencies of the state would not have demanded the shedding of Bourbon blood, though purified by flowing through the veins of an Orleans. Louis XVI. and Philip Egalité were murdered men, but very far from guiltless. How far they were guilty, it became the paramount duty of their immediate descendants to learn, in order that their mistakes might be rectified, and their cruel fate avoided. The lesson has been preached in vain. Where is now the legitimate successor of the sixteenth Louis; where the representative of the house of Orleans?

CHAPTER THE LAST.

Who says that suffering is the monitor of kings? When has it ever proved so? What instruction gained Charles II. from the murder committed at Whitehall? Of what use to James II. were his father's invited misfortunes and his own compelled banishment? Louis XVI. might have never lived, the history of France never been written, for any advantage derived from either by the feeble and effete Charles X. No man living or dead ever passed through such an apprenticeship for the business of his later life as that forced upon Louis Philippe, King of the French, and yet how has the painful lesson been thrown away! Never had prince greater opportunity for the acquirement of the knowledge for the want of which kings fail and command the sympathy of meaner men. The page of history was open before him; the records of his own house were a history in themselves. He had himself been cast upon the world nameless, houseless, the companion of the unfortunate, the associate of the poor. With his own eyes he had witnessed the wrongs of society, with his own ears he had heard its loud and just complaints. Unknown and unrecognised, he had moved against his fellows, and communed with them upon the same low level. Flattery came not to him to beguile, or hypocrisy to mislead his better judgment. He passed into exile with all the experience furnished him by the fate of his family; he issued from it with all the further experience derived from his own personal intimacy with mankind. In vain! Suffering teaches heroism, or it confirms obstinacy.

Poverty closes the heart entirely, or opens it to Paradise. It is now our task to describe the checkered fortunes of Louis Philippe, Count de Neuilly.

Louis Philippe of Orleans, Duc de Valois at his birth, Duc de Chartres on the death of his grandfather, Duke of Orleans on the death of his father, King of the French in 1830, was born at the Palais Royal, October 6, 1773. He was one of five children. His brothers were the Duc de Montpensier, born in 1775, and the Count de Beaujolais, born in 1779; his sisters were Marie Caroline, who died a child, and Eugenie Adelaide, her twin sister, who died at Paris in the winter of 1847. Of this family, Louis Philippe, the first-born, was, a twelvemonth since, the sole survivor. The tutor of all the children was the father's mistress, Madame de Genlis, who appears to have made up for her own misconduct by a scrupulous regard to tbe manners and morals of her pupils. Madame de Genlis, with a strong and well-cultivated mind, was hardly the most fitting person in the world to conduct the education of royal princes. Just before the lady took her youthful charges in hand, Egalité informed her that his eldest boy had given him much pain by acquainting him that he had been "*drumming* at his door all the morning," and by using similar language, indicating the shopkeeper rather than the prince. Madame de Genlis set about crushing the shopkeeper with a vigour that threatened at the same time to stifle nature itself in the character of her pupils. Instead of educating the lads for the great theatre of life, she seems to have been bent upon preparing them for the Théâtre Français. To be born a prince was nothing, unless the prince was sensible of his position, and could act his part. When

Madame de Genlis gave her first lesson to the youthful Louis Philippe, that young gentleman, much to the lady's astonishment, yawned and stretched himself, then threw himself upon a sofa, and perched his legs upon the table. Madame talked sentimentally upon the duties of a prince, and the boy, who, according to the lady, "was as fond of what was reasonable as other children are of what is frivolous," from that moment was cured "of a great many low phrases and of a number of absurd fancies."

A specimen of Madame de Genlis' peculiar system of instruction is worth recording. The mother of her pupils had been staying at Spa for the benefit of her health, and had derived great benefit from the waters of the Sauvenière. Under the guidance of the instructress a *fête* was got up in honor of the event. Near the spring the children constructed a beautiful walk, and otherwise ornamented a very rugged spot. At the end of the walk was a precipice, and beyond that lay a view of great extent and beauty. In the wood, upon a plot of turf, an altar to Gratitude, made of white marble, was raised; on the top of such altar the words "To Gratitude," in very large letters, were written, and below another inscription signified how the children of the Duchess de Chartres had traced the walks and cleared the woods "with more assiduity than the workmen who laboured under their orders." Upon the day of the *fête*, Madame de Genlis invited all the prettiest persons at Spa to come to the fountain at one o'clock in the afternoon, dressed in white; she hired a band of music, and caused the royal children to carry hoes, to signify that they had just finished the walk, which they devoted to their mother; a sentiment which, we are told, "young Louis Philippe expressed with great grace and effect." Then the children disappeared, and the mother, by a circuitous route, was conducted to the altar. There she saw standing four of her children, "forming a charming group," whilst the eldest boy, Louis Philippe again, was seated at the foot of the monument, holding a chisel in his hand, with which he seemed to write on the altar the word "Gratitude." "Every one," naively adds Madame de Genlis, "burst into tears, which proved that the most lively emotions are often produced by the most simple means."

Louis Philippe passed from the hand of his sentimental, but by no means incompetent or unskilful tutor, to step at once into the thorny path of active life. At an early age he entered the army, and on the 20th of November, 1785, inherited the colonelcy of the regiment of cavalry which bore his name. In 1791 we find the Duc de Chartres at Valenciennes, as senior colonel, taking command of the garrison. His attention to military duty had acquired for him the respect of his superiors, and was held up as a pattern to the service. War at this moment had become inevitable. The emigrant nobles, who had left Louis XVI. to make his own terms with his people, had formed an army at Coblentz, and were openly supported by Austria and Prussia. The French Assembly, alarmed by the prospect of invasion, without waiting for attack, resolved to act upon the offensive, and, much against his will, compelled the King, on the 20th of April, 1792, publicly to declare hostilities against Austria and her allies. The campaign was intrusted to Dumouriez, and under this general the Duc de Chartres served. Dumouriez and the young Duc de Chartres were bound together by ties stronger than those that ordinarily attach the soldier to his superior officer. The general had no particular regard for the many-headed master whose orders he obeyed. The Duke, despising the weakness of the King, had no desire whatever to see the monarchy trampled under foot. To preserve the throne in its integrity, and at the same time to give assurance to the people of liberal institutions by taking bodily possession of that throne himself, was an idea worthy of the descendant of the Regent, and as full of promise as of rare temptation. Dumouriez and the Duc de Chartres fought the battles of their country bravely, but the zeal of both found no spur in the love they bore to their immediate employers.

The trial and murder of the King served still further to estrange Dumouriez and his friend from the Assembly, but also put an end immediately to the intentions of the former in favour of the Duke. For the son to aspire to the vacant throne would have been to seal the fate of the father, who had not yet fallen. Even to whisper the desire would have been sufficient to secure the blow which a smaller offence afterwards called down. Dumouriez, in his disgust, contented himself with ostentatiously disregarding the instructions of the Executive Council, and with treating commissioners sent to remonstrate on his disobedience with the most ineffable disdain. Greater prudence would have been more serviceable to his royal *protegé*, who was finally compromised by the general's indiscretion. A defeat, chiefly occasioned by the suicidal rage of the authorities in Paris, who refused to send reinforcements to Dumouriez, brought matters to a crisis. The French commander, burning with vexation and disappointment, proposed to the Austrian colonel to unite with the imperialists, and to march with them upon Paris forthwith. News of his intended desertion reached Paris, and four commissioners accompanied by the minister-at-war, were directed to proceed to the camp to arrest the traitor. The commissioners reached the army on the 2nd of April, 1793, and on the same evening they were quietly arrested themselves by order of Dumouriez. The very next morning the army revolted against their general, and Dumouriez and the young Duke with difficulty escaped with their lives. The Duke pushed on to the head-quarters of the Austrian army at Mons, and, after declining an offer to serve in the ranks of his country's foes, made the best of his way to Switzerland, disguised as an English traveller.

It was not too soon to attempt concealment and disguise. The name of Orleans stood throughout civilised Europe for bloody and unnatural murder. Men shrunk from contact with it, and the very atmosphere was deemed polluted that received the breath of Egalité's unoffending offspring. No wonder that the children themselves were eager to remove from their forehead the sign which made them hateful in the sight of man. The journey to Switzerland was not easy, and the most minute precautions were necessary to avoid detection and insult. Never venturing to appear publicly in the streets or to dine at the *table d' hôte*, Louis Philippe contrived eventually to join his sister and Madame de Genlis at Schaffhausen, and to conduct them in safety to Zurich. At Zurich, the Princess, being recognised in the public square, was openly insulted by an emigrant, who rudely tore away a part of the poor girl's dress with his spur. Almost immediately afterwards, the authorities waited upon the exiles, and told them they must find a resting-place elsewhere. Brother, sister, and governess departed, and secretly retired to Zug, where they took a small house in a secluded situation on the banks of the lake, not far from the town. It was not secluded enough. One night some villains, mistaking the bonnet of the Princess for the Princess herself, threw some heavy stones at the window, which would no doubt have done their work had not Mademoiselle Adelaide fortunately quitted her usual seat for a moment to confer with Madame de Genlis. The notice to quit was emphatic enough. Upon the following morning the ladies sought refuge, under assumed names, in a convent near Bremgarten, and Louis Philippe, the better to insure their safety, became himself a solitary wanderer.

Leaving his sister at the convent, the Duc de Chartres went to Bâle; his means were reduced; he was oblige to sell his horses, and to dismiss all his domestics except one, who had formerly saved his life. Master and servant reached the celebrated *hospice* of St. Gothard, tired and footsore; the Prince rang the bell, and craved refreshment. "There is no admittance here for travellers on foot," was the reply; "certainly not for men of your appearance. Yonder is the house for you," and the monk pointed with his finger to a shed in which some muleteers were eating cheese, and slammed the door in the Prince's face. At Gordona, on another occasion, during a bitter night, Louis Philippe presented himself at a farm-house without luggage, and in somewhat damaged attire. He asked hospitality, and, after much demurring, he was allowed to have a bed of straw in a barn. The future King slept soundly till the break of day, when he awoke to find a young man armed with a gun pacing the floor as sentinel. The appearance of the traveller had excited suspicion in the house, and orders had been given to shoot him if he attempted mischief.

It was whilst pursuing this somewhat ignoble course of life, that a plan was suggested to the young Duke which promised immediate if not lasting relief from his great embarrassment. A gentleman named Chabot-Latour had been invited from Paris to take a professorship in the College of Reichenau. M. Chabot-Latours failed to keep his engagement, and, by the contrivance of the Prince's friends, it was arranged that the Duc de Chartres should appear in the name and place of the absent candidate. The Prince accordingly presented himself for examination, and was unanimously elected, after receiving great commendation for the ability and knowledge he had evinced throughout the ordeal. He was then twenty-two years of age; his salary was about £58 a-year, a larger salary than was usual in Switzerland, and for that sum he taught history, geography, mathematics, and the English language. For the space of one year the Duc de Chartres held the professorship, and none but the director of the institution was aware of the teacher's rank. Louis Philippe was quietly instructing the youth of Reichenau, when he received news of his father's melancholy death, and of his own accession to an an empty blood-stained title. He threw up his appointment at once, and in June, 1794, retired to Bremgarten. He carried along with him an honourable testimonial of the services he had rendered at the academy, and was justly proud of the document when he afterwards sat upon the throne of France, reputed the wisest monarch of his time.

Melancholy and weary of his fate, the exile pined to quit Europe, and in a new world "to forget the greatness and the sufferings which had been the companions of his youth." But he was literally without a farthing. A friend wrote on his behalf to Mr. Morris, who had been ambassador to France from the United States, had been acquainted with Egalité, and was then at Hamburgh, about to return to his native country. Mr. Morris answered the application with promptitude and kindness. He offered the Prince a free passage to America, his services when the exile should arrive there, and, at the same time, he transmitted an order for £100 to defray the expenses of the journey to Hamburgh. The Prince accepted Mr. Morris's friendship in the spirit in which it was offered. "I am quite disposed," he wrote to his benefactor, "to labour in order to make myself independent. I scarcely entered upon life when the greatest misfortunes assailed me; but, thank God, they have not discouraged me. I feel it a great happiness in my reverses that my youth has not given me time to attach myself too much to my position, or to contract habits of life difficult to be broken, and that I had been deprived of my fortune before I was able to abuse or even to use it." It was well and royally said. But how much clearer the intellectual vision of the youth than the maturer eyesight of the man! On the 10th of March, 1795, Louis Philippe quitted Bremgarten, and, travelling still *incognito*, reached Hamburgh at the end of the month.

We have asserted that the opportunities of Louis Philippe for the acquisition of worldly wisdom, from his boyhood upwards, were immense. Let the reader judge as he pursues the singular story. At Hamburgh the Prince missed his friend, who was then employed upon a diplomatic mission in Germany. Some months must elapse before Mr. Morris could return to Hamburgh, and the young adventurer resolved to employ the interval in exploring Northern Europe. The undertaking half a century ago was associated with difficulties unknown to the traveller of to-day. He visited the duchies of Holstein and Schleswig, the island of Zealand, Copenhagen, and Elsinore, and in every place exhibited an honest zeal for information that put suspicion asleep. From Denmark he crossed to Sweden, and thence passed into Norway, making excursions that were remembered long afterwards, to the iron and copper mines of that country. The northward journey did not end even here. The traveller was not content until he had seen the wonders of the Maelström, and had advanced some degrees beyond the Arctic Circle. Returning southwards, the Prince traversed on foot the desert which separates the Northern Ocean from the river Tornea. Fifteen days were occupied in the journey, during which time no other nourishment could be procured than the milk and flesh of the reindeer. Picking up knowledge, and enlarging the range of his acquirements at every step, the youth returned once more to Fredericstadt, in Holstein, at which town he received the gratifying intelligence that the executive directory of France were prepared to grant liberty to his brothers, who had been kept close prisoners since their father's death, upon condition that the Duke of Orleans with them would consent to banishment from Europe. The consent was given as soon as asked, and on the 24th of October, 1796, Louis Philippe landed in Philadelphia; it was not until the 7th of February following that, after a cruel and protracted absence, the three brothers met in the same city, and found in their restoration to one another some consolation for the sufferings long endured by all.

A short visit to the great Washington, then President of the United States, a necessary delay for the arrival of money, and the youths were on their travels again. Arriving at Boston, they learned, to their dismay, that their mother too had been expelled from her native land. Concluding that she would be sent to Cayenne, they determined to reach that colony before her, and proceeded as far as Connecticut on their way. Here they were informed that Spain was her destination. This rendered necessary an alteration of their plans; they would go to Havana, and thence sail direct to Europe. Their road was to New Orleans by the Ohio and the Mississippi, but the winter had set in severely, and the danger and difficulty of the expedition were fearful. So, indeed, they found them. On the Ohio the frost was so bitter that the cider and milk were congealed in the cabin of the boat, although it was heated by a large fire, and by the presence of seven or eight passengers. Four of the boatmen, disabled by cold and fatigue, gave way, and the Princes took their place. Near the point where the Ohio falls into the

Mississippi, at the western extremity of Virginia, matters were even worse, for the travellers having no boatmen with them who knew the river, and could steer the vessel, were obliged, in spite of the cold, to keep watch themselves by day and night. For three hundred leagues at one part of their course they met with but three habitations. After many hardships, from which two of the three adventurers never thoroughly recovered, New Orleans was reached at last, whence they embarked for Cuba on board an American vessel under the Spanish flag. The devoted young men reached Cuba, to be immediately expelled from it by the Captain-General of the island. Orders had been received to deny them hospitality. In their despair the princes resolved to seek shelter in a British colony. They proceeded to the Bahamas, thence to Halifax; and by the kindness of the Duke of Kent, father of our Queen, and then governor of Nova Scotia, were enabled finally to set sail for England. They reached London on the 15th of February, 1800. Their destination, however, was Spain, not England. Obtaining a passage in an English frigate as far as Minorca, they sailed from that island in a Spanish ship to Barcelona. They were now indeed within hail of that dear mother whom they had travelled so far to comfort with their presence; they were, nevertheless, not permitted to land at Barcelona; and the poor lady was not even told that they had reached the harbour on their affectionate pilgrimage. The Princes returned to England, and took up their abode on the banks of the Thames, near Twickenham. Not to remain. The cup of sorrow was full, but did not overflow. The Duc de Montpensier died of consumption, in the arms of his brothers, in 1807, and was buried in Westminster Abbey The funeral was scarcely over before the Count de Beaujolais was attacked with the same disease, and ordered to a warmer climate. Louis Philippe accompanied the invalid to Malta, and reached the island in time to find a final resting-place for the young sufferer. The Count de Beaujolais died at Valetta in 1808. Fortunately for Louis Philippe, he was not left alone in the world. He had still a sister.

After fifteen years' absence brother and sister met again at Portsmouth. The Princess Adelaide had traced the wanderings of the fugitive, after her youngest brother's death, from Malta to Gibraltar, and from Gibraltar to England. She set out to find him. Their meeting is described as most affecting. They vowed to each other never again to separate, and the vow was sacredly kept. In company they proceeded once more in search of their mother. With difficulty they managed to convey a letter to her, fixing a rendezvous at Minorca, and on the 7th of September, 1809, they landed at that island to embrace at last the object of their long and anxious search. After a short sojourn in the island, the three set sail for Palermo, where, on the 25th of the following November, Louis Philippe married the daughter of Ferdinand, King of Naples. In Sicily tranquillity first dawned upon the agitated career of the Duke of Orleans. It was a season of mild repose—a blush of light between the storms. His mother, his sister, and his wife were at his side; children were born unto him; public affairs ceased to harass or depress him: he sought, and found, happiness at the family hearth, where Heaven provides it for the meanest. In the midst of the profound calm there fell a thunderbolt. Napoleon was beaten; Louis XVIII. was restored to the throne of France. Louis Philippe heard the news, and started for Paris that very moment.

Marvellous vicissitudes of life! The man who had been refused his bed of straw at the farmhouse reached the French metropolis, and, scarcely taking time for refreshment, hurried to the Palais Royal to set foot again in his magnificent home. His heart beating high, his soul pierced with a hundred conflicting sensations that expressed themselves in visible tears, the restored heir paced the well-known galleries and visited the well-remembered gardens. The doors of the grand staircase chanced to be opened. The visitor involuntarily entered, but was stopped by a porter still wearing the imperial livery, who said that strangers were not allowed in the private apartments. Louis Philippe, overcome with emotion, fell upon his knees, and in his bewilderment kissed the lowest step of the staircase. He was recognised, and admitted.

Louis XVIII. and Charles X. may be said to have represented the dry sticks of Bourbonism; the sap of the race was gone, the rich blood of Louis Quatorze had ceased to circulate. Whatever was chivalric in the family, whatever heroic, whatever superb, whatsoever could engage the admiration and secure the pride of a people otherwise aggrieved, had departed for ever; whatever was bigoted, oppressive, ignorant, ridiculous, and suicidal, obstinately remained. Louis XVIII. was scarcely on the throne, Louis Philippe hardly housed in the Palais Royal, before intrigues were on foot again to overthrow the old dynasty, and to place the Duke of Orleans at the head of the Constitutional Monarchists. Intriguers on every side were as busy as possible, when the astounding announcement was made that the chained lion at Elba had burst his bonds, and was advancing, with strides such as that lion alone could take, rapidly on Paris. It was enough. Intrigues were postponed for the present. Louis XVIII. as quick as lightning was beyond the frontier. Louis Philippe, accompanied by his family, was again at Twickenham.

Waterloo put matters straight for the Bourbons, had the men been wise enough to keep them so. The first proposition made by the House of Peers on behalf of the restored crown, was that all who had taken any part whatever in the successive revolutions of France should be visited with extreme punishment. Louis Philippe was in his place in parliament when the impolitic measure was proposed. He protested against it loudly and indignantly, and at his instigation the obnoxious motion was rejected without a division. The reader possibly remembers the relative positions of Louis XVI. and Egalité, a generation before. Events repeat themselves. Louis XVIII., considerably disgusted, forbade princes of the blood to appear in the Chamber of Peers unless summoned by special authority. The Duke of Orleans retired into comparative seclusion, and revenged himself upon the court by entering his eldest son as a student in one of the public colleges as a simple citizen. His father had driven his own phaeton, and introduced pantaloons. "I perceive," says Louis XVIII. in his own memoirs, and with touching imbecility, "that although Louis Philippe does not stir, he advances. How must I man age to prevent a man from walking who appears as if he did not make a step? It is a problem which remains for me to solve, and I should be glad not to leave it for solution to my successors." Poor old gentleman! The sum was too difficult both for himself and the brother who succeeded him.

Charles X. was admirably adapted for the task he proposed to himself upon ascending the throne. No one in a shorter time, by any possible manœuvring, could so effectually have ruined his own fortunes and those of all who belonged to him. Power was scarcely in his grasp before Jesuits were installed in office, religious processions revived, and threats held out to all who should dare to question the royal will, or oppose the King's government. After more than a quarter of a century of bloodshed, revolution, anarchy, civil and foreign warfare, this was the result of the great lesson! Humanity sighs as it contemplates the incapacity of dunces in a school where the dullest may find the best instruction, if he will. The people naturally enough refused to be coerced into love of his Majesty's government, and his Majesty, with characteristic obstinacy, declared his resolution "to be unalterable." France had positively to do its work all over again from the very beginning. Revolution had brought the state machine precisely to the point at which revolution had found it in 1792.

France had another struggle for her rights. Fighting again took place in the public streets of Paris, whilst Charles X. was playing a rubber of whist at St. Cloud, and Louis Philippe was nervously watching the issue of a more intricate game at the palace of Neuilly. In the midst of the roar of civil commotion a proclamation was put forth in Paris full of praise of the Duke of Orleans, who it was said would not declare himself, but waited for the expression of the people's wishes. Negotiators soon arrived at Neuilly. The Duchess of Orleans exhibited the greatest indignation when they proposed that her husband should violate his allegiance to his King. Madame Adelaide, the Duke's sister, took another view of the matter. She spoke feelingly when she said, "Let them make my brother a president, a national guard, or anything they please, provided they do not make him an exile or an outlaw." The Duke entered Paris on the 30th of July, 1830, late at night, in a state of painful uncertainty. The friends of a republic had threatened to shoot all who should dare to speak of a monarchy. M. Odillon Barrot, since Prime Minister of Louis Napoleon, to silence all such Republicans, had hit upon a happy sentence, the force of which he has since perhaps found reason to question. "The Duke of Orleans," he said, "is the best of republics." So the Deputies thought, for they created him Lieutenant-General of the kingdom, and the Duke, in accepting the appointment, assured the people that henceforth, at least, "the Charter should be a verity." From the Lieutenant-Generalship to the throne was hardly a step. On Monday, the 9th of August, the great grandson of the Regent grasped the sceptre which for two centuries the family of Orleans had vainly tried to clutch.

In the presence of God, Louis Philippe, King of the French, swore to govern only by the laws, and according to the laws, "*to cause good and exact justice to be administered to every one according to his right, and to act in everything with the sole view to the interest, the welfare, and the glory of the French people.*" It was a great oath, but such as might have been expected from a king cradled in misfortune, and conscious of the crying necessities of the people who had freely elected him to be their chief. His Majesty himself was aware of the magnitude of the obligation, but he confronted it like a man, and had unlimited trust in himself. "I have ratified a great act," he said; "I am profoundly sensible of all the duties it imposes on me. I feel conscious that I shall fulfil them." Who shall say that he overrated the intensity of his feeling at that proud moment of his triumph? Prosperity deadens enthusiasm, and too often blinds the conscience. Louis Philippe, no doubt, took his oath in sincerity, and fell a sacrifice afterwards to his great good fortune.

The reader who shall have gathered from the necessarily hurried narrative which has been placed before him the conviction that from the days of Louis XIV. down to the time of Louis Philippe I., one perpetual struggle existed between a king who aimed at despotism and a people who desired only the subversion of constituted authority, will have received a false impression of the actual case, which he will do well to rectify. It has been asserted also that the secret of France's troubles from the commencement of the present century until this very hour consists in the fact that the rulers of the people, by denying the majority ordinary justice, placed the whole state at the mercy of a minority, who craved not justice but universal anarchy. "The furious," such reasoners say, "might at any time have been disarmed, had monarchs been honest enough to strengthen the hands of the moderate. Louis Philippe knew this, for he said as much when Charles X. opposed himself to the equitable demands of his parliament;" but while we cannot shut our eyes to the fatal consequences of this error as regards the destinies of the House of Orleans, we may remark that nothing would be more unsound, either historically or philosophically, than to confound the outward circumstances of a revolution with the far deeper moral causes which must inevitably have produced it. To a superficial observer the age and infirmities of the King—the recent death of his sister—the hesitation and doubt produced by divided counsels at a moment when the energy and decision of a single man might have stayed the torrent for years, may sufficiently account for the sudden abdication and the inglorious retreat. Had Louis Philippe (it may be said) been ten years younger—had the Prince de Joinville been there—had Marshal Bugeaud been allowed to have his way, would the revolution of February have occurred at all? Very possibly not. But so it is with all great events, whether in the fortunes of empires or of men. The inscrutable decrees of Providence, which regulate the affairs of nations and individuals by the same laws, oftentimes fulfil themselves by means of instruments apparently quite unequal to the importance of the occasion. Men pave the way to their own destruction by a long course of recklessness or vice: rulers let opportunities pass by, or lose the affections of their subjects by selfishness and intrigue; but when at length the downfall of either comes, it often appears to have so little connexion with what has proceeded as to look like the result of a mere oversight or chance. We shall not attempt the task of inquiring by what chain of events or by what series of political errors Louis Philippe managed to destroy the work of thirty years. The true causes of revolutions often lie hidden in those depths of human nature which few politicians take the trouble to explore, but which may nevertheless contain within themselves elements of disorganisation which no human foresight could have been able the control. To have failed in a contest with such antagonists may prove the monarch to have been incompetent, but may not prove that he deserved his fate. The punishment which overtook the ex-King of the French, may be the punishment of an earlier and a worse ambition than that which contrived the fortifications of Paris, or the Spanish marriages. We do not know that the French nation would have fared better under a more liberal monarch than Louis Philippe proved himself, or that, with their present institutions, they are fit for monarchy at all. We should envy no ruler the task of attempting to engraft a shoot of true liberty and manly independence upon that stunted growth of the first revolution which has taken such deep root in the soil of France. How a monarchy is to exist without a middle class to support it, and how a middle class is to be created without giving the people right to dispose of their property as they please, are problems which remain to be solved, but which, we may be sure, contain the secret of the social evils of France.

OCTOBER 23, 1849.

THE DRAMA OF THE FRENCH REVOLUTION.

We call the French Revolution a *Drama*, giving to the term its simplest and most obvious definition. It is difficult to contemplate all the features of that unexpected and extraordinary event, and not to regard it as a dramatic masterpiece performed by the choicest artists to be found in Europe. Our friends across the Channel are without competitors in the histrionic line. They are born actors. French human nature is nature elevated and adorned by art. You see it everywhere —in the open streets, in the Houses of Parliament, in judicial halls, in the smallest boy, in the oldest graybeard, from the *gamin* to the Prime Minister. Life in Paris in anything but the jog-trot vegetating business of life in London. Here we push our way from the cradle to the grave, troubling our heads with no man's business—not courting observation, not striving for effect. There life is a romantic representation of existence, gratuitously offered for the edification or amusement of the world at large. Hence the unapproachable excellence of French vaudevilles, which are but so many daguerreotypes of national manners; and hence also the insipidity of French tragedy, which, scorning to be natural, and striving to be classical, neither satisfies the judgment nor grapples with the heart. Midway, however, between vaudeville and tragedy, modern ingenuity has contrived a species of composition much more suited to the feverish times in which we live than either of the other two. They who have read Dumas and seen Lemaitre know the style. Grand interminable pieces, neither truthfully severe nor painfully familiar; each act a *tableau*, each scene a romance: the *dramatis personæ* made up of the loftiest and the lowest—Kings and Queens mingling with beggars and cutthroats, the vilest jostling against the most heroic, deformity playing the foil to beauty, vice to innocence. Now we are in a palace, now in a hovel; now the great tumble down, and now the humble are uplifted, now you quiver at a hair-breadth escape, now the dance animates or the song soothes your much astonished spirit; from first to last great effects, picturesque situations, unlooked for *rencontres*—endless excitement!

Such a *pièce historique* is the Revolution of 1848; a play with entirely new scenes and decorations, and performed, we may truly say, by the whole strength of the company. No work of fiction coming from the pen of the prolific Dumas, opposed as the brilliant and seductive production may seem to probability and nature, reads half so like a tale of purest fiction as the performance of which we speak. Incongruous as are the scenes, characters, and incidents which that dashing writer brings into his framework, the incongruity looks perfectly symmetrical, by the side of the desperately conflicting and wonderfully opposite events that crowd into the drama under consideration. Dumas is the prince of inventors, but in the height of his audacity he has stopped short of the daring creation which the pen of simple truth has alone authority to write. In his wildest flights the novelist would never have conceived such a programme as that which history enables us to place before him. If it be not so, let the reader judge.

Our first scene is a palace; the period winter; the time morning; the weather cold and miserable. It is 10 o'clock, and the King of France with his wife and family are discovered at the breakfast table. A splendid beginning! Calmness is the prevailing expression of every countenance save one; the King's daughter-in-law looks anxious and disturbed. Well she might be if the audience knew all. Light domestic talk, such as becomes princes and the gilded roof that overhangs them, occupies the moments. You have never seen Royalty so near before; sensible of its grandeur, you gaze in admiration and applaud the unaccustomed sight. Hush! Whilst the lacqueys, dressed in gold and scarlet, move noiselessly about the room, awed by the presence which subdues all lookers-on, a noise is heard without. It becomes more audible by degress. Suddenly the door flies open, and two men enter, paler than ghosts. They are Ministers of State. You learn the fact immediately, or from their haste and horror you would never have suspected it. They have news to communicate. Discontent prevails in the city; the populace are out; the dragoons have surrendered their sabres, the soldiers their arms, within sight of the very apartment in which the King had just now enjoyed his meal, and his daughter-in-law had looked so sad. The reader will note how rapidly the action goes on, how little time is lost. What is to be done? The King is thunderstruck, hesitates for a moment, and then, urged by the Queen, instantly leaves the room. The Queen follows her husband with her eyes from the palace window. She sees him on horseback reviewing the National Guards. She has no fear, neither has he. What more? He returns, accompanied by the man whom, yesterday, to satisfy public clamour, he created Prime Minister. The Minister has power to save his master. You observe at a glance that he is far more anxious to save himself. He craves permission to resign. Permission is granted, when a volley is heard close to their ears. What does it mean! This man will tell you who now enters. The King has a pen in his hand, with which he is about to appoint his new Prime Minister. "Sign not," shouts the last comer—a man of the press, with the face of a student and the spirit of a soldier—"Sign rather your own abdication." The situation is fine. The pen drops from the King's fingers, the speaker takes it up, and quietly replaces it in the Monarch's hand. The audience is already touched. The poor King looks around him for advice; no one offers it: even the Prime Minister of yesterday is dumb; and in another instant the deed is done. The King has abdicated in favour of his grandson. Behind the scenes you hear sounds of tumult and disorder, and your heart is already beating for the issue. The King doffs his robes, places his sword upon the table, and, dressed as a private gentleman, is evidently anxious to depart. The Queen would fain meet the coming danger, but his Majesty has already ordered the carriages. The horses are already put to, but horses and groom are shot by the multitude. A broad path leads from the palace garden, and at the end of it a friendly hand has brought two hired coaches. "Let us go," exclaims the Monarch, and leaning heavily upon the Queen, whose head is high and erect, he hurries on. The coaches are reached; the fugitives escape. They arrive at St. Cloud, at Versailles, but not to stay. On they go, and at half-past 11 o'clock at night they descend at Dreux. At one in the morning they are joined by one of the King's sons, who informs the unhappy pair that the claims of the grandson have been disregarded, and that a Republic has been declared by the people of Paris. It is enough. The King shaves off his whiskers, puts on green spectacles, buries his face in a handkerchief, speaks English, and calls himself Smith. The wind is high, the coast dangerous, embarkation is out of the question at the moment, and before an opportunity offers, the rank of the runaways is discovered. Fortune, however, is with them: they escape capture and put to sea. Protected by Heaven, they reach in safety the hospitable shores of England

Meanwhile what has happened in Paris? The whole city has given way to a handful of rioters—men who meditated an *émeute*, and effected, to their astonishment, an actual revolution. But two individuals upon the side of the King evinced a particle of courage, and these were women—his wife and his daughter-in-law already mentioned. The rest of the city were faithless to themselves as well as to the King. Princes, peers, soldiers, and statesmen, were all sneaking in hiding-places whilst the capital was made over to the mercy of a few dozen incendiaries. The daughter-in-law, seeing the King depart, carries her child to the Chamber of Deputies, and there with womanly courage and queenly dignity vindicates his rights. Her friends entreat her to withdraw. Firm in her purpose, she does not move an inch. She attempts to speak, but is interrupted; and he who interrupts is himself silenced by an armed mob that pours into the hall. The Duchess is forced away, and in that terrible extremity is separated from her child. But the sparrows of the earth are not forgotten. The child is seized by a rough hand, which is strong enough to strike but generous enough to save. The boy is brought to his mother, and mother and son pass from asylum to asylum, chased by sithes, sabres, muskets, and, worse than all, the bloody passions of an infuriated *canaille.* For four days they creep into hiding-places; on the fifth day they are beyond the frontier. Everybody is escaping at the same moment, There is the King's eldest son pale and half naked, throwing aside his tinsel and putting on fustian, looking less than a a man in his fear, trembling with emotion, and finally running like a madman for his life. There are your ministers, of European reputation and wisdom unapproachable, bounding like antelopes, northwards, southwards, "anywhere, anywhere out of the" city! which they, and all the rest, give up to indiscriminate riot. And now the crowning point of our first *tableau* is near. The mob, masters of Paris, are sacking the Tuileries. The choicest movables are broken to atoms; a group take the places which Royalty filled a moment ago at the breakfast table; that is a palpable hit, and brings down laughter on all sides; others are in the wine cellar drinking themselves ten times drunk; others, again, are in the Queen's apartments, defiling that domestic

6

sanctuary. Outside the palace and on the top of it a flag is waved by a dozen men, whose shouts and shrieks invite hundreds, whom you see crawling and clambering up with no earthly object but immediately to slide down again. There is sentiment in all things. The apartments of the poor daughter-in-law are reached, but, strange to say, are respected in the midst of the work of general destruction. Her children's toys are not even touched; the hat and whip of her dead husband are still sacred; the books she had been reading lie open, and they are not even closed. It is an incident that cannot fail to elicit rounds of applause. And whilst anarchy and destruction prevail here, there is equal confusion and danger in the Chamber of Deputies. We have seen the mob forcing their way into that deliberative assembly. Everybody is now rushing to the tribune. Three speakers become marked from the rest; their names are Lamartine, Cremieux, and Ledru Rollin; they gain the popular ear and undertake to establish order—a superhuman responsibility! A Provisional Government is announced, named, and approved on the spot. "To the Hotel de Ville!" exclaims one. "To the Hotel de Ville! respond a hundred; and amidst yells and hootings, cries of "*Vive la Republique!*" "*Vive Lamartine!*" "*A bas tout le monde!*" M. Lamartine sets out for that celebrated building, followed by a train made up of the dregs of a seething metropolis. In the middle of the shouting the curtain falls, and the first act terminates. Search the dramatic annals of the world for such another!

It would not do to cram such action as this into a whole play. They manage more artistically in Paris. Act the second enables us to collect our scattered senses and to breathe. Three days have elapsed since the piece commenced. We are now at the 27th of February, and as the curtain rises for the second time we behold the preparations of a *fête*. After the firing comes a *divertissement*. It is so in all great dramas. The republic is to be proclaimed, and the proclamation is to be made to music, with processions, and all the properties usual in such cases—especially at Astley's. Nothing, to speak honestly, can be more imposing than the exhibition. France is blessed with a republic, and the people are satisfied—that is to say, as satisfied as they can be without money and work. The mob in more senses than one has become its own master. At the same moment that it threw off its monarch it got rid of its employers. What of that! "The republic owes bread and the provision of labour to all her children. She takes the solemn obligation to provide it." The question of work being "of supreme importance," a permanent commission is appointed to enable men to live without working at all. An original idea, not to be found, we believe, in any tragedy or farce. And now all goes merrily on. The high born are down; the low born are up; Jack is as good as his master: Liberty, Equality, and Fraternity are established; every man is to love his neighbour better than himself; selfishness has been put out by an universal extinguisher; a political millennium has been reached by one tremendous effort in a single day. A government, indeed, is hardly required for a people so thoroughly disposed to stifle selfishness and to find pleasure in the comfort and well-doing of one another; but in compliance with antiquated notions a government, as we saw, was formed, and now a National Assembly is summoned. Happy citizens, far removed from despotism, walk about the streets with their hands in their capacious pockets, to gaze upon trees of liberty planted in their honour, and when tired of that, to turn into the theatre gratuitously opened for their amusement. Admirable scenes now take place between the Minister of the Interior and his "emissaries." Perfect liberty being established, the latter are enjoined by M. Ledru Rollin to proceed into the provinces, and to induce the free people of France to elect such representatives as are pleasing in his sight, under pain of his high displeasure; bribery, corruption, and intimidation, old monarchical vices, having become republican virtues under the new *régime*. Whilst the elections proceed we are entertained with more *fêtes* in the capital. As a proof of fraternity, 300,000 soldiers, well armed, assembled in order to be reviewed, and as the sun gleams upon their bayonets, voices innumerable fill the air with praises of this *fête*, strangely called *de la concorde*. The results of the elections are declared. Lamartine, the favorite child of the revolution, is returned for eleven places. The poet, scholar, legislator, is his country's idol. No doubt he will remain so. The august assembly is to meet upon the 4th of May. The Provisional Government have so little to do in a land of universal peace and brotherhood, that on the 30th of April their most important business is to decree "that every representative of the people shall wear a black coat, a white waistcoat with a thrown back collar, black trousers, and a tri-coloured sash adorned with gold fringe." Just before the representatives congregate, we hear that there has been bloodshed in Lyons, on the part of a few ejected fraternals, more devoted to the republic than to life; and under the head of "foreign intelligence," in the daily papers, we ascertain that the nephew of Napoleon Bonaparte, on the preceding 10th of April, was seen walking up and down Regent street, London, dressed as a special constable, under the orders of Major Waller, captain of the division. No time can be given to such trifles. The streets are lined with troops again, the Provisional Government have met, behind them are the members of the National Assembly; trumpets and drums roar forth a martial strain. The glory of republicanism is complete. On they march to the hall of calm deliberation. How magnificent the scene upon which the curtain closes!

Everybody remembers the opening of *Hamlet.* So opens the third act of our revolutionary drama. Instead of the platform before the castle at Elsinore, we have the Mairie of the second *arrondissement;* and in place of "Francisco on his post," we behold a small gentleman in Spectacles, musket on shoulder, walking up and down before a door, to keep out dogs, and to give free entrance to fraternal citizens. All things considered, this is perhaps the best hit in the play. As the curtain slowly rises, you conclude the little gentleman to be an ordinary soldier. You look again. Bless us! it is the Prime Minister of the first act, who took so much care of himself and so little of his master. How intensely dramatic is the situation! That man is a genius; he has written the history of the Empire; he has had the fate of nations oftener than once between the palms of his small hands, and there he stands, leering at poodles out of his large eyes, and pointing his musket at their posteriors as though it were the chief of his accomplishments. Bricklayers and plasterers had been returned to the Assembly, but M. Thiers had failed to find a constituency. We should call all this violent and unnatural at the Adelphi, but, as we said before, French nature is a very extraordinary nature; therefore look on and applaud. We find ourselves again in the House of Parliament, Chamber of Deputies no longer, but National Assembly. Universal suffrage prevails; the people of France are free. There they are, the emancipated millions, represented by a few hundreds of their hearts' own choice. Europe is invited to take cognisance of the fact. A day or two after the meeting of members, the Prefect of Police rises in his place, declares Paris tranquil, and guarantees the continuance of tranquillity. His assurance is received with deafening cheers. Tranquil! Of course it is! Is there anything needed in this world to make men peaceful and contented but self-government and universal suffrage? The only wonder is that a Prefect of Police was required to give the information. The cheers have hardly died away, however, before some curious incidents take place. Next to the possession of freedom, man's greatest enjoyment is to sympathise with the oppressed. The French nation being perfectly comfortable themselves in all their foreign, domestic, and pecuniary relations, resolve to make a formal manifestation of their love for the distressed Poles. The 15th of May is fixed for the demonstration. Twenty thousand men come together on that morning. In lines of thirty-three, with the correctness of organised troops, they march to the Assembly—then in solemn deliberation. Like cats, the nimble sympathisers climb the railings that defend that sacred edifice, and embrace the National Guards who form a protection to the building quite as secure as the *artichauts de fer*. From the railings to the hall itself is but a step and a jump. In an instant the confusion, the din, the rioting of the first act is commenced *de novo*. Fellows with bare brawny arms are waving banners in the centre of the large apartment. Ruffians, innocent of coats and waistcoats, having first invaded the galleries, are sliding down into the space below; and whilst the President's bell is ringing with forty dustman power, a middle-sized individual, with short hair, a long red beard, small inflamed eyes, and blurred face, is flourishing a cane by way of signal to the sympathisers, which they fully understand. In another moment the tumult reaches its height; hands are extended, voices are roaring, pistols are firing, and in the midst of the deafening clamour, a paper is produced which declares "the National Assembly is dissolved." (It had hardly sat a week.) The President—a wise man in his generation—decamps; several members, equally prudent, follow his example; the sovereign people pronounce the government deposed, and name another composed of the brawny arms and waistcoatless bodies already spoken of. The expression of sympathy for the distressed Poles having been made in this singular manner, a body of the sympathisers take forcible possession of the Prefecture of Police. Thither they are followed by one General Bedeau, and six thousand brethren intent upon murder, and are fairly besieged. Two hours are granted for surrender. At the last moment, as the drums begin to beat, as the artillery is pointed, and the soldiers stand to their arms, the sympathisers capitulate on condition that they walk out unmolested. The condition is granted; a way is made for them between the ranks, and to warlike music the third act closes. The joke of this particular portion of the drama is that the Prefect of Police, who guaranteed the continuance of tranquillity, got up the whole affair, and that the very men at whose instigation the government was declared extinct, were members of the government themselves, and its most active limbs. There is no end to the intricacies and staggering incidents of this unparalleled performance.

Act the fourth is a somewhat bloody business, but not without *fêtes* and pleasant episodes to relieve the butchery. The amiable Polish sympathisers having been silenced, and the government restored, the National Assembly proceeds once more to the most pressing business of the country, and holds a long discussion upon the point whether it is advisable to establish the effigy of Napoleon on the cross of the Legion of Honour, or simply to engrave upon that ensign the touching and truthful symbol of a liberated nation, now glaring upon every wall, and expressing the "equality, liberty, and fraternity" of this really happy people. The discussion is scarcely over before it is discovered that the axiom hastily laid down in act the second, to the effect that "the republic owes bread and the provision of labour to all her children," is anything but a self-evident truth or a profitable speculation. The discovery is communicated to the parties chiefly concerned, who get up for the occasion a "*fête des Travailleurs*," and try to vent their indignation at a banquet, precisely as ballet dancers relieve themselves of passion in a *pas*. The *fête*, however, proved a failure. And no wonder! Admission to the feast costs just twopence-halfpenny, and whilst each man's share is but a thin slice of roast veal, some salad, cheese, half a bottle of beer, a glass of wine, and a small glass of brandy, he is further compelled to bring to the banquet his own bread and knife and fork! The elements of success are absent in such melancholy fare. If this be the *feast* of labour, we must not be surprised at the sanguinary aspect of its hideous *fast* that immediately followed it. On the morning of the 22nd of June a decree is published. The unwelcome truth is told, because it can no longer be kept back. Industry cannot support idleness. Mendicancy is social death. Man is born to labour, and no human arrangements can contravene the laws of God. Labour, hitherto pampered by the state, takes alarm, and, well supported, descends into the streets. The clouds never looked so black before, and you preceive that the tragic epoch of this history has come. The dreadful battle,—long postponed—has finally to be fought—foot to foot, and hand to hand; poverty against wealth, despair against content, the reckless spirit of plunder against the tremulous though tenacious spirit of possession. In truth, the fighting is worthy of the desperate struggle, and denotes the mighty interests bound up in it. There is now no childish and unmeaning invasion of the Hall of Assembly. Poverty knows how much depends upon the conflict, and boldly prepares for victory or death. It raises its barricades, it deliberately provides the arms and ammunition, it makes its plans of attack

6*

and defence, and ventures everything, life, limb, wife, and children, in the terrible war for social supremacy. The storm breaks on June 23. It is still violent on the 24th. On Sunday the 25th it has reached its climax; on the 26th there is still work to be done, but on that day all is over. Blood of innocent men has been shed; the lives of the unoffending have been sacrificed; but the interests of society have been vindicated, and the consequences of a huge falsehood palmed upon a credulous people have been once for all brought to naked light. Paris, France, Europe, and civilisation, are rescued; but the lightning that purified the atmosphere has also knocked down the very props upon which the great Republic rested. The self-elected Provisional Government of February has vanished. Liberty with a shriek has quitted the foul soil stained with the blood of fellow citizens. There is a grand moral lesson in Act 4 of our revolutionary drama, and we are sensible of instruction long after the scene closes upon the bloody and humiliating spectacle.

Act 5 begins with a general hornpipe in fetters. The people of Paris are in ecstacies, because they have proclaimed a dictator, established martial law, and see their beautiful city in a state of siege. They could not tolerate the mild yoke of constitutional monarchy; they have lived to ascertain the comforts of unmitigated despotism. On the 27th of June there is but one faith in France, and Cavaignac is its prophet. A Parisian prophet keeps fresh for about six months. Lamartine extinguished Louis Philippe, Cavaignac puts out Lamartine, and, before the play gets very far forward, somebody else no doubt will return the favour to Cavaignac. At the commencement of Act 3 we were shocked to see a Prime Minister doing duty like private Buggins in Birdcage Walk. Act 5 presents us with a demigod, rejected, despised, and forgotten by creatures who were his sworn disciples and worshippers two months before. Don't hiss, we repeat, and say the play's unnatural! We have not undertaken to show you Racine and the unities; but the plot is orthodox and natural enough for all that. At this juncture liberty of person in the city may be pronounced perfect. Bayonets bristle in the air, the streets form an encampment, presses inimical to the government are broken up, and the editors of opposition journals are thrown into prison without benefit of *habeas corpus*. It is a singular fact which philosophers have yet to explain, that every living soul in Paris felt more at his ease, more thoroughly assured of his freedom, and infinitely happier in his mind, whilst submitting to downright slavery, than ever he had been in the heyday of his unquestioned independence. We shall do well to remember the fact when we weep for the blacks. Paris, then, being free to deliberate beyond all doubt, the National Assembly proceeds to arrange the details of the republican constitution. "In the presence of God" (and surrounded by troops) "the Assembly proclaims and decrees" the national laws, and once more dissolves. The frequent repetition of this incident is faulty in a work of art, but we presume it is unavoidable. The new parliament offers some singular features. Marshal Soult—he who fought Wellington—is a candidate at St. Amas, but is beaten by a journeyman cobbler; Lamartine is considered without a claim to the suffrages of any portion of the people; whilst the Regent-street special constable, of whom we had an inkling in an earlier act, is returned for five departments. Positively every act of this wonderful drama is a play in itself. There is no limit to invention—no end to surprise. It is decreed by the constitution, amongst other matters, that France should be governed by a President, chosen, like the members, by universal suffrage. A sort of ballet takes place, called *La Fête de la Constitution*, in which the Statue of the Republic, holding the Constitution in her hand, performs a principal part, and then no time is lost in putting a capital to the shaft of the constitutional column. We were not wrong just now in warning Cavaignac of his insecurity. He was applauded to the skies in June, adored in July; towards the end of November he sufficiently declined to render a vote of confidence, passed by the Assembly, an agreeable acquisition! and in December he puts up for the Presidency to be signally defeated—and by whom? Behold him as he comes upon the stage; notice the ingenious *tableau* as the whole Assembly rises to welcome the tribune, in the person of their constitutional head,—the special constable of Regent-street!

Our play is not yet over, but we drop the curtain for the night. We refer once more to M. Dumas for justification and authority. That daring genius some time since produced in his own theatre a drama which was only half concluded at the close of the sitting. Folks had to pay a second time to ascertain the fate of the hero with whose existence they had the day before been made acquainted. We shall not be blamed for following so illustrious an example.

> "*Five* truths are told
> As happy prologues to the swelling act
> Of the Imperial theme."

Our friends must come again to learn the truths that are behind. They will not regret the trouble. Striking and unequalled as the first part of the "Drama of the French Revolution" assuredly is, we are much mistaken if their astonishment and pleasure are not considerably heightened by the second part yet to be performed.

MARCH 30, 1850.

JOHN HOWARD, THE PHILANTHROPIST.

Conceive a Puritan of the sternest days of Cromwell, dressed in the simple and austere garb of his order, armed resolutely for battle, resolved upon victory, and fighting less for personal triumph than for the glory of God. You have then a picture of John Howard. But remember that the weapons are not of steel, and that the glory by no means consists in the shedding of blood. Howard assailed inhumanity as the Roundhead battled against Royalty; in either case it was war to the last extremity, and the prosecution of work in the spirit of a divinely-appointed missionary.

The name of John Howard stands in England for perfect benevolence. When the public instructor, speaking either from the pulpit or through the press, desires to personify the purest sympathy for human suffering, that name at once occurs to him; but it would be a great mistake to attach the idea of feminine soft-heartedness to efforts as vigorous, as deliberate, and as masculine as ever characterized the movements of intellectual man. The life of Howard is sublime simply because it presents physical weakness overcoming mountains in the pursuit of an end recommended by duty. It is difficult to gather from all that remains to us of Howard's unparalleled career that he was either susceptible by nature or romantic from education and early habit. Poetry had never beguiled him, and fancy slumbered in his mind. Measure him by the vulgar standard, and all the elements of heroism are missing in his composition. Judge him in his own peculiar light, and you may search the annals of heroism in vain for one more illustrious than he.

The date and place of Howard's birth have never been correctly ascertained. It is supposed that he was born at Clapton, in the year 1726. His father had been a merchant, but about the time of his son's birth he retired from business upon a moderate fortune. The mother of Howard died whilst he was still an infant, leaving her offspring sickly, and always ailing, to the care of a farmer's wife, in the village of Cardington, near Bedford, where it would appear the Howards had a small patrimonial estate. The education of the boy was not neglected, but, in spite of good masters, John Howard made no progress in Greek and Latin. "Two circumstances," it has been suggested, "are to be considered in explanation of Howard's inattention to classical studies—First, he felt no vocation to them; Secondly, he was destined to the desk and the Exchange." In simpler language, Howard was a dunce. He was not born for scholarship, as his correspondence testifies; and with that fact before his eyes, Howard senior, in due time, very properly apprenticed his son to Messrs. Newnham and Shipley, wholesale grocers, of Watling street, city. John Howard was still an apprentice when his father died, leaving him, at the age of seventeen, heir to a considerable estate. The boy was already a man in gravity and thought. Purchasing his freedom from his masters he at once set out for France and Italy in search of health and knowledge, and returning home after an absence of a year or two, established himself as an invalid at Stoke Newington, near London. He could not at this period have been twenty years of age, but he was already master of his mind and body. A tendency to consumption rendered it necessary for him to be moderate in his diet: he lived upon fruit, bread, vegetables, and water. Deprived of the usual enjoyments of youth, he sustained himself by religious exercises and the study of the less abstruse branches of natural philosophy. A singular incident during Howard's residence in Stoke Newington furnishes an admirable illustration of his peculiar character. He had reached his twenty-fifth year, and was living in the house of a Mrs. Loidore, the widow of a man who had been clerk in a neighbouring white lead manufactory. Mrs. Loidore was poor, not well-looking, a confirmed invalid, and fifty-two years of age; but John Howard, whilst under her roof, had a severe attack of illness. She tended him as a mother; and upon his recovery, he, in return for her kindness, offered to make her his wife. Mrs. Loidore at first remonstrated with her suitor, and then actually married him. They lived together happily for the space of three years, when Mrs. Howard died. The circumstance needs to be noted. Howard was the son of sickness and misfortune: both partook of his career from the cradle to the grave. His trials—we shall find them to be many—compelled him to seek refuge in piety—piety bade him go forth and struggle for mankind.

Upon the death of his wife, Howard went abroad again; this time he set sail for Portugal. Taken prisoner on the voyage, he was carried into Brest, and there imprisoned. It was his introduction to the gigantic labour of his life. Finally, permitted to return to England upon the understanding that he would go back unless he could obtain a suitable exchange, he not only secured the personal object, but gave himself no rest until he had also obtained the release, upon similar terms, of many of his fellow-sufferers. With this achievement Howard retired in 1756 to the paternal home at Cardington, and for two years occupied himself exclusively in the improvement of his estate, and in the care of the poor by whom it was surrounded. The youthful patriarch, with a full consciousness of what he owed to his people, knew also what was due to their head. Recognizing himself as chief labourer of the vineyard, he exacted duty from every other workman. In 1758 he married again; the match was more suitable than the first, for his wife was but a year younger than himself; but it had also its characteristic incident. John Howard stipulated with Henrietta Leeds before marriage that, "in all matters in which there should be a difference of opinion between them, his voice should rule." Passion in the case of Howard was at all times absorbed by a sense of right.

Before his second marriage, Howard had spent much of his time and fortune in improving the dwellings of the poor on his estate. Henrietta Leeds, with a spirit that answered to his own, shortly after her wedding-day parted with her jewels in order to lay the foundation of a fund for the relief of the sick and destitute. Under the united efforts of this conscientious couple, the poor of Cardington were raised from degradation to comparative comfort. In the course of seven years ignorance and brutality had been cleared from the soil, and morality and social happiness planted in their stead. At the end of this period, however, Mrs. Howard gave birth to a son, and left her husband once more desolate. The love of Howard for his second wife stands apart from every other feeling of his life. The blow sent him weeping to the earth. Years after her death, upon the eve of his departure from England upon one of his humane expeditions, he was walking hand-in-hand with his son in the plantations about Cardington. Suddenly he stopped. "Jack," he faltered to the boy, "in case I should not come back, you will pursue this work or not as you think proper; but remember this walk was planted by your mother, and if you ever touch a twig of it may my blessing never rest upon you."

For eighteen months after his bereavement Howard secluded himself in Cardington, and then had recourse to his usual remedy for sorrow—he travelled again. If gravity had hitherto been the prevailing colour of his mind, it henceforth took a deeper and a holier hue. He lived the life of an ascetic, and his journal is the record of continual and impassioned prayer. After three years' absence Cardington was revisited, and but for an event of ordinary significance which then took place, the pious and well-disciplined Howard might have pursued his journey to the grave unknown to any but the poor who in his neighbourhood were, whilst he lived, the objects of his tenderest solicitude and care. In 1773 he was nominated to the office of sheriff of Bedford. To be appointed to a duty was with Howard to incur the obligation to fulfil it. During the trials of prisoners he sat in court and listened attentively to the proceedings. When the trials were over he visited and inspected the prison. The hideous glare that met him in the felon's cell struck his soul with horror, and revealed to him at once the nature of his mission. The dream of life was at an end, its action had begun. Less with a yearning of human love than with an overwhelming sense of responsibility to his Maker, Howard set about the task of rescuing England from the shame and disgrace that attended her blind and brutal punishment of malefactors. The effort was tremendous; so was the penalty—but the success surpassed both.

It is difficult for us to realize the gigantic nature of the undertaking. The problem of our own day is the punishment of public offenders; but its solution is light and easy compared with the labour that confronted Howard upon the threshold of his extraordinary crusade. We know at least the nature of the sad material with which we have to deal. We have separated and classified the corrupt mass, and rendered it fitting to receive salutary and corrective treatment whenever enlightenment shall have fixed upon the process. We have not removed the guilty from the pale of our sympathies, and given them up to wilful torture and abominable neglect. The transgressors of the law lose the rights of citizenship, but are not deemed in consequence brute beasts. We remember that criminals are men, and that the murderer who forfeits his life to society has still a soul, it may be to be pardoned and redeemed of Heaven. A century ago, and these things were forgotten—if indeed they had ever been known. A more ghastly exhibition than the prison of the last century the mind cannot conceive; the most innocent and unfortunate debtor was thrust into the hole with the most guilty and hardened of cut-throats, and shared the worse fate of the two if he had no means to bribe his gaoler into human charity. Swearing, cursing, blasphemy, and gaming, were the habitual practices of the keepers and the kept; drunkenness was no vice, and the admixture of the sexes no impropriety; religious worship was unknown in a region that seemed cut off from civilization and made over to fiends to govern in the true spirit of Beelzebub; there was corruption from the first official to the meanest gaoler, and more crime within the precincts of the gaol than without. Old criminals corrupted new comers; the governors and their precious crews corrupted all.

Whilst inspecting the prisons of Bedford, Howard had been struck with a strange anomaly. He tells us himself that from its observation he was incited to further activity on behalf of his unhappy clients.

"Some," he says, "who by the verdict of juries were declared not guilty—some on whom the grand jury did not find such an appearance of guilt as subjected them to a trial—and some whose prosecutors did not appear against them—after having been confined for months, were dragged back to gaol, and locked up again until they should pay sundry fees to the gaoler, the clerk of assize, &c."

Howard applied at once to the justices of the county for a salary to the gaoler, who, he contended, ought to be paid by the community and not by the discharged innocents. The justices demanded a precedent for the application, and the good Howard mounted his horse forthwith and proceeded to the neighboring counties in search of one. He not only did not find his precedent, but saw in the course of his progress and search, sights that rendered the Bedford practice a very harmless proceeding indeed, and confirmed his resolution to devote himself henceforward to the reformation of the gaols of England and the world.

One or two specimens of what the inquirer saw will serve for many. He went to Gloucester.

"The castle of that city was in the most horrible condition. It had but one court for all prisoners—only one day-room for males and females. The debtors' ward had no windows, a part of the plaster wall being broken through to let in the light. The night-room (or main) for men felons, though up a number of steps, was found to be close and dark, and the floor so ruinous that it could not be washed. The whole prison was greatly out of repair, while it had not been whitewashed for years. Many persons had died in it the year preceding Howard's visit—a circumstance attributed to a fever engendered by a large dunghill which stood directly opposite to the stairs leading up to the sleeping room. The keeper had no salary—the debtors no allowance of food! The first lived on extortion, the second on charity."

In the episcopal city of Ely,

"The prison was rickety and ruinous—totally unfit for the safe custody of criminals. Of this the wardens were well aware, but instead of strengthening the walls and doors—which would have cost money, and affected the episcopal coffers, they adopted the cheaper plan of chaining the prisoners on their backs to the floor, passing over them several bars of iron, and fastening an iron collar, covered with spikes, round their necks, as well as placing a heavy bar of the same metal over their legs to prevent attempts at escape."

From Ely, Howard proceeded to Norwich. There

"He found the cells built under ground, and the keeper paying 40*l.* a year to the under-sheriff for his situation. The gaol delivery was but once a year; and the allowance for straw for the whole prison was only a guinea per annum."

The felons' gaol at Exeter was a private speculation. As might be expected, the dungeons,

"Though but a few steps under ground, were close, dark, and confined; the windows small, and the whole very unhealthy. An infirmary had been built, but the steps leading up to it were in a ruinous state, and the surgeon told Howard that he (the surgeon) was excused by contract from attending any prisoner in the cells who might be sick of the gaol fever."

From one end of England to the other, from county to county, and from town to town, did Howard travel, in order to drag forth the disgusting mysteries of the British prison house. The first ray of light that burst upon prison gloom was the presence of this Christian man. His informants were his eyes and ears; of all that he heard and saw he made an imperishable note, and whilst he undertook to see justice done by the country to criminals whom he could not otherwise help, he gave freedom in every city to as many as a pecuniary contribution could supply with the liberty of which, guiltless of all crime, they had been wantonly robbed. The fruit of his first great labour was not slow to come.

Upon the conclusion of the survey taken by John Howard of the prisons of England, the House of Commons resolved itself into a committee, in order to ascertain from the philanthropist, who was called to the bar, the actual state of the case. We may conclude that the language of a man in whose stern presence kings were said to quail, and whose indignant soul was overflowing with the wrong it knew, was, if not flattering to Parliament, highly useful for future legislation. The thanks of the Legislature were publicly given at the close of his evidence. In the course of it a characteristic question was addressed to him. A member, surprised at the extent and minuteness of his inspections, inquired at whose expense he travelled. "Howard," says a friend who knew him well, "was almost choked before he could reply."

Having swept the provinces, Howard next turned to the metropolis. We have not space to follow him into the Fleet, the Marshalsea, the King's Bench, the Poultry Comptor, the New Ludgate, and all the other places of detention into which he burrowed, and from which he brought forth for the contemplation of his fellows, misery that the saddest tales of fiction could not parallel. We content ourselves with the announcement that the industry of the individual who never wearied, shamed the parliament into a desire to keep at all events in his track. It is the way of parliaments! Two bills for the better regulation of prisons passed the Legislature in 1774, one on the 31st of March, which abolished all fees, and gave a prisoner his discharge immediately upon acquittal; and another on the 2nd of June, which provided for the whitewashing, cleansing, and ventilation of prisons, for the establishment of infirmaries, and for the erection of dungeons in which even offenders might live. Howard, whose health was always bad, whose days were passed in abstinence and self-denial, was at home paying the penalty of his great exertions when these bills became law; but upon his sick bed he thanked God for his success, and as soon as he recovered, revisited the gaols which he had already examined in every hole and nook—*in order to satisfy himself that the acts were duly and fairly enforced!*

From 1773 to 1775 Howard did not desist from prison inspection. Having exhausted England, he passed into Scotland and crossed into Ireland, in every place acquiring information and accumulating facts for publication. In 1775 he proceeded to the continent, still in furtherance of his mission, halting first in Paris. The French prisons were bad enough, but far superior to those of England. There was at least a motive in the punishment; prisons were for the most part clean and fresh, and food was sufficient and regularly bestowed. The missionary told his business to the authorities and was admitted freely to all public prisons—the Bastille alone excepted. In this his daring love of prison knowledge had nearly caged him for life, but he escaped to be revenged on the French by translating an account of the State prison, secretly published, and obtained by him with the greatest difficulty and trouble. Belgium, Holland, Germany, were all taken in succession, and a mass of materials, the result of enormous labour, unflinching devotion, and great expense, was gathered from every one. To return to England was but to vary the field of exertion. After his first foreign tour,

Howard satisfied himself that improvement had taken root at home, and then he sallied forth again,—this time to Switzerland, but always on the same pious and philanthropic errand. Something of the science of prison discipline was revealed in Switzerland. In his own country Howard had seen the felon thrown into a den, useless to society, fit for nothing but to generate disease, and to hurt all who came within his atmosphere. "*Work* was the principal element of the Swiss system of punishment and reform." The hint was not forgotten.

For three years Howard without resting had occupied himself in collecting information concerning the punishment of offenders, when he resolved to give to the world his great work upon *The State of Prisons.* He had travelled 13,418 miles during the period, and no library could furnish the knowledge which he had stored up. The sensation produced by the book corresponded with its value.

"It had been long and anxiously looked for. The fame of its author's labours—his disinterestedness—the purity of his motives in undertaking such a missionaryship—the courage and devotion with which he had executed it—the sublime confidence in which he had penetrated dark and pestilential dungeons, in order to carry thereunto light and hope; also some intimation of the sterling worth and originality of his private character, had reached, through various channels, the knowledge of his countrymen. The meed of praise, of acknowledgment, was without stint or reservation—was free and full as it was richly merited."

Shortly after the appearance of Howard's volume

it became necessary for the English Government to decide what should be done with the convicts to whom the American war of independence suddenly denied the luxury of transportation. Howard was examined again before a committee of the House of Commons, and, recollecting what he had seen abroad, recommended a house of correction. There was one of some repute in Amsterdam, and Howard offered to visit it in order to ascertain its working. He set out once more. From Holland he proceeded to Prussia, crossed Silesia "through the ranks of the opposing armies of Austria and Prussia," spent some time in Vienna, and then returned by way of Italy. At Rome he desired to see the dungeons of the Inquisition. They were locked, as had been those of the Bastile in Paris; all others opened to him. Having travelled 4,600 miles upon this tour, Howard came homeward again through France. The blessings of the imprisoned followed his course. He had distributed charity whithersoever he went; he had done infinitely more. He had summoned the attention of nations to a subject of human interest in which the happiness and welfare of society are more nearly concerned than the world had ever suspected.

After a short interval of rest, Howard made another home journey in order to learn how far the acts of Parliament of 1774 had succeeded in their objects. "This home journey was, in fact, one of the longest and most laborious which he had yet undertaken, occupying from January to the end of November of the year 1779, in the course of which he traversed almost every county in England, Ireland, and Scotland, travelling to and fro 6,990 miles. The results of all these labours were given to the world at the end of the year." The inspection was satisfactory. "Some of the more flagrant abuses which he had formerly noted had been removed, the spirit of reform was aroused, the gaols were almost universally cleaner, more orderly, more healthy."

We can only indicate the course of his further travels. Every year saw Howard extending the field of his investigation, and amplifying his great knowledge. He had visited the south and centre of Europe; now he travelled to the extreme north. His fame was already universal, much to his annoyance; for no sooner was his approach heralded in any city of Europe, than the prison of that place was brushed up and made to assume holiday attire. To guard against deception he entered Petersburgh alone and on foot. The police, however, discovered him, and the Empress Catherine at once invited the apostle to appear at Court. Howard—Republican and Puritan in every fibre of his heart—respectfully informed the Empress that he came to visit the dungeon of the captive and the abode of the wretched, not the palaces and courts of kings and queens; that his time was limited, and that he must stand excused. He did not go.

It was the boast of Russia, at this time, that capital punishments had been abolished throughout the empire. Howard did not believe it. To satisfy himself, he witnessed the infliction of the ordinary punishment of the knout. A man and woman were brought out. The man received 60 strokes, the woman 25, and then both were conducted back to prison. "I saw the woman," says Howard, "in a very weak condition some days after, but could not find the man any more." He was determined to discover, however, what had become of him, and accordingly he paid a visit to the executioner. Assuming an official tone, he threw the fellow off his guard, and bade him answer without equivocation the questions he had come to put to him. "Can you," he said, "inflict the knout so as to occasion death in a very short time?" "Yes," was the answer. "In how short a time?" continued the questioner. "In a day or two." "Have you ever so inflicted it?"—"I have." "Have you lately?"—"Yes; the last man who was punished by my hands with the knout died of the punishment." "In what manner do you thus render it mortal?"—"By one or two strokes on the sides, which carry off large pieces of flesh." "Do you receive orders thus to inflict the punishment?"—"I do." So much for the Russian boast, and Howard's mode of operation.

Through Russia and Poland, and then home by way of Prussia, Hanover, Holland, and the Austrian Netherlands. In 1783 Howard quitted Falmouth for Spain and Portugal. These countries by no means suffered in comparison with England. The prisons in both were clean, imprisonment for debt had been abolished, the sexes were separated, and criminals alone suffered detention. Returning to England after this tour, Howard published the result of his latest investigations in a second appendix to his great work. Twelve years had passed since he first gave himself up to the absorbing pursuit of his life, and he had taken in turn every country of Europe. He had visited and minutely inspected the gaols of all the chief cities of the continent, he had travelled upwards of 42,000 miles, and he had expended on his travels, and in relieving the poor, the sick, and the friendless, upwards of 30,000*l*. In his 60th year Howard might fairly claim to take his rest. The work, however, that he was born to do was not accomplished.

Towards the end of November, 1785, Howard, anxious, if possible, to discover a remedy for the plague, to which so much of human life was annually sacrificed, quitted his native shores again. His plan was to visit Marseilles, Leghorn, Venice, and Valetta; and then boldly to encounter the scourge itself in the cities of Smyrna and Constantinople. The French, remembering the publication of the pamphlet on the Bastile, forbade his appearance upon the soil of France. Disregarding the interdict, Howard disguised himself and entered Paris. Upon the night of his arrival he was roused from his bed by the police. A lucky thought enabled him to dispose of his visitors for a few minutes, and he seized the opportunity to escape from the capital and to make the best of his way to Marseilles. There he contrived to obtain admission into the lazaretto, and to secure the information for which he came. From Smyrna, where the plague was raging, the resolute pilgrim took his passage to the Adriatic by an infected vessel, with a foul bill of health, in order that he might personally be subjected to the strictest quarantine, and with his own eyes inspect the smallest details of the lazaretto. The sufferings of Howard, his privations and perils whilst in quarantine for 40 days, were fearful; still worse, while he lay consumed by a scorching fever, news came to him that his country was about to raise a monument to his honour, and that his only son, after a short career of the wildest dissipation, had given evidences of downright insanity. His martyrdom had commenced. Chained to his cell, unable to move, even if liberty were accorded him, the afflicted man wrote to his friends in England to take what care they could of his boy until he should return, and as they loved him to prevent the erection of a monument which could not be raised without occasioning him the deepest distress. When Howard finally recovered, and came home again, his first step, after he had satisfied himself of the nature of his son's malady, was to write to the public papers a declaration of his repugnance to the scheme that was intended to do him honour, and an earnest request that no further steps should be taken in the business. The money subscribed for the statue was accordingly returned to the subscribers, or spent in the liberation of poor debtors from gaol.

We have said that sickness and misfortune accompanied John Howard from the cradle to the grave. Whilst he lay in the former, his mother died and left him a sickly child. As he stood on the verge of the latter, his son, the slave of debauchery and vice, perished a raving madman. Let us not stay to make the painful inquiry how far the exertions of the philanthropist may have interfered with the office of the father. It is enough to say, that bereft of domestic happiness, Howard took his last journey, knowing it to be the last. He visited Cardington, provided for the wants of the poor in that neighbourhood, made his will, and parted with his humble friends as a father from his children. His intention was to extend his inquiries on the subject of the plague, and to proceed through Holland, Germany, and Russia to Turkey, Anatolia, Egypt, and the states of Barbary. He departed on the 5th of July, 1789, and got as far as Cherson, in Russian Tartary. There, surrounded by strangers, far away from his country and his home, in the prosecution of his benevolent work, he caught a virulent and infectious fever, and expired. He had marked a spot near the village of Dauphiny, in which, as soon as he was attacked, he expressed a wish to be buried. "Lay me quietly in the earth," he said to one at his bedside, "place a sun-dial over my grave, and let me be forgotten." He died on the 20th of January, 1790, in the 64th year of his age; a benefactor of his kind whose deeds still exercise a mighty influence in the world—a man who had no thought of himself save inasmuch as he could minister to the welfare of his fellows, and who had no thought for them except in obedience to the supreme commandment of God. Not a word of comment need be added. The tale speaks for itself.

SEPT. 11, 1849.

ROBERT SOUTHEY.

CHAPTER THE FIRST.

The life of Robert Southey is a picture the very first sight of which elicits boundless satisfaction; frequent and close inspection qualifies delight; a last and parting look would seem to justify the early admiration. The faults of the subject may therefore be considered secondary and accidental; its merits of the highest order and unimpeachable. So fine a form, perhaps, is seldom disfigured by such uncouth drapery. The vices of Southey's character are the blunderings of the journeyman; its virtues are the perfect work of Nature and of Genius.

We may be justly proud of our late Laureate. Literature does not every day present us with so worthy a son; students who forsake the trodden paths of life to earn their difficult crust by patient spinning of the brain, cannot find a more illustrious example. The pursuit of letters was the business of Southey's life; it was also the first and last joy of his heart. Rather than not at intervals breathe the pure air and partake of the golden light that await the worshipper on the topmost heights of Parnassus, he condescended to work as a bondman, through winter and summer from year to year, on its barren sides. Literature was his glory, and he her pride. Providence, in its bounty, has granted us poets who have put forth a higher note of enchantment; moralists who have preached a more solemn strain; philosophers who have understood more clearly the force of everlasting truths; but in no age have intellectual power and moral worth and social dignity combined to present a finer instance of the literary man.

In early youth Southey took to literatnre as a profession when he might have adopted a more promising calling, and his stedfast adherence to his craft was masculine and perfect. Some men have given utterance to the craving soul in verse immortal as itself, and been satisfied with the loud expression. Others have stolen brief hours from the stern business of life to enjoy a passing gleam of the poet's happiness. But of such it cannot be affirmed that either the pursuit or the communication of knowledge formed the main object of their lives. Southey educated his mind, became a scholar, devoured books with the sole aim and intention of devoting himself to literary dealings. A loving uncle wished him to enter the Church; he sentenced himself to two years' study of the law; but he could not finally bring himself to grasp either divinity or law as his staff, lest haply literature might prove nothing better than a crutch. He declined the one avocation, forsook the other, yet deliberately entered the profession of his own selection with all the resolution and with quite as much of the sense of responsibility that accompany the most conscientious to the pulpit or the bar.

At the age of forty-six Southey began a history of

his life. He registered his recollections from earliest childhood, and communicated them in a series of letters to an old friend. His intention had been to carry those recollections down to the hour of writing, but his heart failed him. The exquisite fragment of autobiography ceases already at Westminster School, and when the lad had hardly attained his fifteenth year. Had Southey found courage to persist in his task, he would have left behind him an autobiography unrivalled for personal and general interest and for its grace and genial style. The few precious sheets that remain exhibit the writer in his most charming aspect. Before he had reached his fortieth year he had proved himself a master of prose. The playful fancy, indicating itself in delicate touches; the marvellous memory, evoking almost from the cradle the most affecting incidents of childhood; the faculty of narrating in the simplest terms the simplest doings of a tranquil life, and of winning and rewarding attention by the very absence of effort—all so characteristic of Robert Southey in his happiest moods—are singularly illustrated in the few but valuable pages of which we speak. Unfortunately, because they are so few, the life of Southey has yet to be written; for we cannot accept the contribution of Mr. Southey's son, important as it is, for more than it pretends to be. The six volumes before us furnish materials for a future structure, but are no more that edifice than so many rows of bricks may be said to constitute the building they must help to raise. The work, edited by the Rev. Charles Cuthbert Southey, professes to give the life of his father, but nothing whatever of that life is to be learnt, except what the reader has skill and judgment enough to gather for himself from *Robert Southey's Letters*, published not unsparingly we grant, but certainly after passing through the hands of one more than ordinarily desirous to present his subject in the fairest light before the world. We will dismiss this portion of our criticism at once, by plainly expressing our regret that the Rev. Mr. Southey has not been spared his delicate and not easy task. We doubt very much whether the son of any man is the fit chronicler of his father's life. We are certain that the son of Robert Southey cannot be just to the public, and not do violence to his own reverential love. We are further convinced that the present biographer, in his very anxiety to reconcile editorial obligations with filial affection, has done great harm to the object that lay nearest his heart. We have to complain in the name of the public, of sins of omission, and of sins of commission on behalf of Robert Southey. At every other page we grow impatient at the absence of all that is required to admit us into recesses which biography undertakes to lay open, and of all comment upon a text that provokes rather than satisfies curiosity, that offers the merest glimpses of matters which it is the chief office of the biographer to bring into the broad day. As frequently are we annoyed by the publication of passages thrown off by their author hastily in early youth—possibly repented of almost as soon as written—often contradicted by passages recurring at a later date, and hardly more essential to a complete understanding of the poet's character than a record of his fractiousness at the interesting time of teething. Robert Southey would have sighed to reperuse the unconsidered utterances of his earlier letters. Why should the reader smile at them? The voluminous collection of epistles for which we are indebted to the indefatigable zeal of the Rev. Mr. Southey, are, we repeat, admirable raw material, as far as they go, for the astute critic and skilful biographer. They ought never to have been thrown in undigested heaps upon the world; nor would they, had the son of Robert Southey been an older man, a more experienced writer, and blessed with good advisers.

Robert Southey was born in the city of Bristol, on the 12th of August, 1774, and was the son of a small tradesman. His childhood, however, was passed, not at home, but in Bath, at the residence of Miss Tyler, his aunt, of whom a speaking portrait is drawn in the biographical fragment. Lament for the ill fortune that induced Southey to cut short that pleasant labour begins as soon as the inimitable Miss Tyler appears upon the scene, and never ceases till the fragment ends. Miss Tyler had a great contempt for Bristol society. She was passionately fond of theatres, and the familiar friend of the great actors who exhibited on the boards of the Bath Theatre—the first establishment of the kind out of London. The gala days of her household were those which found tragedians at her table. Then the lady would assume the appearance and adopt the manners of one who had been bred in the best society, and be equal to her pretensions. Then, too, the best room was opened. At other times Miss Tyler was attired in a bedgown, went about in rags, and lived in the kitchen. But in rags as well as in kitchen, the lady was scrupulously clean; her hatred of dust was a consuming passion; and her notions of uncleanness were as irrational as those of a Hindoo. She once buried a cup for six weeks to purify it from the lips of one who, not being a favourite, was not considered clean. A chair used by an unclean person was invariably dismissed to the garden to be aired. Once a man called upon business, and had the temerity to seat himself in the lady's own chair! The effect of the crime Southey pronounces to have been tremendous. Her features grew tragically fierce; her language became irreverent; her gesticulations were those of one in wild distress, and she lifted up her eyes and hands like a woman lost in hopeless misery or in the last extremity of mental anguish. With this lady Southey lived from the age of two till six. He had no playmates; he was never permitted to do anything in which by any possibility he might contract dirt; he was kept up late at night in dramatic society, and kept in bed late in the morning at the side of his aunt, not daring to make the slightest movement that could disturb her; and his chief pastime—for neither at this time nor at a later period had Southey any propensity for boyish sports—was pricking holes in playbills—an amusement, of course, suggested to him by Miss Tyler, and witnessed by her with infinite delight. As soon as the child could read, his aunt's friends furnished him literature. The son of Francis Newberry, of St. Paul's-churchyard, and the well-known publisher of *Goody Two Shoes*, *Giles Gingerbread*, "and other such delectable histories in sixpenny books for children, splendidly bound in the flowered and gilt Dutch paper of former days," sent the child twenty such volumes, and laid the foundation of a love of books, which grew with the child's growth and did not cease in age, even when the vacant mind and eye could only gaze in piteous though blissful imbecility upon the things they loved.

From *Goody Two Shoes* the advance was rapid and decided. Before the boy was seven years old, he had been to the theatre more frequently than he afterwards went from the age of twenty till his death. The conversations to which he listened were invariably of actors, of authors, and of the triumphs of both; the familiar books of the household were tragedies and "the acting drama." At eight, Beaumont and Fletcher and Shakspeare had been read through. At the same tender age the resolution was first formed to excel in the profession which the child heard extolled for its dignity from morning till night. At first the actors of plays were esteemed beyond all other men; these, in their turn, gave place to writers of plays, whom, almost as soon as he could hold a pen, the boy himself began to emulate. He was not quite nine when he set to work upon a tragedy, the subject being the continence of Scipio. In 1782 he went as day boarder to a school in Bristol, learning from his master, as invariably proved the case with him, much less than he contrived to teach himself. Before he had reached his twelfth year, he had read, with the keenest relish, translations of *Jerusalem Liberated* and the *Orlando Furioso*, and had been entranced with the *Faery Queen* of Spenser—a vision that never yet burst upon the youthful poet's soul but to intoxicate by the brilliant magic of its strains, and to elevate and strengthen by the purity and loveliness of its matchless forms. At thirteen, Southey was not only master of Tasso, Ariosto, and Spenser, but well acquainted also, through translations, with Homer and Ovid. He was familiar with ancient history, and his acquaintance with the light literature of the day was bounded only by the supply. A more industrious infancy was never known; but it was surpassed by the ceaseless energy of youth, which, in its turn, was superseded by the unfaltering and unequalled labour of the man. We intreat the clamourers for the rights of labour to bear in mind the record. No artisan in the workshop, no peasant in the field, no handicraftsman at his board, ever went so young to his apprenticeship, or wrought so unremittingly through life for a bare livelihood, as Robert Southey. Whatever dignity might attach to the vocation, of independence, so called, there was none. Sixty years' continued toil, though they rendered an honest, prudent, honourable and religious man happy and grateful in the midst of suffering and sorrow common to all, yet left him comparatively poor and actually dependent upon the generosity of his country. We dwell upon the fact to console perseverance wherever it may be found, but especially to warn off the mere adventurer from ground on which the wisest and best prepared find it not easy to secure a footing.

Southey tells us himself that he does not remember, in any part of his life, to have been so conscious of intellectual improvement as he was from his twelfth to his fourteenth year, and he attributes his advance as much to constantly exercising himself in English verse, as to any other cause. In truth, he commenced his poetic labours as soon as he was breeched, and in a magnificent fashion that has known no parallel. "The boy is father to the man." The former, at starting, associated poetic fame with the composition of lengthened epics ; the latter could never understand why his contemporaries failed to crown with laurel his protracted narratives in verse. Southey's confidence in his powers was at once the main cause of his great success in literature, and of his failure as a first-rate poet. His ambition sustained him so long as it accompanied efforts to which his genius was equal: it betrayed him into wilful error, and confirmed him in obstinacy whenever it was associated with aspirations which he had no claim to put forth. The heroic attempts made by Southey before he was fairly a schoolboy, astonish by their breadth, and amuse by their boldness. Created for almost superhuman exertion, it would seem that even in petticoats he could hardly think of the lightest of intellectual exercises except as a labour fit for an infant Hercules to grapple with.

At fourteen the young poet was sent to Westminster. He remained at the school four years, when he was dismissed for contributing a sarcastic attack upon corporal punishment to a periodical which he and some of his schoolfellows had set on foot. He returned to Bristol to his aunt in 1792, having formed friendships at Westminster, which, it appears from the present volumes, were a consolation and a blessing to him until his dying hour. One schoolfellow was Mr. Grosvenor Bedford, late of the Exchequer, to whom the bulk of the published correspondence is addressed. Another was the late Mr. C. W. W. Wynn, M.P., who for many years, and until provision was made for Southey by the government, generously allowed his friend an annuity of a hundred and sixty pounds. The lad had scarcely left school before he had the misfortune to lose his father, who died a ruined and broken-hearted man. The kindness of an uncle, however, who had paid Southey's expenses at Westminster, provided for the youthful genius, and he proceeded to Oxford in January, 1793, when he entered at Balliol, having previously been declined at Christ Church on account of his expulsion from Westminster. How close to the French Revolution our hero had arrived the reader will see by the date. He has yet to learn that with the first worthies of that Revolution, and with the cause of civil and religious liberty throughout the world, the author of the satire upon corporal punishment sympathised with all his heart and soul. Southey went to Oxford an honest and a generous-hearted republican; not, be it always remembered, because he had reasoned out his faith and could rest his conviction upon a satisfied judgment, but because his indignant spirit rose naturally against oppression, and because it was the abiding error of a good and virtuous man rashly to obey his impulses whithersoever they might lead, and to be blind to the daily sacrifice which a fine intellect was not too proud to make to most unworthy and unmeaning prejudice. We shall hear more of this hereafter.

It is unnecessary to state that Southey worked hard in his own way whilst he remained at Balliol, but many circumstances combined to bring his residence to a close some time before its natural term. His uncle wished him to go into the Church, as we have said. The nephew had no religious opinions to justify the step, and at no period of his life was he the man to play the hypocrite. In justice to his patron, however, he busied himself with thoughts of a profession, whilst his heart became more and more wedded to a pursuit not yet included in the category of legitimate callings. At first he took to medicine, assiduously attended lectures, and got as far as the dissecting room, where the atmosphere sickened him. It then occurred to him to secure a competency by a stroke. He believed himself entitled to a reversion, and he offered it for sale. No purchaser could be found, and no reversion ever came. Failing here, he applied to one of his friends for official employment in London. Such employment is easier asked than obtained. Nothing seemed left for the adventurer, who had already reached his twentieth year, but emigration or open allegiance to the perilous mistress to whom finally he clung, when Samuel Taylor Coleridge, then an undergraduate at Cambridge, paid a visit to Oxford, was introduced to Robert Southey, and suggested a scheme almost as wild as the brain from which it emanated. The boys, after what they deemed due deliberation, decided upon a plan worthy of Robert Owen. They, and as many brother adventurers as they could collect, would embark for the New World, and establish a community there on a thoroughly Social basis. The world was out of joint, and they would set it right by presenting it for imitation a normal world of intellectual contrivance. All the colonists were to marry forthwith; the ladies were to cook and perform household offices upon their arrival at their destination; the men were to cultivate land by common labour, and, when labour was over, to improve one another and themselves by social converse and literary undertakings. Plans of building were made, the form of the settlement was accurately defined, and nothing was wanting, at all events, to give the scheme a trial, but a sufficient quantity of that base metal, for lack of which the most promising buildings have been doomed to perish melancholy carcases. "Money is a huge evil," writes Southey to a friend; with his head full of plans and his heart occupied with an engagement, sagely contracted in his poverty, with a young lady, to whose sister the equally penniless Coleridge prudently engaged himself, and whose father had lately died, leaving a widow and six children "wholly unprovided for." The "huge evil" was fatal. The grand emigration scheme died where it was born—in the heads of its concoctors. But this was not the worst. Miss Tyler hearing of his Social intentions, and of his love for Miss Fricker, immediately shut her door in her nephew's face, and never opened it to him again.

We dwell upon the early incidents of Southey's career, because they constitute *all* the active incidents of his life. Instructive as the whole story of that life unquestionably is, nothing can be more tranquil than its flow from the hour Southey decided upon his course, and braced himself for a responsibility proudly and deliberately assumed. From the moment he resolved to make literature his sole business, Southey had but one thought—to give dignity to the occupation, and to fulfil every possible duty of his position. The struggle was fraught with action and excitement enough, but they were confined to his own invincible spirit, and were known to the world only when it profited by their admirable results.

There was a feeble effort to try the socialist scheme

in Wales upon a small scale, but the ridiculous character of the whole affair became evident to the young poets the moment they attempted to reduce their plans to practice. The notion of reforming the universe rapidly gave place, as might be expected, in the case of Coleridge as well as Southey, to the more imminent question of providing, without loss of time, for their own daily bread. To obtain necessary food, they started as public lecturers in Bristol—Southey taking up history, according to his bent; and Coleridge dealing with politics and ethics. The historical lectures lasted many months; they were well attended, and brought some money, but not enough to enable Southey to publish a poem which he had written in his nineteenth year, and now ardently longed to bring forth. At the remote period of which we speak there lived a bookseller in Bristol; in the outskirts of that city, in honourable retirement, he still dwells. He has survived his illustrious contemporaries, and lives to find consolation in the recollection of friends who, for fifty years, cherished the remembrance of his serviceable sympathy, and never spoke his name but in grateful affection. Joseph Cottle must by this time have travelled far beyond his threescore years and ten; we record it to the old man's praise, that he came to the rescue of genius in its difficulties, and husbanded for mankind powers that might have been deserted through disappointment, and crushed by despair. Cottle provided for the immediate wants of Coleridge, and offered Southey, much to his astonishment, fifty guineas for his unpublished poem of *Joan of Arc*, with a present of fifty copies for his subscribers. Southey noted the instance as the only one extant of a bookseller proving as inexperienced and as enthusiastic as an author himself.

Joan of Arc was an epic of considerable length, displaying great imaginative powers, a singular mastery of language, and an extraordinary facility of verse. Neither *Joan of Arc*, nor any other poem from Southey's pen, can take its place side by side with the masterpieces of those rare poets whose names become a nation's household words; but the first, and every subsequent metrical composition of the Poet Laureate, exhibited, in a remarkable manner, qualities that obtained for their possessor respect and admiration that will not readily be lost. Vigour, fluency, great skill, a fine ear, a flowing pen, strong perception, great learning, copious and recondite illustration—none of them everyday gifts—were all at the writer's command. One talent was given him in almost fatal exuberance. We have already adverted to it. It unfitted him for the highest excellence, and betrayed him into repeated error. The very abundance of the poetic coin distributed by Southey depreciated its value. The most precious of all metals, as our children may hereafter learn, will suffer from a glut. One stands appalled in the presence of Southey's poetic feats. "Is it not a pity, Grosvenor," he writes to one of his poetic friends, "that I should not execute my intention of writing more verses than Lope de Vega, more tragedies than Dryden, and more epics than Blackmore? The more I write the more I have to write. I have a Helicon kind of dropsy upon me, and *crescit indulgens sibi*." In another letter, written before he was twenty, he remarks that he has accomplished a most arduous task. "I have transcribed all my verses that appear worth the trouble. Of these I took one list—another of my pile of stuff and nonsense—and a third of what I have burnt and lost; upon an average 10,000 verses are burnt and lost, the same number preserved, and 15,000 worthless. *Consider that all my letters are excluded*, and you may judge what waste of paper I have occasioned." A note is added by the editor, to the effect that most of these excluded letters were written in verse, and often *on four sides of folio paper*. Shakspeare has informed us how the poet delivers up his heavenborn fancies, and we believe him. Southey kills faith and makes us infidels for ever. A poet's eye "in fine frenzy rolling" is not the eye with which Robert Southey contemplated his creative work and set about it. "I must fly from thought," he writes to Horace Bedford in 1793, "To-day I begin *Cowper's Homer, and write an ode; to-morrow read and write something else.*' As coolly he expresses himself, nine years afterwards, upon the completion of another long epic. "It was my design to identify Madoc with Mango Capac, the legislator of Peru; in this I have totally failed, therefore *Mango Capac is to be the hero of another poem.*" Writing a thousand lines, or destroying a thousand, the labour was equally effortless. "Yesterday," he tells a friend, "I drew the pen across 600 lines, and am now writing to you instead of supplying their place." But their place will be supplied the moment the letter is despatched, for "the poem goes over for publication very shortly." The fountain can never be exhausted. It is as full, and flows as bountifully in 1809 as in 1793. No merchant ever advised his correspondent more methodically and accurately of the items of a cargo than the Laureate communicates to his brother, on the 25th of November, 1809, the *measurement* of a poem just taken off the stocks. "I have this day finished *Kehama*, having written 200 lines since yesterday morning; twenty-four sections, 4,844 lines; 200 or 300 more will probably be added in course of correction and transcription; and all has been done before breakfast, except about 170 lines of the conclusion." What Southey accomplished, however, difficult as it may be to realise the thought, was but a drop in the ocean compared with the great flood which, in his youth, he had designed to pour from his inexhaustible soul into our sadly parched world. He informs a correspondent, in 1812, what had been his generous intention, had not prudence demanded a sacrifice which it almost broke the poet's heart to make. "I had a design," he says, "of rendering every mythology which had ever extended itself widely, and powerfully influenced the human mind, the basis of a narrative poem. I began with the religion of the Koran, and consequently founded the history of the story upon that resignation, which is the only virtue it has produced. Had *Thalaba* been more successful, my whole design would by this time have been effected; for, prepared as I was with the whole materials for each, and with the general idea of the story, *I should assuredly have produced such a poem every year*." We cannot sympathise with the poet in his bitter regret that the opportunity of fulfilling his object was never permitted him.

But, if Southey in his youth composed with rapidity, and gave free rein to a steed that might have been the better for the curb—if, instead of subjecting his intellect to the rigorous discipline, and to the severe habit of investigation, for want of which his well-intentioned and well-stored mind stumbled so frequently in the dark as he advanced in life—if, we say, instead of doing this, he would read without discrimination, and write without limit, it must not be supposed that the struggling lad had no true sense of the poet's mission. His very reverence for the poetic office induced him to regard as an ordinary pursuit the only serious occupation in life which ceases to be cultivated with success the instant it is brought down to the level of a profession. Industrious from his cradle, he could find happiness only in employment. He was happy beyond expression composing his *Joan of Arc*, though laden at heart with all the cares that can oppress the unfortunate, at the threshold of life. His future was uncertain, his present was one of penury. Whilst the precious sheets were printing, he was walking the streets of Bristol without the means of purchasing a dinner. When he lay down at night with no hope of providing for the necessary food of the 'morrow—if he could not sleep, it was simply because his head was full of the verses, and busy with the incidents that were to be committed to paper with the returning daylight. All that he gained by the publication of *Joan of Arc* was over and over again forestalled by his lodging-house bill for tea, bread and butter, and similar modest fare, but the benefit derived from resolute persistence in the labour that he loved, and prosecuted because it comforted and sustained him, compensated richly for trial and privation, had they been twenty times as terrible as they were. To work was part of Southey's religion.

Shortly after Mr. Cottle's munificent purchase of the copyright of *Joan of Arc*, Southey's uncle, who held a chaplaincy in Portugal, arrived in England. He found his nephew a Unitarian in religion, and a Radical in politics. Moreover, he saw him with no visible means of earning his bread, and yet engaged to be married. The rev. gentleman acted a father's part by the unfortunate. To mend his faith, to improve his politics, and to wean his mind from an "imprudent attachment," he proposed a six months' visit to Portugal preparatory to his adoption of the legal profession, for which pursuit the good uncle undertook to prepare him by a needful supply of funds. To gratify his mother, Southey consented to the trip; but, as soon as his uncle had fixed the day for departure, he himself fixed the same day for his union with Edith Fricker. They married, and parted immediately after the ceremony was performed. Edith was poor, and Southey, who resolved to earn money by the sweat of his brow, feared that she would hesitate to receive funds from one not legally her husband. To remove her scruples, he assumed the right to provide for her wants. "Should I perish by shipwreck," he writes from Falmouth to Mr. Cottle, to the care of whose sisters he had left his maiden wife, "or by any other casualty, I have relations whose prejudice will yield to the anguish of affection, and who will love, cherish, and give all possible consolation to my widow." With these words Southey set sail for Portugal, and his wife, who had persuaded him to go, and cried when he was going, though she would not then have permitted him to stay, meekly retired to her place of refuge, wearing her wedding-ring round her neck.

CHAPTER THE SECOND.

Southey returned from Lisbon after a six months' stay, and proceeded at once to London, with his wife, to study the law. It was an irksome labour to the man to whom untiring industry was the very salt of life. His memory was marvellous from childhood, but he could recollect literally nothing of his legal lore the moment he had closed his books. He states that it was not difficult to master the principles or to understand the facts which such books submitted to his eye, so long as his eye was permitted to rest upon them. That once removed, however, and the whole machinery vanished immediately "like the baseless fabric of a vision." A year of torture elapsed and Southey gave up the profitless pursuit. A second visit was made to Portugal in 1800—this time in company with his wife—for the benefit of his health; and advantage was taken of the sojourn to obtain a thorough acquaintance with Portuguese literature. In 1801, the student and his wife were in England again, with no better prospects than before, but by no means repentant of the past or disheartened for the future. In 1802 comes a glimpse of good fortune, and a blaze of promise. Interest has obtained for the poet the somewhat uncongenial appointment of private secretary to the Chancellor of the Exchequer in Ireland, with a salary of 400*l.* a-year, and he hastens to Dublin to undertake the duties of his office. They are not very arduous, for, to say the truth, he has nothing whatever to do. The Right Hon. Isaac Corry, the minister, his master, alive to the fact, proposes to his secretary the tuition of his son.

The proposition is manfully rejected, and Southey resigns his appointment in a very few months after he had accepted it. He goes back to Bristol nothing regretting that he has thrown up "a foolish office and a good salary," and bravely sets to work for the booksellers. He has "a job in hand for Longman and Rees, which will bring him in 60*l.*, a *possibility* of 40*l.*, and a *chance* of a further 30*l.*" What look out can be more magnificent?

We approach an incident in the poet's life which brings us in presence of one of the finest features of his noble character. While struggling at this time on his own account against wind and tide he became acquainted with the forlorn condition of Mrs. Newton, the sister of Chatterton, who, it will be remembered, was, as well as Southey, a native of Bristol. Mrs. Newton and her family were in great distress, and to provide for their wants Southey undertook, in conjunction with Mr. Cottle, to publish by subscription a complete edition of Chatterton's works. The labour, not a slight one, was conscientiously performed. The edition appeared in three volumes octavo at the end of the year 1802, and Southey and his friend had the extreme gratification of paying over to Mrs. Newton no less than 300*l.* as the produce of their industry. The sum rescued the family from poverty, and made them happy in their latter days. Two years before, Southey, writing to his brother from Portugal, had entreated him to pursue his medical studies steadily, and to rely upon the writer's assistance the moment he was able to afford it. "By the time," he writes, "you have acquired enough previous knowledge I trust some of my eggs will be hatched, so that you may graduate either at Edinburgh or in Germany, as shall appear best. On my return you shall have a home, and I trust more comfortable than any you have yet had. We are rising in the world; it is our turn, and will be our own faults if we do not, all of us, attain that station in the world to which our intellectual rank entitles us."

Note the proud expression of conscious power, and admire the patient, humble perseverance which in Southey's case invariably accompanied it! The ardent poet did not wait until his return to England to advance his brother's interest. During his absence he had completed his poem of "Thalaba." He had fixed its value, and thus he writes to his mother respecting his brother and his composition—

"About Harry, it is necessary to remove him; his room is wanted for a more profitable pupil, and he has outgrown his situation. I have an excellent letter from him, and one from William Taylor, advising me to place him with some provincial surgeon of eminence, who will for a hundred guineas board and instruct him for four or five years. A hundred guineas! Well, but thank God, there is 'Thalaba' ready, for which I ask this sum. I have, therefore, thus eat my calf, and desired William Taylor to inquire for a situation—and so once more goes the furniture of my long expected house in London."

It was not the first time that Robert Southey thus forestalled his earnings. For himself, from the earliest hour of his difficult career until its melancholy close, he never contracted a debt, or permitted one indulgence which his means did not liberally justify; yet his whole battle was fought with a load upon his back which would quickly enough have crushed or disgusted a spirit less brave, less hopeful, less magnanimous than his own. His father died poor, and left his brethren to be advanced by his aid. Southey was never so poor as not to be able to extend it. He was not two-and-twenty when Mr. Lovel, who married his wife's sister, fell ill of fever, died, and left his widow and child without the slightest provision. Robert Southey took mother and child at once to his humble hearth, and there the former found happiness until his death. Coleridge, not sufficiently instructed by a genius to which his contemporaries did homage, in a wayward and unpardonable mood withdrew himself from the consolations of home; and in their hour of desertion his wife and children were saved half the knowledge of their hardships by finding a second husband and another father in the sanctuary provided for them by Robert Southey.

"It is my fate," he writes on one occasion, when asking promotion for his brother in the navy, "to have more claimants upon me than usually fall to the share of a man who has a family of his own; and if Tom's circumstances could be mended by a lift in his profession it would be a relief to him as well as to me." But throughout the whole of his correspondence we cannot detect one impatient murmur at his position, or the least intimation that he regarded the wants of his relatives but as so many responsibilities which it was his duty as well as highest gratification cheerfully to meet. "One reason why my father's expenditure," says the biographer, "was with difficulty kept within his income was that considerable sums were, not now and then, but regularly, drawn from him by his less successful relatives." Most assuredly, Robert Southey worked not the less vigorously and contentedly on that account.

Bearing the fact in mind, however, we shall be able to do justice to the conduct of a man whose sympathies for misfortune stretched further than his own door, and to estimate in some degree the splendid sacrifices which he could also make to friendship. In 1811, his friend William Taylor falls into misfortune. He writes to Dr. Gooch on the subject, proposing that the friends of Taylor should without delay raise a sum sufficient to purchase an annuity, or contribute annually a fixed payment towards their unfortunate friend's support. "I am ready now," he says, "with a yearly ten pounds, or with fifty at once. If more were in my power more should be done; but if his friends do not love him well enough to secure him at least 100*l.* a-year, one way or other, the world is worse than I thought it." Again, a few years afterwards, "Seal up 10*l.*," he writes to Mr. Bedford, "and leave it with Mr. Rickman, directed for Charles Lamb, Esq., from R. S. It is for poor John Morgan, whom you may remember some twenty years ago. This poor fellow, whom I knew at school, and whose mother has sometimes asked me to her table when I should otherwise have gone without a dinner, was left with a fair fortune of from 10,000*l.* to 15,000*l.*, and without any vice or extravagance of his own he has lost the whole of it. A stroke of the palsy has utterly disabled him from doing any thing to maintain himself. In this pitiable case, Lamb and I have promised him 10*l.* a year each as long as he lives. You will understand that this is an *explanation* to you, not an *application.* In a case of this kind contributions become a matter of feeling and duty among those who know the party, but strangers are not to be looked to." In 1821, Mr. May, a gentleman from whom Southey in early life had received substantial service, fell into serious pecuniary difficulties himself. On the 10th of December in that year the poet writes to his old benefactor, entreating him to break away from business, and to put himself in the mail for Keswick, that change of air and scene may assist him in bearing his anxieties, and enable him "to lay in a store of pleasant recollections." At the same time while confessing that it is not often he allows himself to wish the accidents of fortune had been more in his favour, Southey intimates that by the same post he has directed his friend Bedford to transfer to Mr. May 625*l.* in the Three per Cents.—his whole savings! "I wish it was more," are his words, "and that I had more at command in any way. I shall in the spring, if I am paid for the first volume of my History as soon as it is finished. 100*l.* I should, at all events, have sent you then. It shall be as much more as I may receive." We make no apology for dwelling at length upon these circumstances. If biography be not utterly worthless, these illustrations of Southey's character have an inestimable value. Look at him, pen in hand, the indefatigable day labourer in his literary seclusion, with no inheritance but his vigorous intellect, no revenue but such as his well-stored mind and matchless industry can furnish, perfect in the manifold relation of husband, brother, father, friend, and by his chosen labours delighting and instructing the world, as well as ministering to the daily happiness of his needy circle,—Look, we say, and confess that heroism is here which conquerors might envy!

Nor was it alone by gifts of money that Southey evinced the natural goodness of his heart, and his eager desire to benefit his fellow-men. He was never so occupied but that he could find time to guide uninstructed genius through its mazy paths, and, if necessary, to accompany the aspiring and friendless some distance on their critical and uncertain journey. Few things are more affecting than the relations of Southey with the young and ardent poets who at various times applied to him for encouragement and help, and who never approached in fear but to be dismissed with even more than hope and healthy reassurance. A year or two after he had helped to rescue Chatterton's sister from want, poor Henry Kirke White published his small volume of poems, which was at once mercilessly and unjustly attacked by one of the leading Reviews of the day. The pathetic letter which Kirke White addressed to the Review, explaining the peculiar circumstances under which his verses were written, caught Southey's eye, and he wrote immediately to the lad, beseeching him to bear up, to proceed in the road he had taken, and to rely upon the writer's aid if he should think fit to publish again. Kirke White returned a grateful answer to his correspondent, promised to act in conformity with his instructions, and proceeded to Cambridge, where hard work rapidly killed him. What Kirke White could not do for himself Southey accomplished for him after his death. He collected his *Remains*, wrote a brief memoir of his life to accompany them, and vindicated the genius which was extinguished before it had time to secure its immortality.

A melancholy halo surrounds the history of more

than one fine-spirited youth, who, encouraged by the tenderness exhibited for Kirke White, freely communicated to Southey their poetic longings, with the hope of interesting the benefactor on their behalf. In 1813 a lad of the name of Dusautoy, then about seventeen years of age, the son of a retired officer living in Devon, and one of a numerous family, inclosed some verses to Southey, requesting the poet's opinion and advice as to their publication. Southey's answer was to warn and teach forbearance. "Abstain from publication," was the sage advice: "read and write. Shoot at a high mark, and you will gain strength of arm. Precision of aim will come in its proper season." The boy proceeded to Cambridge, Southey having taken some trouble to procure him admission into Emmanuel. In the college examinations he stood the first of his year in classics, and fourth in mathematics; he obtained several exhibitions, and was on the high road to University honours, when he fell a victim to a fever that broke out in the town. "I do not think," says Southey, "there ever lived a youth of higher promise." At one time he intended to publish the student's papers. "In seeking to serve him," he says, "I have been the means of sending him prematurely to the grave. I will at least endeavour to preserve his memory."

The case of Herbert Knowles has a still more painful interest than that of Dusautoy. Knowles was a poor boy of the humblest origin, without father or mother, yet with abilities sufficient to excite the attention of strangers, who subscribed 20*l.* a year towards his education, upon condition that his friends should furnish 30*l.* more. The boy was sent to Richmond

School, Yorkshire, preparatory to his proceeding as a sizar to St. John's, but when he quitted school the friends were unable to advance another sixpence on his account. To help himself Herbert Knowles wrote a poem, sent it to Southey, with a history of his case, and asked permission to dedicate it to the Laureate. Southey, finding the poem "brimful of power and of promise," made inquiries of the schoolmaster, and received the highest character of the youth. He then answered the application of Knowles, entreated him to avoid present publication, and promised to do something better than receive his dedication. He subscribed at once 10*l.* per annum towards the failing 30*l.*, and procured similar subscriptions from Mr. Rogers and the late Lord Spencer. Herbert Knowles receiving the news of his good fortune, wrote to his protector a letter remarkable for much more than the gratitude which pervaded every line. He remembered that Kirke White had gone to the university countenanced and supported by patrons, and that to pay back the debt he owed them he wrought day and night, until his delicate frame gave way, and his life became the penalty of his devotion. Herbert Knowles felt that he could not make the same desperate efforts, and deemed it his first duty to say so. "I will not deceive," he writes in his touching anxiety:—

"Far be it from me to foster expectations which I feel I cannot gratify. Two years ago I came to Richmond totally ignorant of classical and mathematical literature. Out of that time, during three months and two long vacations, I have made but a retrograde course. If I enter into competition for university honours, I shall kill myself. Could I twine, to gratify my friends, a laurel with the cypress, I would not repine, but to sacrifice the little inward peace which the wreck of passion has left behind, and relinquish every hope of future excellence and future usefulness in one wild and unavailing pursuit, were indeed a madman's act, and worthy of a madman's fate."

The poor fellow promised to do what he could, assured his friends that he would not be idle, and that if he could not reflect upon them any extraordinary credit, he would certainly do them no disgrace. Herbert Knowles had taken an accurate measure of his strength and capabilities, and soon gave proof that he spoke at the bidding of no uncertain monitor within him. Two months after his letter to Southey he was laid in his grave. The fire consumed the lamp even faster than the trembling lad suspected.

But we must dwell no longer upon this fair portion of the Laureate's character, though it be the fairest we have it in our power to present. Ebenezer Elliott, the corn-law rhymer, who died the other day, might have told us how much he owed of his success to the judicious, and ever-ready advice of Robert Southey; and Chauncey Hare Townshend still lives to acknowledge such obligations as are due from son to sire. The reader who consults Southey's correspondence will note reiterated instances of goodwill, benevolence, and tenderest sympathy, exercised under circumstances that might easily have framed a sufficient apology for their absence. Let them not be forgotten, when it becomes our duty to present a view of the Laureate, upon which the sun will not be found, perhaps, to shine so clearly and so brightly!

At the age of thirty Southey was fairly in harness, devoting half his time to the booksellers, who furnished him the means of living, and half to the prosecution of his darling pursuits, and to the supposed foundations of his fame. It was his belief that genius had no excuse for follies and eccentricities, which are culpable in dulness, and he would not allow himself the luxury of metrical composition, until the prosaic wants of his household were honestly supplied. Providence has rewarded conscientious industry. The reputation of Southey, curiously enough, rests upon the works he wrote in the discharge of humble duty. It has been already said that the poet went to Oxford liberal in his politics to the last degree. He returned from the University equally enthusiastic. As late as 1804, when he was thirty, we find him complaining that "Pitt will go blundering on till everybody, by miserable experience, thinks him what I always did," and looking to Fox for such advancement as a Ministry could give him. Eight years afterwards, however, upon the assassination of Mr. Perceval, we find Mr. Fox's admirer speaking very much in the strain of Mr. Pitt's supporter; but when, how, or why the important change in Southey's political opinions took place, the editor of these volumes takes no pains to inform us. The secret of his conversion lies, we think, not very deep. The key to that, and to other stranger anomalies, Southey himself liberally places in the hands of all who attentively read his correspondence. We shall have occasion to produce it.

In 1804 Southey took up his abode amongst the mountains of Cumberland, and in the house in which, just forty years afterwards, he closed his active, though tranquil career. From first to last there was but slight variation in the course of his life.

"My actions,' he writes, "are as regular as St. Dunstan's quarter-boys. Three pages of history after breakfast (equivalent to five in small quarto printing); then to transcribe and copy for the press, or to make my selections and biographies, or what else suits my humour, till dinner time; from dinner till tea I read, write letters, see the newspapers, and very often indulge in a siesta. After tea, I go to poetry, and correct, and rewrite, and copy, till I am tired, and then turn to anything else till supper."

The result of his intense and regular application is marvellous. We question whether any writer of any country ever produced so much. The fountain never ceased to flow until, fairly exhausted, it could yield no more. The man had but one brain and but one pair of hands, yet he performed at one time the labour of an academy.

"Last night," he writes to Mr. Bedford, in 1806, "I began the preface to the *Specimens of English Poets.* Huzza! And now, Grosvenor, let me tell you what I have to do. I am writing—1. *The History of Portugal.* 2. *The Chronicle of the Cid.* 3. *The Curse of Kehama.* 4. *Espriella's Letters.* Look you, all these *I am* writing. The second and third must get into the press and out of it before this time twelvemonths, or else I shall be like the civil list. By way of interlude comes in the preface. Don't swear, and bid me do one thing at a time. I tell you I can't afford to do one thing at a time; no, nor two neither: and it is only by doing many things that I contrive to do so much; for I cannot work long at anything without hurting myself, and I do everything by heats: then, by the time I am tired of one, my inclination for another is at hand."

Success or failure, well paid or ill paid, it is all the same. Courage never gives way, perseverance never flags. If the public are slow to appreciate the gigantic epics, posterity will show a juster discrimination. He knows full well that "one overwhelming propensity has formed his destiny, and marred all prospects of rank and wealth; but it has made him happy, and will make him immortal!" If the booksellers will not venture a sixpence upon *Madoc*, is he not revenged by unworthily employing his pen upon labours which they are content to remunerate more handsomely! Another mode of taking vengeance was thoroughly Southeyan. Religiously believing that a second generation would hail a Milton in the writer of *Thalaba*, he resolved not to publish any more corrected editions of his poems during his lifetime, but to leave such corrections of all as would avail to give a second lease of copyright to his children. The demand of a future public would be overwhelming, and thus he would disappoint and agonise the booksellers! And so he went on writing epics!

In 1807, Sir Walter Scott proposed to Southey that he should contribute to the *Edinburgh Review*. Southey's answer intimates how far he had travelled from Edinburgh politics. "To Jeffery, as an individual," he writes in reply, "I shall ever be ready to show every kind of individual courtesy! but of Judge Jeffery, of the *Edinburgh Review*, I must ever think and speak as of a bad politician, a worse moralist, and a critic, in matters of taste, equally incompetent and unjust."

A few months before "something had been picked out of the fire" for Southey, in the shape of a Government pension for "literary services," amounting to 160*l.* per annum clear, and the following year he found a congenial home for his altered sentiments in the *Quarterly*, a periodical mainly established to counteract the influence of the Scottish *Review*, and set on foot at the instigation of the late John Murray.

The pension and the constant and well-remunerated employment provided by the *Quarterly*, removed all anxiety on the score of daily bread. The former enabled the labourer to ensure his life for his family; the latter yielded a sufficient and certain income. The poet's idea of a competency was realised; that is to say, his *latest* idea, for he had many on the subject. In volume i. of the correspondence, when he had nothing at all, earthly happiness meant 100*l.* a-year certain. In volume ii. the prospect enlarged, though still "the views and hopes were bounded to an income of 500*l.*" Happy the genius that could find content within that narrow circle!

CHAPTER THE THIRD.

The mere events of Southey's life, from his thirtieth year until his death, might be told in a paragraph. An extract from his own letter has shown how he passed a day in his happy retirement. One day is a sample of all.

When it is added that he became the tutor of his own sons and the hospitable entertainer of as many visitors to the lakes as came armed with letters of introduction to the poet, some idea may be formed of the demands made throughout life upon his intellect and time. That he should have been able to accomplish so much is miraculous; and yet what he lived to complete constituted but a small portion of the ambitious designs harboured in his restless brain. One intended high achievement is spoken of from the first volume to the last. Every spare moment through long years had been devoted to the collection of materials, which, once marshalled into form, were intended to rival in interest and duration of frame the great memorials of Herodotus and Thucydides. "Hand to mouth work," he writes very early in his career, "is very disheartening, and interferes cruelly with better things. But from my *History of Portugal* I do expect permanent profit, and such a perpetual interest as shall relieve me." Every volume of the correspondence contains a reference to this cherished work. In truth, the constant return of the burden falls on the ear like the mournful strains of a chorus bewailing the impotency of human efforts and the vanity of all sublunary schemes. The work of his life—as if he had not performed the labour of a dozen lives—Southey, dying, left unfinished. When shortly before his death the noble vessel of his mind cracked and gave way, the recollection of his grand design hovered over the splendid ruin as a spirit of consolation and peace. The *History of Portugal* was the day-dream of the old man, when dreams were all that remained to him of the reality of life.

Sir Walter Scott was amongst the best and steadiest friends of Southey. We have seen him anxious to connect him with the *Edinburgh Review.* In 1809 he spoke on his behalf to Canning, who proposed for his friend an appointment in his own department of the value of 300*l.* per annum. Sir Walter on sufficient grounds declined it, and then suggested to Southey a professorship at one of the Universities. Professorships in England "are fenced about with subscription," and in 1809 Southey could not subscribe as readily as he might twenty years afterwards. In 1813, upon the death of Pye, the Poet Laureate, the offer of the vacant appointment was made to Scott, who excused himself "as being incompetent to the task of annual commemoration," but strongly recommended Southey as a fit recipient of the honour. Upon Southey, at Scott's desire, the laurel was accordingly conferred. In 1817 the librarianship of the Advocate's Library at Edinburgh, with a salary of 400*l.* per annum, and a prospect of increase, was offered to the Laureate, but his age—for he had reached his forty-fourth year—his dislike of cities, his comparative freedom from pecuniary anxieties, his love for his chosen profession, disinclined him for removal from Keswick, and he refused. He continued in his old path, writing regularly for the *Quarterly*, publishing at stated intervals his prose and his poetic compositions; increasing his stock of books, and gathering from all imaginable sources an incalculable amount of variegated lore. There are breaks in the placid career, such as occur in the progress of all. One year he loses an infant, of whom he is "foolishly fond;" another year he suffers a more bitter loss in the death of a boy already old enough to give promise of excellence, and to take a lively interest in the pursuits and reputation of his sire and sole instructor. "You know," he writes to Mr. Bedford at the time of this great misfortune, "how much I used to unbend and play with the children in frequent intervals of study, as though I were an idle man. Of this I am quite incapable, and shall long continue so. No circumstances of my former life ever brought with it so great a change as that which I daily and hourly feel, and perhaps shall never cease to feel." He justly estimated the weight of this heavy blow. He never thoroughly recovered it. A few years afterwards additional misery was poured into the cup. Returning from a visit to Holland in 1826, he found his daughter Isabel laid on a bed of sickness, from which she did not rise again. "Well do I, though but a child," writes the biographer, "remember that return, as we hastened to meet him, and changed by our sorrowful tidings his cheerful smile and glad welcome to tears and sadness. It was the first time I had seen sorrow enter that happy home; and those days of alternate hope and fear, and how he paced the garden in uncontrollable anguish, and gathered us round him to prayer when all was over, are vividly impressed upon my mind." The domestic picture gets sadder as time wears on; but upon what earthly tabernacle do the "shades of the prison house" not pensively close? In 1834 Southey's eldest daughter married. "The best days of home were over." Shortly afterwards his son Cuthbert quitted the roof to be prepared for Oxford, and very soon a calamity occurred that made all other sorrows fade in the comparison. The mother of the house was bereft of her reason. The anxieties of the household had told upon a delicate frame, and the sole hope of restoration was instant removal from home. The dreadful journey which poor Lamb oftener than once had taken with his sister, Southey underwent with his Edith. "Forty years," he writes to Grosvenor Bedford from York, "has she been the life of my life—and I have left her this day in a lunatic asylum." In the same brief letter he expresses the resignation of a Christian and the confident courage of a man. "God, who has visited me with this affliction," he says, "has given me strength to bear it, and will, *I know*, support me to the end, whatever that may be. To-morrow I return to my poor children. I have much to be thankful for under this visitation. For the first time in my life (he was sixty years old) I am so far beforehand with the world that my means are provided for the whole of next year, and that I can meet this additional expenditure, considerable in itself, without any difficulty." Again—"Mine is a strong heart. I will not say that the last week has been the most trying of my life; but I will say that the heart which could bear it can bear anything." Much as the heart had been tried, it had not undergone the unrelenting conflict of his mind. The former might well be proof against affliction whilst the latter was already tottering.

In the height of his great affliction—at a time we are told when Southey was working more closely than ever—two letters, in one enclosure, reached his desolate house from the minister of the day. Sir Robert Peel had recommended the Laureate to the king for the distinction of a baronetcy. So little were his affairs known, so creditably and so modestly had he borne himself, that it was generally supposed Southey, with other successful writers of the day, had secured a handsome competency by his labours, and that an accession of rank would be as acceptable an addition to his wealth as it had proved to his brother poet at Abbotsford. In one of the two letters referred to was a formal announcement of His Majesty's intention; the other was a private letter from Sir Robert, requesting Southey to say unreservedly how best the minister might serve him, and so find some consolation himself for the many heavy sacrifices entailed by the possession of office. Southey's reply was like himself. He forwarded to Sir Robert Peel a clear statement of his position, and respectfully declined the proffered distinction. Without loss of time—and, indeed, there was little time to lose, for it was April, 1835—Sir Robert attached his name to a warrant which added 300*l.* annually to the amount of Southey's pension, and made at least one deserving man the happier for his four months' tenure of the reins of power.

In 1837, Mrs. Southey, who had been taken back to Keswick some time before, closed her pitiable existence. For three years she had suffered her terrible affliction, and during the whole of that time Southey had betrayed no loss of power in body or mind. With the death of his wife, however, and with the withdrawal of one great incitement to exertion, he became at once an altered man. At first the indications of change were slight and unobserved. He found it difficult to accommodate himself to his altered circumstances. "There is no one," he mournfully writes, "to partake with me the recollections of the best and happiest portion of my life; and for that reason, were there no other, such recollections must henceforth be purely painful, except when I connect them with the prospects of futurity." His spirits were no longer, as they had previously been, uniformly cheerful; his air and gait gradually parted with their accustomed elasticity. In 1838 a trip to the continent was proposed by a few of his dearest friends. His son, the biographer, formed one of the party, and could not fail to detect a considerable change in his father since they had last travelled in company. His movements were slower; he was subject to strange and unusual fits of absence, and he exhibited an indecision in his manner and an unsteadiness in his step that had nothing in common with the vigour and firmness that belonged to the spirit and flesh of Robert Southey. As the party proceeded on their journey the signs of mental decrepitude became more painful. He would continually lose his way in the most familiar places, and, being narrowly watched by his child in consequence, would now smile at his errors as if to cloak their origin, and now openly confess an affecting consciousness of his revealed infirmities. We have omitted to say that, in addition to his other writings, Southey invariably kept a minute record of all that he saw on his travels. What he did not do in the way of composition it is difficult, in truth, to say. We half suspect, from an intimation in the volumes before us, that he even kept faithful copies of his countless letters. His last journal, containing an account of the tour of which we speak, is but too accurate an index of the condition of mind under which it was composed. It breaks off abruptly when about two-thirds of the tour were completed, and shows a gradual but perceptible change in the hand-writing—"a change which, as his malady crept on, became more and more marked, until in some of the last notes he ever wrote the letters are formed like the early efforts of a child." The continental journey, as we have said, took place in 1838. At the close of that year we find the shaken man, then in his sixty-fifth year, residing for a time with Mr. Bowles. In 1839, and on the 5th of June, Southey married Mr. Bowles' daughter. The biographer contents himself with a simple announcement of the fact. We follow his example.

On his way home to Keswick, after his marriage, Southey passed a few days in London. No doubt any longer existed of his melancholy decline. The vigour of his faculties was gone. His body was thin and shrunk, his animated face had lost its fire, his intellect had no vestige of its former clearness. A friend who visited him noticed, in the course of conversation, an obvious confusion of ideas. "He lost himself for a moment; he was conscious of it, and an expression passed over his countenance which was exceedingly touching—an expression of pain and also of resignation." The friends of the poet attributed his ailments to repeated attacks of influenza, from which he had repeatedly suffered. Nearly half a century of incessant mental toil could give a more rational solution of the utter wreck. The candle had burnt to the socket—the brain was exhausted—the intellectual fibre was utterly worn out. He soon ceased to work at all; and for Southey to cease from labour, was to be deprived of reason, strength, and life. What else should keep that eager soul and body from its blissful occupations? And, in very truth, when reason had taken its last and everlasting leave, when the body had become inert, and when life itself hung by the slenderest thread, the shadow of things past remained, and the temple was not wholly unconscious of the glories that were once enshrined there. While one spark of reason lingered Southey would still talk of work that could no longer be done, of the resumption of labours, that had been laid aside for ever, and even when the black night came at last, and memory, utterly extinguished, could no longer brood upon its pleasures, the poor bereft scholar would still walk round his library, gaze intently on his darling books, take them down mechanically, affect to read them, and put them back again unread. For one sad year there was an utter blank—and then he died. He fell asleep on the 21st of March, 1843, and he lies in Crosthwaite churchyard with his children who preceded him, and with their mother, his own faithful Edith. "One circumstance," says his son, "connected with the last years of his life deserves to be noticed as very singular. His hair, which was previously almost snowy white, grew perceptibly darker, and I think, if anything, increased in thickness and a disposition to curl." The livery of toil had been thrown off in the solemn hour of mental blindness and repose.

The reader will have remarked that we have endeavoured to place before him, in the whole course of our narrative, the representation of Southey the man, rather than of Southey, poet, philosopher, and politician. It is not without deliberation that we have hitherto included in the picture the private rather than the public aspect of this great character. When Sir Robert Peel informed Southey of his having "advised the King to adorn the distinction of baronetage with a name the most eminent in literature," he truly added, that the name "had claims to respect and honour which literature alone can never confer," and that it was the minister's aim to mark his gratitude "for eminent services rendered, not only to literature, but to the higher interests of virtue and religion." Southey by his life adorned the literary profession, and for the sake of literature let his great example persuade the world to judge more tenderly of its gifted teachers, and induce the instructors to merit public respect and approbation by the practice of virtues that embellish the lowliest pursuits and give grace to the highest. True nobility dwelt in the quiet retreat among the Cumberland mountains. No English gentleman ever fulfilled the duties of his station more perfectly than the humble master of Greta-hall. It could not be said that the literary man was without *status* in society so long as Southey lived to prove that patient drudgery is still consistent with the daily exercise of all domestic virtues. Who should deny *his* social position, or refuse to acknowledge as an equal, the man who in learning and genius was superior to thousands, and in the ordinary relations of life was inferior to none?

We have already adverted to the style and character of Southey's poetical compositions. His protracted epics will certainly not assume the high classical place of which he believed them worthy. Beauties they have, which the intelligent will not be slow to appreciate; but they lack the divine element which alone enables human thoughts to take root for ever in the souls of the multitude. They were poured forth too easily, too rapidly, too voluminously, too much at the will of the writer, who never waited for the bidding of the Muse, but constituted himself her remorseless master. Southey's notions of rhythm, too, stood always in the way of popularity. Verse he contended should adapt itself to the requirements of the narrative, and in his adaptations he not seldom bewildered and distressed his readers. The violence of his transitions is sometimes wholly insupportable. Again, the subjects of Southey's principal metrical compositions were as unfavourable to success as his peculiar rhythmical views. They were foreign to the sympathies of his readers, and no amount of genius could bring them home to their hearts. At one period of his life he made the fearful resolution to render every mythology which had extended itself widely and powerfully influenced the human mind the basis of a narrative poem. Fortunately for himself, he was prevented so dreary an undertaking. As it is, his unpleasant heathenish discourses excite no living interest in the mind, and indicate nothing so much as his own utter ignorance of the machinery that constitutes the moving springs of passion in the people. The minor compositions of Southey are here and there of exquisite beauty, though even among these prolixity becomes too often a fault. Where prolixity is absent the short poetical effusions are perfect.

The remarks that apply to his poems may be extended to Southey's prose. His shortest productions are his best. The *Life of Nelson* will be cherished by his countrymen long after his interminable histories will be forgotten by all the world. Charming as his prose style unquestionably is—clear, masculine, and to the point—it is too often thrown away on subjects of little or no interest to the public, and, like his verse, becomes diffuse from the vastness of the writer's knowledge and his abiding inability or unwillingness to keep back his acquisitions and to exhibit the results of his great learning rather than the learning itself. We have a notable instance of this infirmity in the most entertaining and characteristic of all his works. *The Doctor*, full of quiet, delicious humour, most agreeable in style and manner, and overflowing with quaint learning of every kind, too frequently stops on his journey to dip into one of the most commonplace books which his industry contrived to fill, and with which his friends since his decease have astonished the public. How often the good Doctor's quotations are without any interest whatever, and how often their actual merit has nothing to do with the matter in hand, we need not inform those who are acquainted with this grotesque production. Had the Doctor given himself time to think, he would certainly have kept much of his erudition out of sight, and not been a whit the less welcome for presenting his cheerful mind and happy countenance, without his clogs and incumbrances.

It is impossible to deny that the grave and fatal fault of Southey's character was want of reflection. It is painful to note the countless evidences of the failing. Never has there been so clear a proof given of the worthlessness of inordinate labour unaccompanied by the constant exercise of superintending judgment. Southey gave so much time to the minds of other men that he seems never to have had a moment to look into his own. Nothing thoroughly distinct and perspicuous can be ascertained of either his political or religious convictions, and solely because neither the one set of views nor the other was based upon well matured principles, or resulted from a severe, though absolutely essential, process of thought. Southey retreated from hard mental discipline. His likes and his dislikes depended upon no fixed rules, but partook of the nature of his own mixed temperament. He is not, it is true, all things to all men, but all men and all things before finding acceptance with him must adapt themselves to his prejudices and prepossessions. Hence at different times of his life, we find him a freethinker, a Unitarian, an orthodox believer, and a heterodox churchman; a socialist, a republican, a determined opponent of Roman Catholic claims, a stickler for the rights of conscience, a party man, a Tory, and a merciless castigator of the powers that were. Is it not extraordinary that, possessing an astounding memory from his childhood and no ordinary powers of perception, he could by no ingenuity grasp the principles of law and was forced to give up the study in disgust? It would be inexplicable but for the acknowledgment, made over and over again in these volumes, that Southey hated science and scientific men, and therefore shrunk from a pursuit that brought him continually in contact with the objects of his dislike. "I once passed an evening," he writes, "with Professor Young at Davy's. The conversation was wholly scientific. . . . Generally speaking I have little liking for men of science. Their pursuits seem to deaden the imagination and *harden the heart*." Again, in a letter to Mr. Townsend:- "As a geologist you will enjoy one more pleasure than I do, who am ignorant of every branch of science. Mineralogy and botany are the only branches which I wish I had possessed. . . . These two sciences add to our out-door enjoyments and have no injurious effects. *Chymical and physical studies seem, on the contrary, to draw on very prejudicial consequences.* Their utility is not to be doubted; but *it appears as if man could not devote himself to these pursuits without blunting his finer faculties*." Once more, with reference to the great Sir Humphrey Davy—"These scientific men are, indeed, the victims of science; they sacrifice to it their own feelings and virtues and happiness." Can any conclusions be more monstrous, or indicate more certainly utter want of reflection upon the part of the man bold enough to utter them?

The prophecies of a sworn hater of science do not stand much chance of fulfilment, and those of Southey have had no better fate than might have been expected. He began to prophesy in 1803, when he announced that "the *Edinburgh Review* would not keep its ground." Half a century has elapsed, and the *Review* still flourishes. About the same time he proclaims that "The Protestant dissenters will die away. Destroy the test and you kill them." In 1851 the race is not extinct. No old lady looked for the destruction of the world by an earthquake with half the dread that Southey throughout his life contemplated the overthrow of Monarchy in his native land. He is for ever crying "Wolf," but the beast never comes. "The more I see, the more I read, and the more I reflect," he writes in 1813, "the more reason there appears to me to fear that our turn of revolution is hastening on." Two years afterwards the prospect is blacker still. "The foundations of Government are undermined. The props may last during your lifetime and mine, but I cannot conceal from myself a conviction that at no very distant day the whole fabric must fall." What scientific man, however "hard-hearted," would have ventured to propose the remedy against revolution which suggested itself to the poet in 1816? "The only remedy," he writes to Mr. Rickman "(*if even that be not too late*), is to check the press. . . . My measures would be to make transportation the punishment for sedition, and to *suspend the habeas corpus*, and thus I would either have the anarchists under way for Botany Bay or in prison within a month after the meeting of Parliament." It is nothing to Robert Southey that revolution does not come. The longer it tarries the more he raves. "There is an infernal spirit abroad," he writes in 1820, "and crushed it must be. The question is, whether it will be cut cut short in its course or suffered to expend itself like a fever. In the latter case we shall go on, through a bloodier revolution than that of France, to an Iron military Government—the only possible termination of Jacobinism." In 1823 the vision becomes more distinct and gloomy. The *clairvoyant* is in a state of ecstacy, and thus proceeds:—"The repeal of the Test Act will be demanded, and must be granted. The dissenters will get into the corporations. Church property will be attacked in Parliament. Reform in Parliament will be carried; and then

—Farewell, a long farewell to all our greatness." Southey once lit his fire with Euclid. Had he spared that inoffensive volume he might have found reward in the perusal of its calm and elementary truths. He was 55 years old when the Catholic Relief Bill passed. During its discussion he prophesied some of its results:—"The Protestant flag will be struck, the enemy will march in with flying colours, the Irish Church will be despoiled, the *Irish Protestants will lose heart, and great numbers will emigrate, flying while they can from the wrath to come.* These are my speculations," he says, adding with singular *naïveté*, "partaking perhaps of the sunshine of a hopeful and cheerful disposition." 1829 came and went; 1832 arrived, but still Robert Southey would not be comforted. "The direct consequence of Parliamentary reform must be a new disposal of church property, and an equitable adjustment with the fundholders—terms which in both cases mean spoliation;" therefore Southey is not indisposed to pray that "The cholera morbus may be sent us as a lighter plague than that which we have chosen for ourselves." The King threatens to make Peers! "Nothing, then, remains for us but to await the course of revolution. I shall not live to see what sort of edifice will be constructed out of the ruins, but I shall go to rest in the sure confidence that God will provide as is best for his church and people." It was well said, but Southey did not go to rest yet. A year later and he is prophesying away more lugubriously than ever. "I am not without strong apprehensions," he writes on the 6th of March, 1838, "that before this year passes away London will have its Three days!" Oh, had he but lived till 1848 and seen his London enjoying its *one* day—on the 10th of April!

Had Southey been less a hater of science he would have done greater justice to his own honest and thoroughly humane disposition. Had he conceived less loftily of his own unassisted and undisciplined powers, he would have been answerable for fewer errors of judgment, for which his heart was in no way responsible. By his extreme and almost fanatical views of society and government, put forth in the *Quarterly Review* and in other works, Southey evoked a spirit of dislike in the nation which his honest intention and true regard for the interests of his country might well have spared him. Because his convictions gushed vehemently from uninstructed feeling, and could never appeal to a satisfied judgment, they lacked in their expression the dignity of reason and the moderation of truth. The laughers were all against him and revelled in his inconsistency. And how frequently did inconsistency appear? Fresh from an attack upon Byron, whom he branded as chief of the Satanic School and reproached for his want of reverence, he wrote his own *Vision of Judgment*, which for irreverent and daring dealing with the mysteries ot Heaven can hardly be surpassed. Groaning in one breath over the ignorance of the people, he denounced in another all London universities and mechanics' institutes. Protesting against the crude theories of all political economists, he oftener than once suggested economical schemes, even more impracticable and absurd than his first boyish plan of rescuing society by means of Pantisocracy. One day he walks into Rowland Hill's chapel, and is shocked by the absence of the decorum and ceremonial observances that belong to his own orthodox and established church; the next he is proposing open air preaching, and a departure from custom and order at which decent dissenters themselves would stand aghast.

No words can express the thorough contempt which Southey felt for political economists, and no language, we fear, can make known his own great want of acquaintance with the first principles of government. What shall be said of the statesman who eternally laments the glaring fact, that public opinion has finally become the law of administration in England, instead of directing all his energies towards the elevation of that opinion by the wide dissemination of education and of every known means of social improvement? What shall be said of the politician who in the maturity of his years, and in the height of a popular struggle, in which the cause of the people was hallowed by justice, boldly announced that concession to the multitude and their political advancement were impossible, because "in divinity, in ethics, and in politics *there can be no new truths*;" and because "in any well-ordered state" it is impossible for the masses to have too little authority, independence, and power? What idea can we have of the reasoning faculties of the philosopher and the divine —for Southey wrote *Books on the Church*, and was deeply read in divinity—who saw growing around him institutions for dispelling ignorance and imparting useful knowledge, and yet could discern "in all these things nothing more than a purpose of excluding religion, and preparing the way for the overthrow of the Church?" We have said that the key to Southey's inconsistencies lies open in these volumes. Let the reader take it up, and unlock more of a good man's intellectual failings if he is so disposed. We have revealed enough. But before we part company with Robert Southey, let us take together, in charity, one final glance into the little room where sits the grey-haired man, "working hard and getting little—a bare maintenance, and hardly that; writing poems and history for posterity with his whole heart and soul; one daily progressing in learning, not so learned as he is poor, not so poor as proud, not so proud as happy." Great men have invited him to London, and he is now answering the invitation. The thought of the journey plagues him. "Oh dear, oh dear!" he writes, "there is such a comfort in one's old coat and old shoes, one's own chair and own fireside, one's own writing desk and own library—with a little girl climbing up to my neck and saying 'Don't go to London, Papa, you must stay with Edith'—and a little boy whom I have taught to speak the language of cats, dogs, cuckoos, jackasses, &c., before he can articulate a word of his own—there is such a comfort in all these things, that *transportation* to London seems a heavier punishment than any sins of mine deserve." Gently let us close the door upon such happiness.

THE AMOURS OF DEAN SWIFT.

GREATER men than Dean Swift may have lived. A more remarkable man never left his impress upon the age, immortalised by his genius. To say that English history supplies no narrative more singular and original than the career of Jonathan Swift, is to assert little. We doubt whether the histories of the world can furnish for example and instruction, for wonder and pity, for admiration and scorn, for approval and condemnation, a specimen of humanity at once so illustrious and so small. Before the eyes of his contemporaries, Swift stood a living enigma. To posterity he must continue for ever a distressing puzzle. One hypothesis—and one alone—gathered from a close and candid perusal of all that has been transmitted to us upon this interesting subject, helps us to account for a whole life of anomaly, but not to clear up the mystery in which it is shrouded. From the beginning to the ending of his days Jonathan Swift was more or less MAD.

Intellectually and morally, physically and religiously, Dean Swift was a mass of contradictions. His career yields ample materials both for the biographer who would pronounce a panegyric over his tomb, and for the censor whose business it is to improve one generation at the expense of another. Look at Swift with the light of intelligence shining on his brow, and you note qualities that might become an angel. Survey him under the dark cloud, and every feature is distorted into that of a fiend. If we tell the reader what he was, in the same breath we shall communicate all that he was not. His virtues were exaggerated into vices, and his vices were not without the savour of virtue. The originality of his writings is of a piece with the singularity of his character. He copied no man who preceded him. He has not been successfully imitated by any who have followed him. The compositions of Swift reveal the brilliancy of sharpened wit, yet it is recorded of the man that he was never known to laugh. His friendships were strong, and his antipathies vehement and unrelenting, yet he illustrated friendship by roundly abusing his familiars, and expressed hatred by bantering his foes. He was economical and saving to a fault, yet he made sacrifices to the indigent and poor sternly denied to himself. He could begrudge the food and wine consumed by a guest, yet throughout his life refuse to derive the smallest pecuniary advantage from his published works, and at his death bequeath the whole of his fortune to a charitable institution. From his youth Swift was a sufferer in body, yet his frame was vigorous, capable of great endurance, and maintained its power and vitality from the time of Charles II. until far on in the reign of the second George. No man hated Ireland more than Swift, yet he was Ireland's first and greatest patriot, bravely standing up for the rights of that kingdom when his chivalry might have cost him his head. He was eager for reward, yet he refused payment with disdain. Impatient of advancement, he preferred to the highest honours the state could confer, the obscurity and ignominy of the political associates with whom he had affectionately laboured until they fell disgraced. None knew better than he the stinging force of a successful lampoon, yet such missiles were hurled by hundreds at his head without in any way disturbing his bodily tranquillity. Sincerely religious, scrupulously attentive to the duties of his holy office, vigorously defending the position and privileges of his order, he positively played into the hands of infidelity by the steps he took, both in his conduct and writings, to expose the cant and hypocrisy which he detested as heartily as he admired and practised unaffected piety. To say that Swift lacked tenderness, would be to forget many passages of his unaccountable history that overflow with gentleness of spirit and mild humanity; but to deny that he exhibited inexcusable brutality where the softness of his nature ought chiefly to have been evoked—where the want of tenderness, indeed, left him a naked and irreclaimable savage—is equally impossible. If we decline to pursue the contradictory series further, it is in pity to the reader, not for want of materials at command. There is, in truth, no end to such materials.

Swift was born in the year 1667. His father, who was steward to the Society of the King's Inn, Dublin, died before his birth and left his widow penniless. The child, named Jonathan, after his father, was brought up on charity. The obligation due to an uncle was one that Swift would never forget, or remember without inexcusable indignation. Because he had not been left to starve by his relatives, or because his uncle would not do more than he could, Swift conceived an eternal dislike to all who bore his name, and a haughty contempt for all who partook of his nature. He struggled into active life, and presented himself to his fellow men in the temper of a foe. At the age of fourteen, he was admitted into Trinity College, Dublin, and four years afterwards, as *a special grace*—for his acquisitions apparently failed to earn the distinction—the degree of Bachelor of Arts was conferred upon him. In 1682, the year in which the war broke out in Ireland, Swift, in his twenty-first year, and without a sixpence in his pocket, left college. Fortunately for him, the wife of Sir William Temple was related to his mother, and upon her application to that statesman the friendless youth was provided with a home. He took up his abode with Sir William in England, and for the space of two years laboured hard at his own improvement, and at the amusement of his patron. How far Swift succeeded in winning the good opinion of Sir William may be learnt from the fact that when King William honoured Moor Park with his presence, he was permitted to take part in the interviews, and that when Sir William was unable to visit the King, his *protégé* was commissioned to wait upon his Majesty, and to speak on the patron's authority and behalf. The lad's future promised better things than his beginning. He resolved to go into the church, since preferment stared him in the face. In 1692 he proceeded to Oxford, where he obtained his Master's degree, and in 1694, quarrelling with Sir William Temple, who coldly offered him a situation worth 100*l.* a year, he quitted his patron in disgust, and went at once to Ireland to take holy orders.

He was ordained, and almost immediately afterwards received the living of Kilroot, in the diocese of Connor, the value of the living being about equal to that of the appointment offered by Sir William Temple.

Swift, miserable in his exile, sighed for the advantages he had abandoned. Sir William Temple, lonely without his clever and keen-witted companion, pined for his return. The prebend of Kilroot was speedily resigned in favour of a poor curate, for whom Swift had taken great pains to procure the presentation; and with 80*l.* in his purse, the independent clergyman proceeded once more to Moor Park. Sir William received him with open arms. They resided together until 1699, when the great statesman died, leaving to Swift, in testimony of his regard, the sum of 100*l.* and his literary remains. The remains were duly published and dedicated to the King. They might have been inscribed to his Majesty's cook, for any advantage that accrued to the editor. Swift was a Whig, but his politics suffered severely by the neglect of his Majesty, who derived no particular advantage from Sir William Temple's "remains."

Weary with long and vain attendance upon Court, Swift finally accepted at the hands of Lord Berkeley, one of the Lords Justices of Ireland, the rectory of Agher and the vicarages of Laracor and Rathbeggan. In the year 1700 he took possession of the living at Laracor, and his mode of entering upon his duty was thoroughly characteristic of the man. He walked down to Laracor, entered the curate's house, and announced himself "as his master." In his usual style, he affected brutality, and having sufficiently alarmed his victims, gradually soothed and consoled them by evidences of undoubted friendliness and good will. "This," says Sir Walter Scott, "was the ruling trait of Swift's character to others; his praise assumed the appearance and language of complaint; his benefits were often prefaced by a prologue of a threatening nature." "The ruling trait" of Swift's character was morbid eccentricity. Much less eccentricity has saved many a murderer in our days from the gallows. We approach a period of Swift's history when we must accept this conclusion, or revolt from the cold-blooded doings of a monster.

During Swift's second residence with Sir William Temple, he had become acquainted with an inmate of Moor Park, very different to the accomplished man to whose intellectual pleasures he so largely ministered. A young and lovely girl—half ward, half dependent in the establishment—engaged the attention and commanded the untiring services of the newly-made minister. Esther Johnson had need of education, and Swift became her tutor. He entered upon his task with avidity, condescended to the humblest instruction, and inspired his pupil with unbounded gratitude and regard. Swift was not more insensible to the simplicity and beauty of the lady, than she to the kind offices of her master; but Swift would not have been Swift had he, like other men, returned everyday love with ordinary affection. Swift had felt tender impressions in his own fashion before. Once in Leicestershire he was accused by a friend of having formed an imprudent attachment, on which occasion he returned for answer, that "his cold temper and unconfined humour" would prevent all serious consequences, even if it were not true that the conduct which his friend had mistaken for gallantry had been merely the evidence "of an active and restless temper, incapable of enduring idleness, and catching at such opportunities of amusement as most readily occurred." Upon another occasion, and within four years of the Leicestershire pastime, Swift made an absolute offer of his hand to one Miss Waryng, vowing in his declaratory epistle, that he would forgo every prospect of interest for the sake of his "Varina," and that "the lady's love was far more fatal than her cruelty." After much and long consideration, Varina consented to the suit. That was enough for Swift. He met the capitulation by charging his Varina with want of affection, by stipulating for unheard-of-sacrifices, and concluding, with an expression of his willingness to wed, "*though she had neither fortune nor beauty*," provided every article of his letter was ungrudgingly agreed to. We may well tremble for Esther Johnson, with her young heart given into such wild keeping.

As soon as Swift was established at Laracor, it was arranged that Esther, who possessed a small property in Ireland, should take up her abode near to her old preceptor. She came, and scandal was silenced by a stipulation insisted on by Swift, that his lovely charge should have a matron for a constant companion, and never see him except in the presence of a third party. Esther was in her seventeenth year. The vicar of Laracor was on his road to forty. What wonder that even in Laracor the former should receive an offer of marriage, and that the latter, wayward and inconsistent from first to last, should deny another the happiness he had resolved never to enjoy himself? Esther found a lover whom Swift repulsed, to the infinite joy of the devoted girl, whose fate was already linked for good or evil to that of her teacher and friend.

Obscurity and idleness were not for Swift. Love, that gradually consumed the unoccupied girl, was not even this man's recreation. Impatient of banishment, he went to London, and mixed with the wits of the age. Addison, Steele, and Arbuthnot became his friends, and he quickly proved himself worthy of their intimacy by the publication, in 1704, of his *Tale of a Tub.* The success of the work, given to the world anonymously, was decisive. Its singular merit obtained for its author everlasting renown, and effectually prevented his rising to the highest dignity in the very church which his book laboured to exalt. None but an inspired madman would have attempted to do honour to religion in a spirit which none but the infidel could heartily approve.

Politicians are not squeamish. The Whigs could see no fault in raillery and wit that might serve temporal interests with greater advantage than they had advanced interests ecclesiastical; and the friends of the Revolution welcomed so rare an adherent to their principles. With an affected ardour that subsequent events proved to be as premature as it was hollow, Swift's pen was put in harness for his allies, and worked vigorously enough until 1709, when, having assisted Steele in the establishment of the *Tatler*, the vicar of Laracor returned to Ireland and to the duties of a rural pastor. Not to remain, however! A change suddenly came over the spirit of the nation. Sacheverell was about to pull down by a single sermon all the popularity that Marlborough and his friends had built up by their glorious campaigns. Swift had waited in vain for promotion from the Whigs, and his suspicions were aroused when the Lord Lieutenant unexpectedly began to caress him. Escaping the damage which the marked attentions of the old government might do him with the new, Swift started for England in 1710, in order to survey the turning of the political wheel with his own eyes, and to try his fortune in the game. The progress of events was rapid. Swift reached London on the 9th of September; on the 1st of October he had already written a lampoon upon an ancient associate! and on the 4th he was presented to Harley, the new minister.

The career of Swift from this moment, and so long as the government of Harley lasted, was magnificent and mighty. Had he not been crotchetty from his very boyhood, his head would have been turned now. Swift reigned. Swift was the government; Swift was Queen, Lords, and Commons. There was tremendous work to do, and Swift did it all. The Tories had thrown out the Whigs, and had brought in a government in their place quite as Whiggish, to do Tory work. To moderate the wishes of the people, if not to blind their eyes, was the preliminary and essential work of the ministry. They could not perform it themselves. Swift undertook and accomplished it. He had intellect and courage enough for that, and more. Moreover, he had vehement passions to gratify, and they might all partake of the glory of his success; he was proud, and his pride revelled in authority; he was ambitious, and his ambition could attain no higher pitch than it found at the right hand of the prime minister; he was revengeful, and revenge could wish no sweeter gratification than the contortions of the great who had neglected genius and desert, when they looked to them for advancement, and obtained nothing but cold neglect. Swift, single-handed, fought the Whigs. For seven months he conducted a periodical paper, in which he mercilessly assailed, as none but himself could attack, all who were odious to the government, and distasteful to himself; not an individual was spared whose sufferings could add to the tranquillity and permanence of the Government. Resistance was in vain; it was attempted, but invariably with one effect—the first wound grazed, the second killed.

The public were in ecstacies. The laughers were all on the side of the satirist, and how vast a portion of the community these are, needs not be said. But it was not in the *Examiner* alone that Swift offered up his victims at the shrine of universal mirth. He could write verses for the rough heart of a nation to chuckle over and delight in. Personalities to-day fly wide of the mark; then they went right home. The habits, the foibles, the moral and physical imperfections of humanity, were all fair game, provided the shaft were dipped with gall as well as venom. Short poems, longer pamphlets,—whatever could help the Government and cover their foes with ridicule and scorn, Swift poured upon the town with an industry and skill that set eulogy at defiance. And because they did defy praise, Jonathan Swift never asked and was ever too grand to accept it.

But he claimed much more. His disordered yet

exquisite intellect acknowledged no superiority. He asked no thanks for his labour, he disdained pecuniary reward for his matchless and incalculable services—he did not care for fame, but he imperiously demanded to be treated by the greatest as an equal. Mr. Harley offered him money, and he quarrelled with the minister for his boldness. "If we let these great ministers," he said, "pretend too much *there will be no governing them.*" The same minister desired to make Swift his chaplain. One mistake was as great as the other. "My Lord Oxford, by a second hand, proposed my being his chaplain, which I, by a second hand, refused. I will be no man's chaplain alive." The assumption of the man was more than regal. At a later period of his life he drew up a list of his friends, ranking them respectively under the heads, "Ungrateful," "Grateful," "Indifferent," and "Doubtful." Pope appears among the grateful, Queen Caroline among the ungrateful. The audacity of these distinctions is very edifying. What autocrat is here for whose mere countenance the whole world is to bow down and be "grateful!"

It is due to Swift's imperiousness, however, to state that, once acknowledged as an equal, he was prepared to make every sacrifice that could be looked for in a friend. Concede his position, and for fortune or disgrace he was equally prepared. Harley and Bolingbroke, quick to discern the weakness, called their invulnerable ally by his Christian name, but stopped short of conferring upon him any benefit whatever. The neglect made no difference to the haughty scribe, who contented himself with pulling down the barriers that had been impertinently set up to separate him from rank and worldly greatness. But, if Swift shrank from the treatment of a client, he performed no part so willingly as that of a patron. He took literature under his wing, and compelled the government to do it homage. He quarrelled with Steele when he deserted the Whigs, and pursued his former friend with unflinching sarcasm and banter, but at his request Steele was maintained by the government in an office of which he was about to be deprived. Congreve was a Whig, but Swift insisted that he should find honour at the hands of the Tories, and Harley honoured him accordingly. Swift introduced Gay to Lord Bolingbroke, and secured that nobleman's weighty patronage for the poet. Rowe was recommended for office, Pope for aid. The well-to-do, by Swift's personal interest, found respect, the indigent, money, for the mitigation of their pains. At Court, at Swift's instigation, the Lord Treasurer made the first advances to men of letters, and by the act made tacit confession of the power which Swift so liberally exercised for the advantage of everybody but himself. But what worldly distinction, in truth, could add to the importance of a personage who made it a point for a Duke to pay him the first visit, and who, on one occasion, publicly sent the Prime Minister into the House of Commons, to call out the First Secretary of State, whom Swift wished to inform that he would not dine with him if he meant to dine late?

A lampoon directed against the Queen's favourite, upon whose red hair Swift had been facetious, prevented the satirist's advancement in England. The see of Hereford fell vacant in 1712. Bolingbroke would now have paid the debt due from his government to Swift, but the Duchess of Somerset, upon her knees, implored the Queen to withhold her consent from the appointment, and Swift was pronounced by Her Majesty as "too violent in party" for promotion. The most important man in the kingdom found himself in a moment the most feeble. The fountain of so much honour could not retain a drop of the precious waters for itself. Swift, it is said, laid the foundations of fortune for upwards of forty families who rose to distinction by a word from his lips. What a satire upon power was the satirist's own fate! He could not advance himself in England one inch. Promotion in Ireland began and ended with his appointment to the Deanery of St. Patrick, of which he took possession, much to his disgust and vexation, in the summer of 1713.

The summer, however, was not over before Swift was in England again. The wheels of government had come to a dead lock, and of course none but he could right them. The Ministry was at sixes and sevens. Its very existence depended upon the good understanding of the chiefs, Bolingbroke and Harley, and the wily ambition of the latter, jarring against the vehement desires of the former, had produced jealousy, suspicion, and now threatened immediate disorganization. A thousand voices called the Dean to the scene of action, and he came full of the importance of his mission. He plunged at once into the vexed sea of political controversy, and whilst straining every effort to court his friends, let no opportunity slip of galling their foes. His pen was as damaging and industrious as ever. It set the town in a fever. It caused Richard Steele to be expelled the House of Commons, and it sent the whole body of Scotch peers, headed by the Duke of Argyll, to the Queen, with the prayer that a proclamation might be issued for the discovery of their libeller. Swift was more successful in his assaults than in his mediation. The Ministers were irreconcilable. Vexed at heart with disappointment, the Dean, after his manner, suddenly quitted London, and shut himself up in Berkshire. One attempt he made in his strict seclusion to uphold the government and save the country, and the composition is a curiosity in its way. He published a proposition for the exclusion of all dissenters from power of every kind, for disqualifying Whigs and Low Churchmen for every possible office, and for compelling the presumptive heir to the throne to declare his abomination of Whigs, and his perfect satisfaction with Her Majesty's present advisers. Matters must have been near a crisis when this modest pamphlet was put forth, and so they were. The intrigues of Bolingbroke had triumphed over those of his colleague, and Oxford was disgraced. The latter about to retire into obscurity addressed a letter to Swift, entreating him, if he were not tired of his former prosperous friend, "to throw away so much time on one who loved him as to attend him upon his melancholy journey." The same post brought him word that his own victory was won. Bolingbroke triumphant besought his Jonathan, as he loved his Queen, to stand by her Minister, and to aid him in his perilous adventure. Nothing should be wanting to do justice to his loyalty. The Duchess of Somerset would be reconciled, the Queen would be gracious, the path of honour should lie broad, open, and unimpeded before him. Bolingbroke and Harley were equally the friends of

Swift. What could he do in his extremity? What would a million men, taken at random from the multitude, have done, had they been so situated, so tempted? Not that upon which Swift, in his chivalrous magnanimity, at once decided. He abandoned the prosperous to follow and console the unfortunate. "I meddle not with Lord Oxford's faults," is his noble language, "as he was a Minister of State, but his personal kindness to me was excessive. He distinguished and chose me above all men when he was great." Within a few days of Swift's self-denying decision Queen Anne was a corpse, Bolingbroke and Oxford both flying for their lives, and Swift himself hiding his unprotected head in Ireland amidst a people who at once feared and hated him.

During Swift's visit to London in 1710, he had regularly transmitted to Stella, by which name Esther Johnson is made known to posterity, an account of his daily doings with the new government. The journal exhibits the view of the writer that his conduct invariably presents. It is full of tenderness and confidence, and not without coarseness that startles and shocks. It contains a detailed and minute account, not only of all that passed between Swift and the government, but of his changeful feelings as they arose from day to day, and of physical infirmities, that are commonly whispered into the ear of the physician. If Swift loved Stella in the ordinary acceptation of the term, he took small pains in his diary to elevate the sentiments with which she regarded her hero. The journal is not in harmony throughout. Towards the close it lacks the tenderness and warmth, the minuteness and confidential utterance, that are so visible at the beginning. We are enabled to account for the difference. Swift had enlarged the circle of his female acquaintance whilst fighting for his friends in London. He had become a constant visitor, especially at the house of a Mrs Vanhomrigh, who had two daughters the eldest of whom was about twenty years of age, and had the the same Christian name as Stella. Esther Vanhomrigh had great taste for reading, and Swift, who seems to have delighted in such occupation, condescended, for the second time in his life, to become a young lady's instructor. The great man's tuition had always one effect upon his pupils. Before Miss Vanhomrigh had made much progress in her studies she was over head and ears in love, and, to the astonishment of her master, she one day declared the passionate and undying character of her attachment. Swift met the confession with a weapon far more potent when opposed to a political foe than when directed against the weak heart of a doting woman. He had recourse to raillery, but, finding his banter of no avail, endeavoured to appease the unhappy girl by "an offer of devoted and everlasting friendship, founded on the basis of virtuous esteem." He might with equal success have attempted to put out a conflagration with a bucket of cold water. There was no help for the miserable man. He returned to his deanery at the death of Queen Anne with two love affairs upon his hands, but with the stern resolution of encouraging neither, and overcoming both.

Before quitting England he wrote to Esther Vanhomrigh, or Vanessa, as he styles her in his correspondence, intimating his intention to forget every thing in England and to write to her as seldom as possible. So far the claims of Vanessa were disposed of. As soon as he reached his deanery he secured lodgings for Stella and her companion, and reiterated his determination to pursue his intercourse with the young lady upon the prudent terms originally established. So far his mind was set at rest in respect of Stella. But Swift had scarcely time to congratulate himself upon his plans before Vanessa presented herself in Dublin, and made known to the Dean her resolution to take up her abode permanently in Ireland. Her mother was dead, so were her two brothers; she and her sister were alone in the world, and they had a small property near Dublin, to which it suited them to retire. Swift, alarmed by the proceeding, remonstrated, threatened, denounced—all in vain. Vanessa met his reproaches with complaints of cruelty and neglect, and warned him of the consequences of leaving her without the solace of his friendship and presence. Perplexed and distressed, the Dean had no other resource to than to leave events to their own development. He trusted that time would mitigate and show the hopelessness of Vanessa's passion, and in the meanwhile he sought, by occasional communication with her, to prevent any catastrophe that might result from actual despair. But his thoughts for Vanessa's safety were inimical to Stella's repose. She pined and gradually sank under the alteration that had taken place in Swift's deportment towards her since his acquaintance with Vanessa. Swift, really anxious for the safety of his ward, requested a friend to ascertain the cause of her malady. It was not difficult to ascertain it. His indifference and public scandal, which spoke freely of their unaccountable connexion, were alone to blame for her sufferings. It was enough for Swift. He had passed the age at which he had resolved to marry, but he was ready to wed Stella provided the marriage were kept a secret and she was content to live apart. Poor Stella was more than content, but she over-estimated her strength. The marriage took place, and immediately afterwards the husband withdrew himself in a fit of madness, which threw him into gloom and misery for days. What the motives may have been for the inexplicable stipulations of this wayward man it is impossible to ascertain. That they were the motives of a diseased, and at times utterly irresponsible, judgment, we think cannot be questioned. Of love, as a tender passion, Swift had no conception. His writings prove it. The coarseness that pervades his compositions has nothing in common with the susceptibility that shrinks from disgusting and loathsome images in which Swift revelled. In all his prose and poetical addresses to his mistresses there is not one expression to prove the weakness of his heart. He writes as a guardian—he writes as a friend—he writes as a father, but not a syllable escapes him that can be attributed to the pangs and delights of the lover.

Married to Stella, Swift proved himself more eager than ever to give to his intercourse with Vanessa the character of mere friendship. He went so far as to endeavour to engage her affections for another man, but his attempts were rejected with indignation and scorn. In the August of the year 1717, Vanessa retired from Dublin to her house and property near Cellbridge. Swift exhorted her to leave Ireland altogether, but she was not to be persuaded. In 1720, it would appear that the Dean frequently visited the recluse in her retirement, and upon such occasions Vanessa would plant a laurel or two in honour of her guest, who passed his time with the lady reading and writing verses in a rural bower built in a sequestered part of her garden. Some of the verses composed by Vanessa have been preserved. They breathe the fond ardour of the suffering maid, and testify to the imperturbable coldness of the man. Of the innocence of their intercourse there cannot be a doubt. In 1720, Vanessa lost her last remaining relative—her sister died in her arms. Thrown back upon herself by this bereavement, the intensity of her love for the Dean became insupportable. Jealous and suspicious, and eager to put an end to a terror that possessed her, she resolved to address herself to Stella, and to ascertain from her own lips the exact nature of her relation with her so-called guardian. The momentous question was asked in a letter, to which Stella calmly replied by informing her interrogator that she was the Dean's wife. Vanessa's letter was forwarded by Stella to Swift himself, and it roused him to fury. He rode off at once to Cellbridge, entered the apartment in which Vanessa was seated, and glared upon her like a tiger. The trembling creature asked her visitor to sit down. He answered the invitation by flinging a packet on the table, and riding instantly away. The packet was opened; it contained nothing but Vanessa's letter to Stella. Her doom was pronounced. The fond heart snapped. In a few weeks the hopeless, desolate Vanessa was in her grave.

Swift, agonised, rushed from the world. For two months subsequently to the death of Vanessa his place of abode was unknown. But at the end of that period he returned to Dublin calmer for the conflict he had undergone. He devoted himself industriously again to affairs of State. His pen had now a nobler office than to sustain unworthy men in unmerited power. We can but indicate the course of his labours. Ireland, the country not of his love, but of his birth and adoption, treated as a conquered province, owed her rescue from absolute thraldom to Swift's great and unconquerable exertions on her behalf. He resisted the English government with his single hand, and overcame them in the fight. His popularity in Ireland was unparalleled, even in that excited and generous-hearted land. Rewards were offered to betray him, but a million lives would have heen sacrificed in his place before one would have profited by the patriot's downfall. He was worshipped, and every hair of his head was precious and sacred to the people who adored him.

In 1726, Swift revisited England, for the first time since the death of Queen Anne, and published, anonymously as usual, the famous satire of *Gulliver's Travels.* Its immediate success heralded the universal fame that masterly and singular work has since achieved. Swift mingled once more with his literary friends, and lived almost entirely with Pope. Yet courted on all sides he was doomed again to bitter sorrow. News reached him that Stella was ill. Alarmed and full of self-reproaches, he hastened home to be received by the people of Ireland in triumph, and to meet—and he was grateful for the sight—the improved and welcoming looks of the woman for whose dissolution he had been prepared. In March, 1727, Stella being sufficiently recovered, the Dean ventured once more to England, but soon to be resummoned to the hapless couch of his exhausted and most miserable wife. Afflicted in body and soul, Swift suddenly quitted Pope, with whom he was residing at Twickenham, and reaching his home, was doomed to find his Stella upon the verge of the grave. Till the last moment he continued at her bedside, evincing the tenderest consideration, and performing what consolatory tasks he might in the sick chamber. Shortly before her death part of a conversation between the melancholy pair was overheard. "Well, my dear," said the Dean, "if you wish it, it shall be owned." Stella's reply was given in few words. "*It is too late.*" "On the 28th of January," writes one of the biographers of Swift, "Mrs. Johnson closed her weary pilgrimage, and passed to that land where they neither marry nor are given in marriage," the second victim of one and the same hopeless and consuming passion.

Swift stood alone in the world, and for his punishment was doomed to endure the crushing solitude for the space of seventeen years. The interval was gloomy indeed. From his youth the Dean had been subject to painful fits of giddiness and deafness. From 1736, these fits became more frequent and severe. In 1740, he went raving mad, and frenzy ceased only to leave him a more pitiable idiot. During the space of three years the poor creature was unconscious of what passed around him, and spoke but twice. Upon the 19th of October, 1745, God mercifully removed the terrible spectacle, from the sight of man, and released the sufferer from his misery, degradation, and shame.

The volumes which have given occassion to these

remarks are a singular comment upon a singular history. It is the work of a Frenchman who has ventured to deduce a theory from the *data* we have submitted to the reader's notice. With that theory we cannot agree; it may be reconcileable to the romance which M. de Wailly has invented, but it is altogether opposed to veritable records that cannot be impugned. M. de Wailly would have it that Swift's marriage with Stella was a deliberate and rational sacrifice of love to principle, and that Swift compensated his sacrificed love by granting his principle no human indulgences; that his love for Vanessa, in fact, was sincere and ardent, and that his duty to Stella alone prevented a union with Vanessa. To prove his case M. de Wailly widely departs from history, and makes his hypothesis of no value whatever, except to the novel reader. As a romance, written by a Frenchman, *Stella and Vanessa* is worthy of great commendation. It indicates a familiar knowledge of English manners and character, and never betrays, except here and there in the construction of the plot, the hand of a foreigner. It is quite free from exaggeration, and inasmuch as it exhibits no glaring anachronism or absurd caricature, is a literary curiosity. We accept it as such, though bound to reject its highest claims. The mystery of Swift's amours has yet to be cleared up. We explain his otherwise unaccountable behaviour by attributing his cruelty to prevailing insanity. The career of Swift was brilliant, but not less wild than dazzling. The sickly hue of a distempered brain gave a colour to his acts in all the relations of life. The storm was brewing from his childhood; it burst forth terribly in his age, and only a moment before all was wreck and devastation, the half-distracted man sat down and made a will, by which he left the whole of his worldly possessions for the foundation of a lunatic asylum.

October, 3, 1850.

REMINISCENCES OF COLERIDGE AND SOUTHEY, BY JOSEPH COTTLE.

READER! imagine a pious Boswell, and you have good Joseph Cottle before you. "Never, my dear sir," said Dr. Johnson, in one his admonitory epistles to the obsequious Bozzy, "never take it into your head to think that I do not love you; you may settle yourself in full confidence both of my love and esteem. I love you as a kind man, I value you as a worthy man; and hope, in time, to reverence you *as a pious man.*" The condition unfortunately wanting in the personal character of the biographer of the greatest of lexicographers is found in the memorialist of one of the noblest philosophers whom the world has seen. There is much that is kind in Cottle, more that is worthy, and a good deal that is unquestionably religious. Boswell was polite, affable, and courteous to a fault; Cottle is all three short of the fault. Bozzy, a gentleman and lawyer, lived for the acquaintance and friendship of the eminent and learned of his generation. Cottle, beginning life as a bookseller, seems to have as eagerly pursued such friendships, discriminating only between those a Christian conscience might lawfully approve and those it was in duty bound to reject. Boswell, certainly not a poet, published, nevertheless, in imitation of his superiors, "The Club at

Newmarket," a tale in verse; Cottle, by no means destined to live as a darling of the muses, presents us, in emulation of his more highly-gifted companions, with his "Hymns and Sacred Lyrics," 12mo, half-bound. Bozzy, from the multitude of his attachments, distinguished one that he might link for ever his little soul with that of a giant. Cottle identifies his small history with the career of a master mind towering high above contending intellects. Both are anxious to commemorate their heroes and themselves; both take the same means, both are in a measure faithful to a duty arduous though self-imposed. Boswell never hesitates to display the human weaknesses of the god he worships; but he exhibits the foibles only to magnify the virtues, and rather than these should suffer, is always ready to immolate himself. Cottle is equally candid; but less for the sake of his hero than for the cause of religion, which is dearer to him even than his idol;—the one thinks of nothing but his mighty subject—the other, as the Wesleyans would say, is ever anxious to "*improve*" it. In one part of his work, the ecstatic Boswell tells us he can compare his biography to nothing but the Odyssey: the episodes may be interesting and instructive, but the hero is never out of sight and always in the foreground. In the first line of his book, the more collected Cottle prepares us for a sublimer vision; he assures us that it is with "a *solemnised* feeling" that he enters on his reminiscences, and that his task is something better than that of admiring the eloquence, extolling the genius, and forgetting the failings of Samuel Taylor Coleridge.

It is astonishing how much you may abuse a man if you will but do it in a reverent spirit, and, as it were, for the good of the object abused. You may fill three-fourths of a professed panegyric with absolute censure, provided the latter proceed from pious lips and from the depths of a self-constituted converted heart. Joseph Cottle reminds us at every step of those very good-natured friends who are always saying unkind things with a view to one's peace of mind and eventual improvement. You invite an old acquaintance to your hospitable board; you give him of food the best, of welcome the heartiest; you suffer the cloth to be removed, only that it may lead to the presence of more genial things, and forthwith your old acquaintance dilates upon the sinfulness of men in general, and upon your own backslidings in particular. Anger is impossible, wrath is out of the question. If you remonstrate, the speaker avows that if his love were less his reserve would be greater—if your interests, temporal and eternal, were not as lead upon his heart, he would eschew your wine and walnuts and make you over to the fiend for ever. We confess that we are not altogether comfortable in witnessing the *tête-à-tête* conferences, the domestic passages, revealed in the present volume. The faults of Coleridge are not unknown—they were many and grievous; but it is hardly the office of the friend of half-a-century to disseminate them after death, upon the plea of pious obligations. There is sometimes as much piety in drawing down the veil upon the infirmities of departed genius, as in ruthlessly upraising it, especially if the hand concerned has grasped, day after day, for fifty years, in confidence and friendship, the other's palm, that now lies withered and cannot help itself. Critics and historians have a duty to perform, stern often and unacceptable; they know their work, and do not shrink from it. Friendship, too, has its privileges and rights. Joseph Cottle, you should not be ashamed of them. One such privilege—not the least—is to keep buried in your bosom, for your own instruction if you will, the heavy faults committed in the flesh by him you loved, but now irreparable and punishable elsewhere. We know true piety is anxious to communicate its warnings and examples to mankind; but, have no fear! angels will close their eyes the while you lock such secrets in your breast.

Now, nobody must dislike Cottle in consequence of these remarks. On the contrary, the reader must love Cottle. He is as good-hearted and as well-meaning a creature as ever breathed. He is an old man, a patriarch in these times, and a living familiar of those whose names have already become classical in the English tongue. Charles Lloyd, Robert Lovell, Sir H. Davy, Hannah More, Robert Hall, Charles Lamb, Robert Southey, and Samuel Coleridge, were youthful and aspiring when Cottle was young, helping some, counselling others, and admiring all. Of that friendly and illustrious group who, united by sympathy and the like pursuits and faith, fought their way to victory and fame under a galling fire of ridicule and scorn, and of whom the grey and honoured Wordsworth stands, alas! the sole survivor,* Joseph Cottle was the beloved associate and the chosen counsellor. Cottle took care of Coleridge and Southey, when to take care of these men meant

* Wordsworth has since departed, but Joseph Cottle still lives on. August, 1851.

nourishing and sustaining glorious spirits in the bleak hour of poverty, obscurity, and neglect. The claim upon our gratitude can never be forgotten. The reader must remember it when he grows angry with the biographer for revealing so much that is ugly of that friend from whom the world has gathered so much that is beautiful; and, moreover, let him bear in mind, that the Octogenarian is without one spark of malice in his whole composition. "It is not a light *motive*," he tells us, "which could have prompted him, when this world of 'eye and ear' is fast receding, while grander scenes are opening, and so near! to call up almost long-forgotten associations, and to dwell on the stirring by-gone occurrences that tend, in some measure, to interfere with that calm which is most desirable, and best accords with the feelings of one who holds life by such slender ties." What that motive is, we have already said. We can hardly allow it to justify all that it would excuse; but it absolves the writer at least of a malicious intent, which, in truth, is simply impossible in the case of Joseph Cottle. The utter absence of anything approaching cruelty, or even worldly-mindedness, is marvellous throughout his long career. His was the weakness of being too easy. We shall proceed to give instances of the failing, at all times and in all men amiable. Meanwhile, to guard our author against wholesale condemnation at the outset, let us afford him the benefit secured by the poet for the farmer of Tilsbury Vale:—

"You lift up your eyes, but I guess that you frame
A judgment too harsh of the sin and the shame;
In him it was scarcely a business of art,
For this he did all in the *ease* of his heart."

The introduction of Coleridge and Southey to their present biographer, fifty-seven years ago, is amusing in the extreme. To many of our readers the circumstances connected with it must be well known. For the sake of the ignorant we will more particularly refer to them. At the close of the year 1794, Mr. Cottle, then living in Bristol, informs us that a clever young Quaker, of the name of Lovell, just then married to a certain Miss Fricker (whose sisters, by the way, became afterwards respectively the wives of Coleridge and Southey), waited upon him with the intelligence that a few friends from Oxford and Cambridge were about to sail with him to the banks of Susquehanna, in America, for the purpose of forming a social colony, in which there was to be a community of property, and where *all selfishness was to be proscribed.* The adventurers were to be tried and incorruptible characters, and, as Joseph Cottle fulfilled both conditions, he was affectionately invited by his visitor to become one of the immaculate society of Pantisocritans. The party already engaged in the enterprise were four—Lovell, the quaker; Coleridge, from Cambridge; and Southey and George Burnet, from Oxford. Bristol was the point of embarcation, and the youthful founders of the new system were expected shortly to arrive there. Joseph had a humble opinion of his merits, and expressed himself unworthy to join the sacred brotherhood; but, to use his own words, "he had read so much of poetry, and sympathised so much with poets in all their eccentricities and vicissitudes, that to see before him the realisation of a character which in the abstract most absorbed his regards, gave him a degree of satisfaction which it would be difficult to express." Accordingly, he requested Lovell to introduce his friends as soon as they should appear; and, before they appeared, gratified his love for poets in the abstract by perusing the verses which had already fallen from the pens of the unfledged enthusiasts. Southey was the first to arrive. "Never," says Cottle, "will the impression be effaced produced on me by this young man. Tall, dignified, possessing great suavity of manners, an eye piercing, with a countenance full of genius, kindliness, and intelligence, I gave him at once the right hand of fellowship, and to the moment of his decease the cordiality was never withdrawn." Next came Coleridge; his eye, brow, and forehead indicating at once the commanding genius of the man. Interview rapidly followed interview, only to increase the first impression of admiration and respect. A touching proof of the perfect self-denial of these young men, who were bent upon nothing short of the regeneration of the world, is given by Cottle at starting. It will be seen that their whole intercourse with the bookseller was directed by a benevolent wish to increase his intellectual and social enjoyments. "Each of my new friends," he naively informs us, "*read me his productions. Each accepted my invitations* (!), *and gave me those repeated proofs of good opinion*, ripening fast into esteem, that I could not be insensible to the kindness of their manners, which it may truly be affirmed infused into my heart a brotherly feeling, that more than identified their interests with my own." Poor Cottle!

The bookseller introduced his new acquaintances to several friends, and we are not surprised to learn from him that the philosophers found Bristol "a very pleasant residence," and, gratified by his invitations and attention, contented themselves with preaching of the delights of Pantisocracy, without taking any steps whatever to put their sermons into practice. The inquisitive and philosophic mind takes pleasure in following the career of the purely philanthropic and humane. It will be pleased to trace the course of the Pantisocritans. Cottle grew uneasy as the period arrived for the sailing of the ship, which was not yet engaged, and for the departure of the adventurers, who were resolved to go, having no means to set out. In the height of his apprehension and distress, however, a letter reached him from one of the regenerators of the society, strikingly characteristic of all modern reformers, which brought tears of joy and gratitude to the eyes of the bookseller, and assured him that he was not yet to be robbed of the society of those from whom he had learned to derive so much of his happiness. The letter was as follows:—

"My dear Sir,—Can you conveniently lend me five pounds, as we want a little more than four pounds to make up our lodging bill, which is indeed much higher than we expected; seven weeks, and Burnet's lodging for twelve weeks, amounting to eleven pounds.

Yours affectionately,

"S. T. Coleridge."

"Never," exclaims the good Cottle, "did I lend money with such unmingled pleasure, for now I ceased to be haunted day and night with the spectre of the ship! the ship! which was to effect such incalculable mischief!" The money given, the giver waited upon the receiver. The Pantisocritan was in a desponding mood.

Cottle, "to keep up his spirits," recommended him to publish a volume of his poems. The regenerator answered with a smile of scorn. He had offered his poems to the booksellers in London, and the majority would not even look at them. One, after diligently reading them, offered six guineas for the copyright. "Poor as I was," said the reformer, "I refused to accept the offer." Cottle offered twenty guineas at once. "It was very pleasant," says the guileless old gentleman, "to observe the joy that instantly diffused itself over his countenance." It was, in fact, too much for Cottle. "Come, I will make it thirty," said the enthusiastic tradesman, "and you may have the money when you will." "The silence and the grasped hand," says our dear friend, "showed that at that moment one person was happy." But Cottle is by no means content to make one person happy at a time. Off he goes to the other Pantisocritan, and, out of breath, tells him he has given his friend thirty guineas for one volume of poems, and he will give him the like sum for another. The effect of the offer may be anticipated. "He cordially thanked me, and instantly acceded to my proposal."

Before the tangible advantages of Mr. Cottle's friendship the hairbrained scheme of the Susquehanna banks faded gradually away. Moreover, the learned youths who proposed to establish peace all over the world could not live peacefully among themselves. First, Coleridge quarrelled with Lovell, and then he quarrelled with Southey. That ponderous but restless genius, never at ease with itself, could not adapt itself to the ways of others. Coleridge could not be happy in his youth any more than he was tranquil and contented in his meridian.

As a boy, he pined for the solitudes of America; as a man, for vastness greater than the earth could give. The spirit, tremendous in its powers, and divine in its longings, was discontented and wretched in its bondage. Hence, the singular and humiliating contradiction presented in his character; the greatness and the smallness continually clashing and contrasting; the magnificent and gorgeous visions of the gifted dreamer now placing him at the front of his contemporaries, now the small and pitiful doings of the man banishing him to the lowest seat in the company.

It is, perhaps, unnecessary to state that Coleridge received his thirty guineas a very long time before Cottle saw his poems. In the mildest possible way, we are assured, and we believe our informant, for it is the scrupulous Cottle himself, the bookseller communicated to the poet the grievous complaints of the printer; but the answers received were those of injured innocence and offended virtue. Still there was noble forgiveness at the heart of the Pantisocritan, as the following moving epistle, written in the midst of the printing annoyances, abundantly testifies:—

"Dear Cottle,—Shall I trouble you (I being over the mouth and nose in doing something of importance at Lovell's) to send your servant into the market and buy a pound of bacon and two quarts of broad beans; and when he carries it down to College-street, to desire the maid to dress it for dinner, and tell her I shall be home by 3 o'clock?

"Yours affectionately,

"S. T. C."

The American delusion abandoned, Coleridge without any reasonable means of keeping a wife, married. The less able Coleridge became to provide for his establishment, the more necessary it was for the indefatigable Cottle to look after him. "When a common friend familiarly asked Coleridge how he was to keep the pot boiling when married? *he very promptly answered that Mr. Cottle had made him an offer, and he felt no solicitude on the subject.*" The offer was one guinea and a half for every 100 lines he might present in blank verse or rhyme. Of course, many guineas and a half were dissipated before the publication of a single line. Still Cottle complained not. Nay, to console and sustain his debtor, he on one occasion sent him a kind invitation to dinner, which the messenger, not finding Coleridge at home, inconsiderately brought back. Coleridge heard of the occurrence, and concluding that the letter could refer only to one subject, returned an answer to the invitation, thanking God for his dispensations, but asserting his belief that he should have thanked Heaven more had he been born a shoemaker, and not a poet; imprecating his fate, and upbraiding poor Cottle for unkindness which he would have died rather than commit, and imputing to him motives to which his heart was altogether a stranger. "My happiest moments for composition are broken in upon by the reflection that I must make haste! I am too late! I am already months behind! I have received my pay beforehand! . . I have not seen the note, but I guess its contents. I am writing as fast as I can. Depend upon it, you shall not be out of pocket by me."

"At the receipt of this painful letter," beautifully

proceeds Cottle, "my first care was to send the young and desponding bard some of the precious metal, to cheer his drooping spirits, to inform him of his mistake, and to renew my invitation." Shortly afterwards came a proposition from the poet. He desired to publish a pamphlet on a subject of importance connected with the city of Bristol. All he asked was three guineas for the copyright, the first sheet to be delivered on Thursday, the second on Monday, &c. The pamphlet never appeared, but "I presented Mr. C. with the three guineas," says poor Cottle in a note. It would be an endless task to narrate all the exquisite pecuniary adventures with which Mr. Cottle's very amusing volume abounds. They are not confined to the earliest period of the bookseller's acquaintance with the bard, but they are dotted here and there through the whole course of their friendship. The following is very instructive in its way:—

"During the delivery of one of his lectures it was remarked by many of Mr. Coleridge's friends, with great pain, that there was something unusual and strange in his look and deportment. The true cause was known to few, and least of all to myself. At one of the lectures, meeting Mr. Coleridge at the inn door, he said, grasping my hand with great solemnity, 'Cottle, this day week I shall not be alive.' I was alarmed, but, speaking to another friend, he replied, 'Do not be afraid. It is only one of Mr. Coleridge's odd fancies.' Afterwards he called me on one side, and said, 'My dear friend, a dirty fellow has threatened to arrest me for 10*l*.' Shocked at the idea, I said, 'Coleridge, you shall not go to goal while I can help it,' and immediately gave him the 10*l*."

The Cottle family were doomed to be victimised, it

would seem, by the too facile *protégé* of the bookseller. On one occasion Cottle ventured to entreat for copy, which the printer imperiously demanded. Coleridge excused himself on the plea that he was wholly absorbed in the interest and affairs of Cottle's brother. Hear the biographer!

"My brother, when at Cambridge, had written a Latin poem for the prize,—the subject, *Italia Vastata*, —and sent it to Mr. Coleridge, with whom he was on friendly terms, in manuscript, requesting the favour of his remarks, and this he did *about six weeks before it was necessary to deliver it in.* Mr. Coleridge, in an immediate letter, expressed his approbation of the poem, and cheerfully undertook the task; but, with a *little* (oh! gentle Cottle!) of his procrastination, he returned the manuscript, with his remarks, *just one day after it was too late to send the poem in!*"

The intellectual and social existences of Samuel Taylor Coleridge were as distinct as two parallel streams flowing side by side, but never joining. The anomalies of human nature, whilst they solemnly testify to the fact of our fallen condition, give us no clue to reconcile or repair them. The most learned and devout of the present generation humbly acknowledge for their teacher, master, counsellor, and guide, the man who knew not what domestic virtue means, what social obligations lawfully impose; the slave who gave himself up to a degrading passion and sacrificed for it all that men are accustomed to hold most dear on earth. The means of enriching himself by honest labour were prodigally given him, yet he preferred to manly exertion the ignoble idleness of the pitied mendicant. He received single pounds in charity, when he might have commanded hundreds as the just payment of his honourable toil. He knew not the sanctity of a pledged word. Engagements deliberately undertaken were given up without a thought. If he contracted to deliver a lecture, the chances were as much against as in favour of his appearing before the crowded audience assembled to listen to the teacher who spoke as one inspired. It was nothing that Coleridge had sold his tickets and been paid for them. The additional fact was not worth a straw in the calculation. And, then, as to his home! What shall be said of the man whom a faithful friend, smitten by his negligence and wilful perseverance in a life-destroying habit, thus ventures to address?—

"Your wife and children are domesticated with Southey. He has a family of his own, which, by his literary labour, he supports, to his great honour; and to the extra provision required of him on your account he cheerfully submits; still, will you not divide with him the honour? You have not extinguished in your heart the father's feelings. Your daughter is a sweet girl. Your two boys are promising, and Hartley, concerning whom you once so affectionately wrote, is eminently clever. These want only a father's assistance to give them credit and honourable stations in life. Will you withhold so equitable and small a boon? Your eldest son will soon be qualified for the university, where your name would inevitably secure him patronage, but without your aid how is he to arrive there? And, afterwards, how is he to be supported? Revolve on these things, I entreat you, calmly on your pillow."

Such is the picture presented of Samuel Taylor Coleridge, looking upon the man from the ordinary social eminence from which we are accustomed to contemplate our fellow mortals. It is far different when we ourselves look up and behold the gifted spirit placed far above humanity, on " a heaven-kissing hill." The profoundest thought, the most subtle and extended learning, the most delicate and discriminating taste, were but secondary characteristics of the great philosopher to whom learning came in humility, wisdom with the confession of ignorance, to receive the lessons which poured from his soul with an aim, a fulness, a scope, an originality and force that have never been surpassed in modern times, if even they have been equalled in antiquity by the great oracles of the Academy and the Porch. We have read of none simply human whose simple conversation has been so marvellously rich and beautiful as that which is described to us by listeners who have left the sage's footstool to become, as it is said, "fresh and independent sources of moral action in themselves upon the principles of their common master." It is not our business to account for the phenomena afforded in the character of Coleridge. Intellectually a giant, and morally a dwarf, the chief personage of Mr. Cottle's book affords ample room for hypothesis and psychological investigation. Let them be pursued. It is sufficient for benevolence to know, that before his final departure from the earth, Samuel Taylor Coleridge wrestled successfully with a vice that at one period of his life threatened to master and destroy him, and that, beginning the world as a Socinian, he quitted it a humble and devoted Christian believer.

We have left ourselves but little space to speak of

one who, inferior to Coleridge in genius, immeasurably excelled him in all that goes to constitute the perfect social being. Robert Southey is distinguished as the most eminent *littérateur* of his country. His writings are as varied as his acquirements; both are of the highest order. He knew more of many things than any of his contemporaries; and few have written so much and so well with so little reason for regret and self-reproach. He gave a dignity to periodical literature, which under his hand established "a local habitation and a name" that cannot but prove highly serviceable in the present hour, when readers are accustomed to take their intellectual food in the smallest quantities, and so many purveyors are abroad to administer unwholesome portions. The beauty of Southey's prose style is admitted by those who deny him high rank as a poet; but even as a poet Southey has committed to posterity productions high above mediocrity. The purpose of his writings, whether in verse or prose, is always the highest and the noblest. His productions are as pure as his conversation was manly and his life virtuous. He regarded religion with the reverence of a child, and excluded from the pages which he circulated for the delight and edification of his fellows, all that was unworthy the man, responsible to his God and fitted for immortality. In the midst of a puerile, fantastic, and meaningless literature, such as that to which many of our popular writers have doomed us, we miss the masculine and invigorating pen of Robert Southey.

We owe it to Mr. Cottle to state that throughout his volume not one syllable of violated confidence appears with reference to Southey, when such violation is calculated to do harm to the memory of his departed friend. From the time that he first shook hands with the Pantisocritan in Bristol, to the mournful hour when Southey gazed upon his oldest and dearest friends without the power of recognising them, the friendship of the biographer and the author suffered no flaw. The flow of their intercourse was equable, and as fresh in the sunset as in the dawn. "Southey," says Cottle, writing to John Foster in 1842, "spent a week with me four or five years ago, when he manifested the same kind and cordial behaviour which he had uniformly displayed for nearly half a century, and which had never during that long period been interrupted for a moment. Nor was steadfastness in friendship one of his least excellencies. From the kindliness of his spirit, he excited an affectionate esteem in his friends, which they well knew no capriciousness on his part would interrupt; to which it might be added, his mind was well balanced, presenting no unfavourable eccentricities, and but few demands for the exercise of charity. Justly, also, may it be affirmed, that he was distinguished for the exemplary discharge of all the social and relative virtues,—disinterestedly generous, and scrupulously conscientious, presenting in his general deportment courteousness without servility, and dignity without pride. There was in him so much kindliness and sincerity, so much of upright purpose and generous feeling, that the belief is forced on the mind that, through the whole range of biographical annals, few men endowed with the higher order of intellect have possessed more qualities commanding esteem than Robert Southey, who so happily blended the great with the amiable, or whose memory will become more permanently fragrant to the lovers of genius or the friends of virtue."

Coleridge and Southey are but two of a distinguished multitude. Of many dear to the lovers of English literature and science the pages of Joseph Cottle abound with pleasing anecdote and agreeable reminiscences. We refer our readers to them, and shake the venerable and chatty Joseph warmly by the hand.

NOVEMBER 3, 1847.

THE LIFE OF JOHN KEATS.

It is the old story! We are again summoned to admire where once we despised. The citizens of Bristol erect a monument to the memory of Chatterton, who, to save himself from death through hunger, took poison, and was thrown, pauper-like, into the burying ground of Shoe-lane workhouse, London. Keats, spurned and persecuted in his lifetime, is welcomed today, and from his distant grave begins to influence thought in the land of his birth, which he quitted in proud, but intolerable despair. The instances are two out of many. The tale did not begin with "the marvellous boy, the sleepless soul, that perished in his pride;" it has not ended with Adonais, whose soul—

> "Like a star
> Beacons from the abode where the eternal are."

Our present task is a simple one. We cannot recall genius from the tomb to witness the final triumph of its long suffering, and to console itself for its wrongs in the consciousness of our remorse. We may in the public market-place do justice to the citizen whom we ostracised in ignorance and hooted forth in folly.

John Keats was born under an unlucky star. He was beset with evil influences from the moment that he felt his own great strength. Had he been suffered to walk alone, unaided but by the might of his spirit, he would never have been struck down on the way by the fury of men who were waging war to the death against his associates. Keats at starting was the victim of a quarrel between parties who, like most antagonists, were wrong and were right in their respective grounds of opposition. The chosen or forced companions of Keats, when, as a mere boy, he resolved to dedicate his life to the service of poetry, were unfortunately members of a school. Unfortunately, again, the sharpest and cleverest critics of the day were members of another. The author *Comus* himself would not have escaped Scot-free from the encounter. Keats might have sung as an angel, and his voice would have made no impression upon ears that listened to nothing but the promptings of an internal and most vindictive rage.

There is much to be said for and against the belligerents. It is not to be denied that if the critics of the early part of the century were vicious beyond all bounds, the objects of their attack were but too often ridiculous past all hope. The very worthy and, in their way, highly respectable gentlemen who, at the time of Keats' appearance upon the stage, had formed themselves into a snug coterie, and under the unpoetical title of "Cockneys," forced public attention to a most ridiculous expression of many rare and noble sentiments, invited satire and laid themselves fairly open to the assaults of the evil-disposed. Grown-up men are not suffered, in the heart of our practical and manly nation, to play the parts of children. Even the madness of our poets must have its method, or be dismissed to the asylum. What could be done with a small family of lyrical aspirants who employed the muse in writing sonnets to one another, and the greengrocer in preparing crowns of ivy for mutual coronations? How was it possible to avoid a laugh at the amiable simplicity of inveterate Londoners, who converted Primrose Hill into Parnassus, and deliberately walked to the Vale of Health at Hampstead—not for health, but inspiration? Two of the earliest productions of poor Keats indicate, in their very titles, how thoroughly he had identified himself at starting with the puerilities of his friends. One is suggested by sleeping in Mr. Leigh Hunt's pretty cottage on the Hampstead Road; the other owes its origin to a neighbouring paddock. Hunt, Hazlitt, Shelley, and Godwin, were the backers of the boy when he stripped, with a lion's heart, to fight his great battle for fame; and never had mortal deeper reason to pray heaven to save him from his friends. The greatness of the names are beyond all doubt; so is the fact that in the year 1817, or thereabouts, they were sounds to alarm the rising generation, and the veriest bugbears of society. A letter of recommendation from any one of the four was a certain passport, not to neglect—that might have been borne—but to persecution and insult. The failings—the vices, if you will—of one and all were visited on the head of their unfortunate *protégé*, whoever he might be. Keats, chivalrous to a fault, cannot be said to have been caught when his sympathies urged him to the side of individuals whom, in his soul, he believed to be cruelly oppressed.

The critics were far from blameless. They revelled wantonly in their strength, and took unfair advantage of the time. The peace of Europe, the triumph of order, the frightful remembrance of the French Revolution, the downfall of the Corsican despot, gave extraordinary power to the pen advocating Conservatism, and opposing the designs of Democracy. The friends of Keats were politicians as well as poets; one, indeed, the chief and most affectionate, was suffering in prison the penalty of excessive liberality which had been betrayed into a libel upon the then Prince Regent. There can be no doubt whatever that the literary critic, assuming the sword of the political partisan, struck at the fantastic poet through the heart of the uncompromising Radical, and mocked the writing chiefly because he hated the man. The temptation to crush was immense, but the mode of attack was, after all, cowardly. Society, but too willing to stigmatise the conscientious Reformer, needed not the instigations of falsehood to bring its whole scorn to bear upon a few well-meaning and high-hearted, although, in many respects, misguided men. Crimes were imputed to harmless dreamers in the Hampstead fields, in the existence of which the accusers themselves never believed. Practices were hinted at too monstrous for belief—if anything can be too monstrous for prejudice to credit and enjoy. The responsibility and gravity of the literary judge utterly gave way before the necessity of silencing an enemy to Church and State. You opened the critic's pages for a touch of his quality, and found him belabouring, with a heavy cudgel, an unhappy devil lying already half crushed under his foot.

In such a state of things Keats rose—an undoubted poet. Do not question the fact with the evidence you have around you. It is the spirit of Keats that at the present moment hovers over the best of our national poesy, and inspires the poetic genius—such as it is—of our unpoetic age. Had he lived, he would eventually have towered above his contemporaries; dying before he was twenty-six years of age, he took his place at once among the examples whom he so passionately loved, and the models he so successfully imitated, and so closely approached. *Endymion*, full of faults, overflows with as many beauties, and both are stamped with greatness. The most unsparing reviewer of the time was not half so conscious of the many defects of this extraordinary composition as the author himself, who, at the beginning of his career, entered upon a system of self-tuition, the effects of which are strikingly apparent at its close, although the interval is spanned by a very few months.

"Knowing within myself," says Keats in his preface to *Endymion*, "the manner in which this poem has been produced, it is not without a feeling of regret that I make it public.

"What manner I mean will be quite clear to the reader, who must soon perceive great inexperience, immaturity, and every error denoting a feverish attempt rather than a deed accomplished. The two first books, and indeed the two last, I feel sensible are not of such completion as to warrant their passing the press; nor should they, if I thought a year's castigation would do them any good. It will not; the foundations are too sandy. It is just that this youngster should die away; a sad thought for me, if I had not some hope that, while it was dwindling, I may be plotting and fitting myself for verses fitter to live.

"This may be speaking too presumptuously, and may deserve a punishment; but no feeling man will be forward to inflict it; he will leave me alone, with the conviction that there is not a fiercer hell than the failure in a great object. This is not written with the least atom of purpose to forestall criticisms, of course, but from the desire I have to conciliate men who are competent to look, and who do look, with a jealous eye, to the honour of English literature. The imagination of a boy is healthy, and the mature imagination of a man is healthy, but there is a space of life between in which the soul is in a ferment, the character undecided, the way of life uncertain, the ambition thick-sighted; thence proceeds mawkishness, and all the thousand bitters which those men I speak of must necessarily taste in going over the following pages. I hope I have not, in too late a day, touched the beautiful mythology of Greece, and dulled its brigthness, for I wish to try once more before I bid it farewell."

Such was the honest declaration, and such the simple and masculine strength of a mere youth in his earliest adventure; but it did not save him from the wrath he anticipated and deprecated. Even at this distance of time, it is not without a smarting sense of pain that the lover of Keats takes up *Endymion* and becomes conscious of the many opportunities for ridicule which the poem presents, but which tenderness and a simple desire for the honour of the national literature would have known how to appreciate. The intoxication of an imagination that scorned, in its joyous delirium, the promptings of reason and judgment, is visible throughout; but the luxuriance of the highest poetic faculty was in itself a pledge sufficient of the poet's future eminence. For the reasons already given, the essential beauty of the structure was overlooked by the arbiters of the day in their eagerness to expose the grotesqueness, and, it may be, the absurdity of the ornament. It was a huge mistake, but time alone was required to correct it. To attempt the annihilation of genius because of its exaggerations and imperfections, is the most fruitless of all efforts. The exuberant tree must not be upbraided with sterility because it needs pruning. In his choice of a subject we believe Keats to have been unfortunate. Against the opinion of his present biographer we are disposed to assert that his first steps would have been safer had they been not on classic ground. Unacquainted with Greek, and deriving his inspiration and knowledge not directly from the primitive sources, a tone and stamp were given to characters and subjects that startled by their novelty, and provoked irresistible mirth from the associations which they suggested. Scholars were offended, and the uninitiated were puzzled. Whilst *Lemprière's Dictionary* lent blocks, John Keats furnished the clothing. The skeleton of Pagan mythology looked strange enough in its modern garb, and the kindly disposed might be pardoned for their smile of wonder as they watched the august visitor of antiquity taking his splendid airing in the Hampstead fields. The minor faults of the composition were certainly not few. It was evident to the lightest reader that the author of *Endymion*, instead of adapting rhymes to his subject, very frequently indeed compelled his subject to bend obsequiously to his rhymes. The effect of this high dereliction of the poet's sacred duty is too visible.

But sum up all the vices of style, and all the faults inseparable from the nature of the subject, and there remains behind a poem that will live, because it bears the impress of undoubted originality and power, and is redolent of the stuff which makes Milton and Johnson, Fletcher and Shakspeare, the household gods they have become.

The affecting modesty of the preface to *Endymion* was not crushed by the fate to which the poem itself was immediately doomed. The *Quarterly* and *Blackwood* fell upon Keats as an infuriated bulldog might fasten upon the neck of some lone child. A letter, signed " J. S." appeared in the *Morning Chronicle* of October 3, 1818, remonstrating against the tyranny of the reviewers, and an eager friend sent the newspaper to Keats to console the stricken poet in his misfortune. Hear the poet's answer :—

"*9th Oct.*, 1818.

"My dear Hessey.—You are very good in sending me the letter from the *Chronicle*, and I am very bad in not acknowledging such a kindness sooner. Pray, forgive me. It has so chanced that I have had that paper every day. I have seen to-day's. I cannot but feel indebted to those gentlemen who have taken my part. As for the rest, I begin to get a little acquainted with my own strength and weakness. Praise or blame has but a momentary effect on the man whose love of beauty in the abstract makes him a severe critic on his own works. My own domestic criticism has given me pain without comparison beyond what *Blackwood* or the *Quarterly* could inflict; and also, when I feel I am right, no external praise can give me such a glow as my own solitary re-perception and ratification of what is fine. 'J. S.' is perfectly right in regard to the 'slip-shod *Endymion*.' That it is no fault of mine. No; though it may sound a little paradoxical, it is as good as I had power to make it by myself. Had I been nervous about it being a perfect piece, and with that view asked advice and trembled over every page, it would not have been written; for it is not in my nature to fumble. I will write independently. I have written independently, *without judgment;* I may write independently, and *with judgment,* hereafter. The genius of poetry must work out its own salvation in a man. It cannot be matured by law and precept, but by sensation and watchfulness in itself. That which is creation must create itself. In *Endymion* I leaped headlong into the sea, and thereby have become better acquainted with the soundings, the quicksands, and the rocks, than if I had stayed upon the green shore, and piped a silly pipe, and took tea and comfortable advice. I was never afraid of failure; for I would sooner fail than not be amongst the greatest."

Hear this sagacious detector of personal weakness, this proudly humble man again! He is writing to his brother in America:—

"—— My poem has not at all succeeded. In the course of a year or so I think I shall try the public again. In a selfish point of view I should suffer my pride and my contempt of public opinion to hold me silent, but for your and Fanny's sake I will pluck up my spirit and try it again. I have no doubt of success in a course of years if I persevere; but I must be patient."

And yet again!—

"—— I have proceeded pretty well with *Lamia*, finishing the first part, which consists of about 400 lines. I have great hopes of success, because I make use of my judgment more deliberately than I have yet done; but in case of my failure with the world, I shall find my content."

In the year 1820, less than two years after the publication of *Endymion*, the poem of *Hyperion* appeared with other compositions. The journey was all but accomplished. The earlier poems of Keats had exhibited striking vigour shrouded in obscurity, and the sinews of thought, though sadly encumbered with fervid mystification. A leap of years had been made in the interval. For simplicity, beauty, grandeur, and the deepest pathos, *Hyperion* is scarcely to be surpassed in the language. With one spring the rejected, but inspired boy, had placed himself where he had long hoped and prayed to be. "I think," he says in one of his letters, "I shall be among the English poets after my death."

Keats wrote no more! On the 23rd of February, 1821, he died at Rome—not "snuffed out by an article," as the tradition goes, but the victim of a disease which had already destroyed his mother and his younger brother. It may be seen from the glimpses we have given above that the effect of malignity was not to depress the poet, but rather to rouse him, as a criticism had already roused Byron, to the vindication of his genius, and to the putting forth his strength. There was nothing of death in the arrows that came from the reviewer's quiver. Had no "article" ever been written, we question whether Keats, with his foredoomed tendency to physical decay, could at any time of his life have passed muster at a life insurance office; consumption had marked him for her own. He lingered but little, and, after death, the only wonder was that he had lingered so long. Who knows how closely allied, in the case of Keats, were the mother's inheritance and his own intellectual pre-eminence.

The personal history of poor Keats may be summed up in a few lines. His father was in the employ of Mr. Jennings, a livery-stable keeper in Moorfields, and, marrying his master's daughter, became a partner in the business. He died from the fall of a horse in the year 1804, and at the early age of thirty-six. His mother, "a lively and intelligent woman, was supposed to have prematurely hastened the birth of John by her passionate love of amusement." She died of consumption in the year 1810. His brothers were—George, older than himself, and Thomas, younger. He had also a sister, youngest of all. The elder brother married and settled in America; the younger died of consumption in the poet's arms. The devotion of John Keats to this suffering invalid, during the whole of his protracted illness, constitutes a fair feature in his short and fiery life. The poet was born on the 29th of October, 1795. When about five years old he was sent, with his brothers, to the school of Mr. Clarke at Enfield, and he quitted the school after the death of his mother, when he had reached his fifteenth year. His pursuits at school are thus described:—

"After remaining some time at school with Mr. Clarke, his intellectual ambition suddenly developed itself; he determined to carry off all the first prizes in literature, and he succeeded; but the object was only obtained by a total sacrifice of his amusements and favourite exercises. Even on the half-holidays, when the school was all out at play, he remained at home translating his *Virgil* or his *Fenelon.* It has frequently occurred to the master to force him out into the open air for his health, and then he would walk in the garden with a book in his hand. The quantity of translations on paper he made during the last two years of his stay at Enfield was surprising. The twelve books of the *Æneid* were a portion of it; but he does not appear to have been familiar with much other and more difficult Latin poetry, nor to have even commenced learning the Greek language. *Tooke's Pantheon, Spence's Polymetis,* and *Lemprière's Dictionary*" (slender furnishing surely) "were sufficient fully to introduce his imagination to the enchanted world of old mythology. . . . He does not seem to have been a sedulous reader of other books, but *Robinson Crusoe* and *Marmontel's Incas of Peru* impressed him strongly, and he must have met with Shakspeare, for he told a schoolfellow considerably younger than himself, 'that he thought no one could dare to read *Macbeth* alone in a house at two o'clock in the morning.'"

When Keats quitted school, in 1810, he was apprenticed for five years to Mr. Hammond, a surgeon of Edmonton. From Edmonton he passed to London to walk the hospitals. He became in time a qualified practitioner, but not before the Muse had won him over to her side, and the acquaintance of the gentlemen to whom we adverted at the commencement of this article had, by their countenance, example, and support, induced him to prefer the path of letters to the doctor's surgery. In 1818 *Endymion* was published; in 1820 *Hyperion* and other poems; and very shortly afterwards he ruptured a bloodvessel, took to his bed, and rose from it to lie down again soon afterwards for ever. Despairing of restoration at home, in company with a devoted attendant and friend, Mr. Severn, the artist, Keats set out for Italy. He visited Naples and Rome; in the latter city placed himself under the care of Sir James Clark, then practising in Rome, but very soon sank under the melancholy and pitiless disease to which two members of his family had already fallen victims.

Connected with his illness and death may be mentioned two incidents that for the living reader contain a mournful and a striking interest. Amongst the earliest friends of Keats were Haydon, the painter, and Shelley, the poet. When Keats was first smitten, Haydon visited the sufferer, who had written to his old friend, requesting him to see him before he set out for Italy. Haydon describes in his journal the powerful impression which the visit made upon him—"the very colouring of the scene struck forcibly on the painter's imagination. The white curtains, the white sheets, the white shirt, and the white skin of his friend, all contrasted with the bright hectic flush on his cheek, and heightened the sinister effect; he went away, hardly hoping." And he who hardly hoped for another, what extent of hope had he for himself? From the poet's bed to the painter's studio is but a bound for the curious and eager mind. Keats, pitied and struck down by the hand of disease, lies in paradise compared with the spectacle that comes before us—genius weltering in its blood, self-destroyed because neglected.

Pass we to another vision! Amongst the indignant declaimers against the unjust sentence which criticism had passed on Keats, Shelley stood foremost. What added poignancy to indignation was the settled but unfounded conviction that the death of the youth had been mainly occasioned by wanton persecution. Anger found relief in song. *Adonais: an Elegy on the Death of John Keats*, is amongst the most impassioned of Shelley's verses. Give heed to the preface:—

"John Keats died at Rome, of a consumption, in his twenty-fourth year, on the — day of ——, 1821, and was buried in the romantic and lovely cemetery of the Protestants in that city, under the pyramid which is the tomb of Cestius, and the massy walls and towers, now mouldering and desolate, which formed the circuit of ancient Rome. The cemetery is an open space among the ruins, covered in winter with violets and daisies. *It might make one in love with death to think that one should be buried in so sweet a place.*"

Reader, carry the accents in your ear, and accompany us to Leghorn. A few months only have elapsed. Shelley is on the shore. Keats no longer lives, but you will see that Shelley has not forgotten him. He sets sail for the gulf of Lerici, where he has his temporary home; he never reaches it. A body is washed ashore at Via Reggio. If the features are not to be recognised, there can be no doubt of the man who carries in his bosom the volume containing *Lamia* and *Hyperion.* The body of Shelley is burned, but the remains are carried——whither? You will know by the description, "The cemetery is an open space among the ruins, covered in winter with violets and daisies. *It might make one in love with death to think that one should be buried in so sweet a place.*" There he lies! Keats and he, the mourner and the mourned, almost touch!

September, 17, 1849.

SPORTING IN AFRICA.*

JOHN BRIGHT should be in ecstasies! Roualeyn Gordon Cumming, after five years absence from his native land, returns to help the member for Manchester to abolish the game laws. What will be the use of laws for the preservation of game when the game itself is repudiated? *Five Years of A Hunter's Life* has already reached a second edition. Two editions more will about exhaust the sporting readers of the United Kingdom; and what sportsman then, what individual with a blush of shame in his fallen nature, will survey a poor partridge with a nobler sentiment than he regards the barn-door fowl? We dare the British lion to spend his magnificent energies in running a timid unresisting hare off his agitated legs the instant he ascertains how the unaided pluck of one man has extinguished the supremacy of his African prototype. As easily imagine that England's admired aristocracy will pass their holydays in catching flies and flaying earwigs, as suppose that they will condescend to cowardly battues, having learnt how the uncaged lion himself may be met on equal terms, and vanquished bravely, as a king should be. It is time to enlarge the sphere of our recreations. In all that concerns our daily occupations

* Times, Sep. 19, 1850.

we have been marching of late in seven-leagued boots. With respect to our manly pleasures we are still in swaddling clothes. In the days of railroads and electric telegraphs, marine and earthly, it is really too derogatory to human dignity to gallop after a harmless puss, with the view of giving fire to the blood of the undignified pursuer. We have never awakened to the fact before, so complacently does wonder sleep upon the neck of custom. Roualeyn the First opens our eyes with his rifle, and it will not be that potentate's fault if we lazily close them again.

It is not, however, without an alarming sense of inability that we presume to deal with the adventures of Roualeyn Gordon Cumming, prince of hunters, conqueror and autocrat of all the beasts. We are conscious of our great audacity in venturing even to quote the achievements of a hero, now for the first time in his life weeping because there are no more animals to vanquish, and desolate because the megatherium was disposed of before he took to shooting. What can the feeble quill say of a gentleman who quitted Great Britain that he might take part in a war against savages, and bade adieu to civilization and the Cape, because warring with mere men yielded no relish to his splendid and bloody ambition? With what spirit shall we address ourselves to the labours of a fellow Christian who seriously informs us, that "the sweetest and most natural sounds" he ever heard were the bellowings of a whole troop of hungry lions, to which he listened in the depths of a forest at the dead hour of midnight, "unaccompanied by any attendant, and ensconced within 20 yards of the fountain" which the said lions were awfully approaching; that it was "a joyful moment" to him when, on another occasion, he found himself face to face with a maddened lioness, and he "at once made up his mind that she or he must die"—the chances being twenty to one at the moment in favour of the brute? How can we assimilate our notions of things in general with those of an individual who gravely assures us that "lion hunting may be followed to a certain extent with comparative safety," and that nothing more is required of "him who would shine in the overpoweringly exciting pastime of hunting this justly celebrated king of beasts," than "a tolerable knowledge of the use of the rifle, and acquaintance with the disposition and manner of lions (!), perfect calmness and self-possession (! !), and a recklessness of death (! ! !) ?" To speak the plain truth, Mr. Roualeyn Gordon Cumming's ideas of enjoyment are so very peculiar, and the coolness with which he talks of things unpleasant is so absolutely frightful, that a flesh and blood reviewer is about as much at home with him as the adventurous editor of a weekly newspaper found himself the other day deciding, with bludgeons on either side of him, between the respective merits of the amiable Tipton Slasher and the not less redoubtable Bendigo.

We are not too proud to acknowledge our utter incapacity in the presence of a personage who cannot close his eyes o' nights for the intense amusement he derives from a mad chorus of leopards, elephants, and hyenas, all screaming within a few yards of his dormitory; who mourns for a gun that bursts in his hands "as David mourned for Absalom;" who "takes coffee" and then "rides for a leopard;" who closes a chapter of his journal and tumbles into his hole with a memorandum, that "lions roar about the camp all the evening" jotted down in the temper of an elderly gentleman closing his diary with the unexciting remark, "thermometer 53 in the shade;" who discovers to his horror the corpse of a faithful follower half eaten up by a lion, and endeavours "to divert his mind" by starting at once "in quest of elephants;" who takes to crocodile shooting as a recreation after sterner sport as a man inclines to a rubber after chess; who "ends a grim lion's career with a single ball behind the shoulder, cutting the main arteries close to the heart," and then affectingly "plucks a lock of hair" from the beloved one's mane, that he may wear it close to his bosom in everlasting and tender remembrance: who, struggling with a hippopotamus in the water, expresses "his great astonishment," as he might have done had he been struggling with a new-born babe, that "he could not guide the monster in the slightest; but she continued to splash and plunge and blow, and make her circular course, carrying him along with her as if he were a fly on her tail;" who "could not die happy" until he had slaughtered an elephant, and who positively describes as "pleasant work" an encounter with one of the giants of the forest, in the course of which the mighty beast received "35 balls, all about and behind his shoulders," and receiving them was fain to reduce his furious pace "to a very slow walk," for "blood flowed from his trunk and all his wounds, leaving the ground behind him a mass of gore; his frame shuddered violently, his mouth opened and shut, his lips quivered, his eyes were filled with tears;" who chases rhinoceros as boys run after butterflies, and who cannot for the life of him conceive that "the coward exists not prepared to die" any moment for a lovely and glorious land uninhabited by any but savage beasts and equally wild and less governable men.

Travellers tell strange tales, especially just now, of Africa. The last accounts furnished by the explorers into the far interior make known the startling fact, that the country, instead of being as supposed a worthless desert, is a land of snowy mountains, great rivers, and inhabited not by negroes but by people as white as ourselves. According to Mr. Cumming, the portion of Africa to which he confined his exploits, is quite as remarkable as himself—and that is saying much. A bite of a dog, as everybody knows, is nothing to laugh at in England; in Africa a snake may "spit his poison into the eye of a marksman, and yet never interfere with his skill in drawing his bow." One night, whilst Roualeyn was occupied "bagging buffaloes, rhinoceros, koodoos, zebras, and other game, a horrid snake," writes the hunter, "flew up at my eye and spat poison into it. Immediately I washed it well out at the fountain. I endured great pain all night, but the next day the eye came all right." In Africa you may live in the water and take no harm, suffer acute rheumatism and experience no inconvenience, lose all your strength and yet not be in the slightest degree feeble. "On the 15th," it is written in Roualeyn's diary, "I felt very ill, but in the forenoon I went down to the river, where I shot two sea-cows. In the evening, feeling worse I bled myself, but strong fever was on me all night."

Three days afterwards the writer's state of health was no better:—

"On the 18th I felt extremely weak and nervous from the fever and the quantity of blood which I had lost, insomuch that I started at my own shadow, and several times sprang to one side when the leaves rustled in the bushes. I walked along the bank of the river with my gun loaded with small shot, intending to shoot a partridge for my breakfast. Presently I came upon the fresh dung of bull elephants, and at the same moment my people at the waggons saw two old bulls within 200 yards of them; and the wind being favourable they walked unsuspiciously. *After a very short chase I succeeded in killing both*

In Africa, too, horses fall upon the top of the rider and hurt him as much as the horse at Astley's hurts Mr. Widdicomb, when, at the word of command, the trained Arab steed quietly lets himself down and dies for a feed of corn in the arena. Guns burst in the African hunter's hand and lead to no unsatisfactory results; disease visits him only to strengthen, and suffering comes really to add to the physical and moral enjoyment,

External nature keeps up the African standard. African "peals of thunder are the most appalling, the most fearful" Mr. Cumming ever heard; "the forked lightnings" is to match; "the terrific hailstorms" are "such as I had never before witnessed:" the size of the stones rendering the boasted "large as an egg" of our oldest rural inhabitant simply ridiculous. We have rained ladybirds and frogs in Kent and Surrey before now, but the first flight of locusts beheld by our hunter makes us blush for the national vermin.

"On they came like a snowstorm, flying slow and steady, about a hundred yards from the ground. I stood looking at them until the air was darkened with their masses, while the plain on which we stood became densely covered with them. Far as my eye could reach—east, west, north, and south—they stretched in one unbroken cloud, and more than an hour elapsed before their devastating legions had swept by." On the earth, or in the air—birds, beasts, or insects—it is all the same. "The most extraordinary and striking scene as connected with beasts of the chase" that Mr. Cumming had ever beheld, was a herd of *springboks* covering miles of ground. "To endeavour to form any idea of the amount of antelopes which he that day beheld were vain; but he has, nevertheless, no hesitation in stating that some hundreds of thousands of springboks were that morning within the compass of his vision."

It was on the 23d of October, 1843, that Mr. Cumming quitted Grahamstown on his first sporting tour. Instead of a dogcart he drove a waggon drawn by many oxen; his ordnance consisted of three double-barrelled rifles by Purday, William More, and Dickson, of Edinburgh; three stout double-barrelled guns for rough work; much lead; many bullet moulds, powder flasks, and shooting belts; hundreds of pounds of gunpowder; thousands of gun flints, and tens of thousands of percussion caps. The waggon was laden with baggage, provisions, and general stores; the saddlery was made up of two English hunting saddles, common saddles for servants, and one pack saddle to convey venison to camp. Of horses at starting the hunter had but two; of servants and attendants but four; and of cash in hand exactly 200*l*. Equipped as he was, Mr. Cumming "considered himself prepared to undertake a journey of at least 12 months among Boers or Bushmans, independent of either."

As Mr. Cumming receded from the Cape his sport became more exciting and his danger greater. Proceeding northward from the abode of civilization through the haunts of semi-barbarous tribes, he worked his way up to the unvisited and dreaded domains of the fraternity whose representatives in England are contemplated with greatest advantage and pleasure through iron bars and in trebly-locked dens. Beginning with harmless and timid deer, he closes his marvellous career with foot to foot conflicts with the wildest and bloodiest of beasts. Van Amburgh was a poor apprentice compared with our hero. The American drew the teeth of innocent cubs and lashed them into fear of man. The Briton presented himself alone in the primeval forest as champion of human kind, and dared any ten of its horrid inhabitants to contest the belt with him. What battles he fought we tremble to think of. What victories he won the native rulers in those distant parts will never cease to remember. We trust they will remember them with gratitude and love. Whatever slaughter may have been committed in their ranks, none was inflicted in vengeance. Isaac Walton himself never fondled a worm or gazed upon the hysteric breathings of a gasping fish with half the tenderness felt by Gordon Cumming as often as he raised his faithful "Purday" and unerring "Dickson of Edinburgh." "On the 23d," we find it written in his diary,

"I stood up in my hole at dawn of day. After I had proceeded a short distance, I perceived the head of an old bull looking at me over a small rise on the bushy plain. The head disappeared. On gaining the rise I again saw the handsome head, with its strangely hooked, fair set horns, gazing at me from the long grass some hundred yards in advance. He had lain down. I held as though I had intended to go past him; but before I neared him he sprang to his feet, and endeavoured to make off from me." The heart of the hunter was pierced. Hear how he proceeds! "*Poor old bull! I at once perceived that it was all over with him.*" Yes, there was little doubt of it. "I walked up to within 80 yards of him, and sent a bullet through his heart." Another case of bull occurs. Gazing one morning from his hole, the anxious hunter perceives a fine brindled bull gnoo dashing into the waters of a fountain within 40 yards of him, followed by four tearing, fierce-looking wild dogs. "All the four had their heads and shoulders covered with blood, and looked savage in the extreme; their eyes glistened with ferocious glee. My anxiety," Mr. Cumming goes on, "to possess this fine old bull, and also a specimen of the wild dog, prevented my waiting to see more of the fun." Much against the promptings of his nature, for "he could not help feeling very reluctant to fire at the jolly hounds," the sportsman fired at the gnoo and at the largest hound right and left. His aim was good in all respects—too good for the distressed and mourning hunter. As to the hounds, he "could not divest himself of the idea that they deserved a better recompense for the masterly manner in which they had pursued their desperate game;" and for the unhappy gnoo—but here are Mr. Cumming's admirable reflections on his end at full:—

"Poor old bull! I could not help commiserating his fate. It is melancholy to reflect that in accordance with the laws of nature such scenes of pain must ever be occurring; one species, whether inhabiting earth, air, or ocean, being produced to become the prey of another. At night I watched the water with fairish moonlight, and shot a large spotted hyena."

We listen to a martyr philosopher!

We cannot drag ourselves away from the constantly recurring instances of Mr. Cumming's morbid yet most becoming sensibility. Chasing a herd of giraffes he contrives to turn the finest cow out of the herd. Note the animated and considerate pursuit:—

"Finding herself driven from her comrades and hotly pursued, she increased her pace, and cantered along with tremendous strides. In a few minutes I was riding within five yards of her stern, and, firing at the gallop, I sent a bullet into her back. Increasing my pace, I next rode alongside, and placing the muzzle of my rifle within a few feet of her, I fired my second shot behind the shoulder. Dismounting, I hastily loaded both barrels, putting in double charges of powder. In a short time I brought her to a stand in the dry bed of a watercourse, where I fired at fifteen yards, aiming where I thought the heart lay, upon which she again made off. Having loaded I followed. Once more I brought her to a stand, and dismounted from my horse."

"The reader will conclude that when the giraffe and Mr. Cumming are face to face, and there is no escape for the beautiful runaway, that the hunter's first thought and act tend to destruction. Not in the least. His soul is overflowing with emotion at the instant. The spotted creature has one shot in her back, another behind her shoulder, a double charge from two barrels as close to her heart as circumstances will permit; but the uppermost sentiment in the mind of the pursuer is one of almost unutterable affection. The giraffe drops at last, a sacrifice to affection. "There," exclaims Nimrod, with the outburst of a lover, "there we stood together, alone in the wild wood. I gazed in wonder at her extreme beauty, while her soft dark eye, with its silky fringe, looked down imploringly at me, and I felt a pang of sorrow, in this moment of triumph, for the blood I was shedding. Pointing my rifle towards the skies I sent a bullet through her neck." This it is to be "sacrificers, not butchers, Caius Cassius!"

There are drawbacks to all sublunary enjoyments—even to a hunter's life in the far interior. "It often happened," quietly writes Mr. Cumming—"when I had lain down for the night with no other roof above me than the vaulted conopy of heaven, that my placid slumbers were rudely disturbed by rain falling like a waterspout on my face. Such events as these were extremely disagreeable,"—we intreat the reader's attention to the profound humility of the word,—*extremely disagreeable*, more especially when it came down so heavily as to preclude the possibility of maintaining our usual watchfires. In weather like this the prowling tyrant of the forest is ever most active in his search for prey, and our ears were occasionally greeted with the deep-toned voice of troops of lions, as attracted by the smell of our beef they prowled around our encampments."

Can it be possible that Mr. Cumming regards it as

a special providence and a reward of merit that he was permitted "to leave the red deer, which he loved to follow in his native land," in order to enjoy recreation such as this? Altogether "a nicht wi' Cumming" must have been about as dismal a pastime as the mere pleasure-seeker can conceive. Shortly after the hunter had taken to his *al fresco* couch on the 12th of March, he states that—"Two porcupines came grunting up to him, and stood within six feet of where he lay. About midnight," he proceeds, "an old wildebeest came and stood within 10 yards of me, but I was too lazy to fire at him. All night I heard some creature moving in the cracked earth beneath my pillow, but, believing it to be a mouse, I did not feel much concerned about the matter. I could not, however, divest myself of a painful feeling that it might be a snake." And, therefore, by way of forgetting the incident entirely, our admirable friend wrapped his blanket round his body and lulled himself to sleep. While taking his breakfast next morning, Mr. Cumming, who awoke much refreshed from invigorating slumbers, observed his men carrying a very large serpent. On approaching their master's bedding "they had discovered the horrid reptile sunning itself on the edge of the blanket, until on perceiving them it glided in beneath it." All that Mr. Cumming has further to say on the subject, is to describe its character for the benefit of any comparative anatomist to whom the information may be interesting. "It was a large specimen of the black variety of the puff adder, one of the most poisonous serpents of Africa, death ensuing within an hour after its bite."

Serpents have no chance at any time with the hero

of Altyre. His encounter with a boa shows what may be done in a case of extremity. One day, following the track of one of his monsters, he suddenly detected an enormous old rock snake stealing in beneath a mass of rock beside him. This would not do at all. The hunter was desirous to preserve the skin, and for the reptile to sneak away in so uncivil and inhospitable a fashion was a breach of good manners not to be forgiven. To shoot the boa would have been to spoil the cuticle. Our hunter proceeded with more discretion. He cut a tough stick about eight feet long, lightened himself of his shooting belt, and then went to work. Our readers will appreciate the delicacy with which we request Mr. Cumming to finish the story in his own words:—"Seizing him by the tail (!)" so runs the account—

"I tried to get him out of his place of refuge; but I hauled in vain, he only drew his large folds firmer together; I could not move him. At length I got a strip of hide round one of his folds, about the middle of his body, and Kleinboy (his attendant) and I commenced hauling away in good earnest."

We stop for a moment to inform the reader that an engraving in volume 2, page 128, represents Mr. Cumming and the boa at this critical period of their playful controversy, and that too much praise cannot be given to the boa, all Mr. Cumming's explanations notwithstanding, for his evident self-denial and devotion to the cause of manly sport throughout the whole proceeding.

"The snake," proceeds the journal, "finding the ground too hot for him, relaxed his coils, and suddenly bringing round his head to the front he sprang out at us like an arrow, with his immense and hideous mouth opened to its largest dimensions, and before I could get out of his way he was clean out of his hole, and made a second spring, throwing himself forward about eight or ten feet, and snapping his horrid fangs *within a foot of my naked legs;* I sprang out of his way, and getting a hold of the green bough I had cut I returned to the charge. The snake now glided along at top speed; he knew the ground well, and was making for a mass of broken rocks where he would have been beyond my reach; but before he could gain this place of refuge I caught him two or three tremendous whacks on his head. He, however, held on, and gained a pool of muddy water, which he was rapidly crossing, when I again belaboured him, and at length reduced his pace to a stand. We then hanged him by the neck to a bough of a tree, and in about fifteen minutes he seemed dead; but he again became very troublesome during the operation of skinning, twisting his body in all manner of ways. This serpent measured fourteen feet."

We cannot pretend to accompany Mr. Cumming through all his sublime and unparalleled achievements. It is sufficient to state that the combat just recorded is but an insignificant episode in the fearful history of adventure and bloodshed in which the author of the volumes before us found himself engaged during the space of five years. The Knight of Altyre entered the dark forests of Africa, there planted his standard, and gaily proclaimed battle *à l'outrance* against all comers. No tournament of old ever witnessed such foes, such fights, such spoils,—antelopes, lions, crocodiles, elephants, leopards, giraffes, wild dogs, big buffaloes, overgrown hippopotami, in tens, in twenties—yea, in fifties, answered the Scotchman's challenge, and united to attest the strength of his heart and the stony firmness of his brave right hand. What the Society for the Prevention of Cruelty to Animals will think of the business we will not venture to guess. Might we advise the members of that gentle institution, we would humbly suggest to them to regard it as a dream and a fable. The hunter himself tells us that one night his sleep was harassed by distressing dreams. He dreamt that lions were scouring the world in search of him. Starting in the hole which served him for a bed, he uttered a loud shriek and could not recollect in what part of the world he stood. He heard the rushing of light feet, as of a pack of wolves, close on every side of him, accompanied by the most unearthly sounds. In the next moment, to his horror, he saw himself surrounded by savage wild dogs, chattering and growling. They might be counted by scores. There was not a moment for consideration. Eternity yawned before the hunter, but his presence of mind came when the frightful dream had passed away. He knew that a human voice had power over the beasts of the earth, that a resolute bearing could appal the fiercest. Drawing himself up to his full height, he waved his large blanket with both hands, and addressed his savage assembly, as Demosthenes before him had overtopped the raging waters of the sea. The effect was electrical and decisive. The dogs acknowledged the supremacy of man, and retired to a respectful distance. Under the peculiar circumstances of a hunter almost alone in African forests it is easy to believe that dreamland and the land of reality lie very often in close proximity—that the confines of both cease to be discriminated and are not unfrequently interchangeable. Let the Society aforesaid, then, be comforted. For our part we know not scepticism. They of weaker faith may do homage to their incredulity, and still exhibit no want of charity towards Roualeyn Gordon Cumming, by accepting one half of his work as gospel, and attributing the rest to the suppers of underdone lions, which are clearly as inimical to quiet repose as Welch rabbits and pork.

CHANTREY THE SCULPTOR.

FRANCIS CHANTREY was a poor boy. His father rented a small farm at Jordanthorpe, near Sheffield, and died when his son was only 12 years of age. The widow in the first year of her bereavement, married again, taking unto herself as husband—much to the disgust of her son, who would never call his mother by the name she had acquired on her second marriage—a farm servant of her own, by name Job Hall. Francis, after the manner of step-sons, was quickly placed in a grocer's shop in Sheffield, but after a few weeks' misery behind the counter he was removed, at his own earnest request, and apprenticed to "Robert Ramsay, of Sheffield, in the county of York, carver and gilder," the contents of whose shop-window had caught the eye of the grocer's boy and communicated, as is the wont of such instruments, potently and mysteriously with his genius. Ten pounds were paid at the binding, and the apprenticeship was for a long seven years. The date of the indenture is Sept. 19, 1797, when Chantrey was 16 years old.

Mr. Ramsay, besides being a carver in wood, was also a dealer in prints and plaster models. Chantrey at once set about imitating both. He began to work the moment he set foot in the carver's shop, and he ceased his labors only when he died. In a former brief notice of his character we have called attention to the thoroughly English qualities, in virtue of which Chantrey won his way to renown. His example is valuable chiefly in this regard. His patience, industry, and steady perseverance achieved everything for him that he subsequently won. His biographers (Mr. Holland as well as Mr. Jones) place Chantrey upon a pedestal somewhat too high for his deserts. We presume the amiable fault is inevitable in all biographical attempts. The hero must transcend all former heroes, or the scribe is at fault. But, in truth, there is no occasion to demand for Chantrey more than he may lawfully aspire to. His countrymen are not slow to recognise claims so valid and so well understood. Chantrey's genius was not overwhelming or astonishing; his compositions had nothing in them of high imagination and of strictly called poetic elevation. But for simplicity, beauty, and truth, his works are not to be surpassed; and they evoke admiration and applause as the undoubted, though unpretending, triumphs of a gifted mind well disciplined in the school from which no genius, however lofty, can skulk without peril of misadventure. In Ramsay's shop, Chantrey copied the prints, worked at the carvings, cleaned pictures, and tried his 'prentice hand as a modeller upon the face of a fellow-workman. He did more. At a trifling expense he hired a small room, to which he retired to spend every hour he could call his own in modelling and drawing. "It was often midnight," writes Mr. Holland, "before he came home; but neither master nor servant ever suspected he had been anywhere but in his obscure studio, drawing, modelling, or poring over anatomical plates." He was still an apprentice when he made the acquaintance of Jonathan Wilson, the medal engraver. In the old High-street of Sheffield was a low gloomy shop, called "Woollen's Circulating Library." "In a back chamber of these premises," Mr. Holland informs us, "night by night, towards the close of his apprenticeship, did young Chantrey and his friend Wilson devote themselves to the pencil, their principal exercise being to copy the drapery of a series of French prints of statuary." Subsequently meeting Mr. Raphael Smith, "the distinguished draughtsman in crayon," at his master's house, and growing impatient of wood-carving, Chantrey induced Mr. Ramsay to cancel his indentures two years before his term of apprenticeship expired. A friend advanced £50 to effect his release, and freedom being obtained, Chantrey, then in his 21st year, made the best of his way to London. Reaching that scene of his future greatness, he called immediately upon an uncle and aunt, both living in the service of Mrs. D'Oyley, in Curzon-street, Mayfair, and that lady, much to her credit, gave the young artist a room over her stable to work in, and requested his uncle to see him daily supplied with a necessary knife and fork.

At Mrs. D'Oyley's, Chantrey was still a man of all work, cleaning the pictures in that lady's house, and occupying himself now with painting and now with sculpture, yet doubtful as to which pursuit he should finally and exclusively devote his powers. A very few months after taking up his residence in Mayfair we find the active youth back in Sheffield upon a flying professional visit, making the most of his advantages at this as at every later period of his life. Mr. Holland has fished from the *Sheffield Iris* of April 22, 1802, a characteristic advertisement referring to this artistic speculation, much too good to be lost:—

"F. Chantrey, with all due deference, begs permission to inform the ladies and gentlemen of Sheffield and its vicinity, that during his stay here he wishes to employ his time in taking of portraits and crayons and miniatures, at the pleasure of the person who shall do him the honour to sit. F. C., though a young artist, has had the opportunity of acquiring improvement from a strict attention to the works and productions of Messrs. Smith, Arnold & Co., gentlemen of eminence. He trusts in being happy to produce good and satisfactory likenesses; and no exertion shall be wanting on his part to render his humble efforts deserving some small share of public patronage. Terms—from two to three guineas. 24, Paradise-square."

The advertiser was not without custom. Indeed, Sheffield had patronised his exertions in this direction before, and Mr. Holland enumerates as many as seventy-two portraits still to be found in Sheffield and the neighborhood, all painted by Chantrey before he forsook the brush for the chisel. Among the seventy-two are portraits of Chantrey's old schoolmaster; of James Montgomery, the poet; of an old man, whose canvass announces that the work is "done by Francis Chantrey, a self-taught youth, of Norton parish;" of a cutler, who paid Chantrey the first guinea he received for the exercise of his pencil; and of an ambitious confectioner, who gave the artist £5 and a *pair of top boots!* for a likeness "in oil, of the brownish tint, rather tamely executed."

Two years elapsed from the first visit to Sheffield, and Chantrey had made sufficient progress in sculpture to justify a more ambitious appeal to the patronage of his fellow-townsmen. The *Sheffield Iris* of Oct. 18,

1804, is again the vehicle of his humble petition for work. Thus runs the advertisement;

"SCULPTURE AND PORTRAIT PAINTING.

"F. Chantrey respectfully solicits the patronage of the ladies and gentlemen of Sheffield and its environs in the above arts, during the recess of the Royal Academy, which he hopes to merit from the specimen he has to offer to their attention at his apartments, No. 14 Norfolk-street. As models from life are not generally attempted in the country, F. C. hopes to meet the liberal sentiments of an impartial public."

There were Sheffield gentlemen ready to be done in plaster, as there had been cutlers and confectioners willing to be immortalized in oils. Moreover, there was a laudable desire to push native talent, and Chantrey was fairly taken by the hand by the men of Sheffield. A correspondent of a local journal called attention to the genius which providence had unexpectedly raised in the land of hardware, and the first opportunity was seized to bring its capability publicly to the test. A monument was to be raised to the memory of the late vicar of Sheffield, in 1805, and Chantrey, then 24 years old, was selected for the work. So successful was the artist on this occasion, that Montgomery, in alluding to his achievement, prophesied that "his genius would not only confer celebrity on the little village of Norton, the place of his birth, but reflect glory on his native country itself." Three years after this performance, Chantrey sent for exhibition to Sheffield "a gigantic head of Satan," modelled in the room over the stable in Mayfair, and remarkable not only as an indication of the sculptor's powers, but as the harbinger of all his subsequent success. Flaxman, who had seen and admired this head at the Exhibition of the Royal Academy, recommended Chantrey for the execution of the busts of four admirals required for the Naval Asylum at Greenwich. This commission led immediately to others. Painting was given up. The professional visits to Sheffield were also abandoned; no further advertisements were inserted in the *Sheffield Iris.* Chantrey married, and received substantial coin with his wife. Mrs. D'Oyley's butler was comfortably warm in respect to the things of this life; and when he gave his daughter to his nephew, he added a sum sufficient to enable the latter to build himself a studio, and to take a position worthy of his prospects. From first to last, Chantrey received of his wife's money considerably more than £10,000; and of all artists that ever lived Chantrey knew best how to turn such gifts of fortune to good account.

Francis Chantrey, like Byron, rose one morning and found himself famous. In the year 1811 he had six busts in the Exhibition; and one of these was the head of Horne Tooke, which brought commissions, according to Chantrey's own account, amounting to 12,000*l.* It is very likely that with this enormous success, acquired through the instrumentality of the radical philologer, Chantrey's own radicalism began to decline. The sculptor was a furious democrat in his early struggles, sneered at the reigning family, and roared for sir Francis Burdett. As he invested his thousands in the Three per Cents, the respectability of existing institutions visibly increased. A more gentlemanly old Tory never lived than Chantrey at the age of 60.

In 1811, over fifteen competitors, Chantrey was selected to execute a statue of George III. for the city of London. From that year until 1817 he commanded in his profession. By universal consent he was allowed to be unequalled in his time as a modeller of busts, and nothing, indeed, can surpass the force, the truthfulness, and simplicity of these works. In 1817 he was elected an associate of the Royal Academy, and executed the exquisite monument of "The Sleeping Children," now in Litchfield cathedral. Mr. Holland is very much distressed because it has been contended that the sole merit of the *design* of this monument does not rest with Francis Chantrey; and he takes infinite pains to prove the contrary. Mr. Holland however, might have spared his indignation and his trouble. There is no doubt that Stothard's pencil gave Chantrey the original sketch for this lovely work of art; the sketch is in existence, and will ,we believe, be shortly published in Stothard's life. It is equally certain that the snow-drops placed in the hands of the younger sister were a poetic and affecting suggestion of Allan Cunningham. But what then? Look at Stothard's drawing, and compare it with the grace, feeling and irresistible beauty of the sculptured monument. It matters little who designed the sketch, while the marble remains to attest the power, perception, and matchless skill of the mind that gave it glowing life. No eye that has ever gazed upon those artless forms has cared to look beyond them or to inquire too curiously into their origin. They speak, silently sleeping, sufficient for their creator. What sculptor of Chantrey's day could have wrought such work had the whole Academy combined to furnish him with a subject?

From 1817 untill his sudden death in 1841, Chantrey's career was one of wonderfully profitable occupation and accumulating triumphs. Four monarchs sat to him, and the list of remarkable persons whose faces he perpetuated in marble is much too long to be enumerated here. The last bust on which Chantrey wrought with his old spirit, and the last which he touched with the chisel, was that of Queen Victoria, now at Windsor, justly regarded by Prince Albert as the best existing bust of Her Majesty. The last bust modelled by Chantrey was that of Lord Melbourne, but upon this the sculptor labored with his own hand very little indeed. His strength was failing him at the time, and the noble sitter was himself suffering from ill-health. Indeed, we have reason to know that while Lord Melbourne would invariably quit the studio in Eccleston-street with a sad conviction of the sculptor's waning faculties, Chantrey himself would at the same time commiseratingly deplore to his friends the visible decline of a statesman's once clear and active intellect. Neither suspected his own trouble, but both regarded the other as passing rapidly into a state of hopeless mental decrepitude.

Chantrey had a dread of modelling horses, and made more of one horse than Ducrow ever made out of his whole stud. The first "horse commission" was the George IV. for the marble arch; the second, Sir Thomas Munro, for Madras; the third, the Duke of Wellington, for the city. Of these unquestionably the finest is the Munro; but all the horses are from the same model. In the first two no difference whatever is made in the animals; in the Duke of Wellington's case the head of the horse is altered, but in other respects the steed is that mounted by Sir Thomas and the

King; and no other. For George IV. Chantrey received 9,000*l.*, and profited 3,000*l.*; for Monro, he was paid 7,000*l.*, and profited as much; for the Duke of Wellington his charge was 10,000*l.*, and by this he must have gained at least 5,000*l.* In his later years the sculptor became greedy of commissions and money, and anxious to secure everything. He was eager for the Wilkie statue, and eagerer still for the Glasgow Wellington statue; but the Glasgow people, having a laudable fear of the old horse, took refuge in Marochetti.

These and other points to which no reference is made in Mr. Holland's book are of interest in estimating the character and claims of Francis Chantrey. It is worthy to be noted—for, certainly, the discovery would never be made by an inspection of his works—that Chantrey's vision was very imperfect. Of the right eye he had no use whatever; yet he was an excellent shot. Of reading, he had none. His education had been of the very humblest; yet no one would have accused him of ignorance on any matter. He had surprising tact, a singular faculty of observation, admirable facility of acquiring knowledge in his daily walks, and perfect skill in concealing his poverty. He was brought up, the son of a working man, first in a poor cottage, then in a carver's shop; but he was at ease in the society of princes, and his manner was as far removed from obsequious flattery as from vulgar rudeness. He had a fine and frank independence which endeared him to his inferiors, and gave dignity to his professional character in the eyes of those above him. It will hardly be said that Chantrey during the whole of his professional and highly "respectable" life was disposed to disturb the many useful institutions of his country; but one very important institution he failed to support by any extensive personal co-operation. It is a fact, that except to be married, or to put up a monument, Chantrey never was inside a church in his life. Mr. Holland complains that Mr. Jones in his *Recollections* has made no mention of Chantrey's visits to a place of worship; but we confess that this is somewhat hard upon Jones, who has made mistakes enough, as we all know, without being forced into others against his will. If any one is to be blamed for Jones' silence in this respect it is certainly not the biographer; and Mr. Holland would seem to be of that opinion when he very properly vindicates the character of Bacon, the sculptor, and shows how a man may humbly fulfil the not very irksome public duties of a Christian without the smallest sacrifice of his pretensions to eminence in art.

In his will Chantrey provided that the whole of his large fortune, amounting, we believe, to £90,000, should, at the decease of his widow, become the property of the Royal Academy, for the purpose of purchasing "works of fine art of the highest merit in painting and sculpture," but only such as shall have been entirely executed "with-"in the shores of Great Britain;" the "wish and intention" of the artist being "that the works of art so purchased shall be collected for the purpose of forming and establishing a public national collection of British art in painting and sculpture." One or two minor bequests are of a curious nature. As a mark of his regard for the long services of his old lieutenant, Allan Cunningham, Chantrey stipulated in his will that the latter should be entitled to receive a legacy of £2,000 upon his superintending the completion of the Wellington statue. Allan attended to the important work up to the day of his death, but he died before the statue was completed, and—whatever may have been the intentions of the testator—his family lost the money. Another bequest was a gift of £50 per annum, "to be paid to a schoolmaster, under the direction of the vicar or resident clergyman, to instruct 10 poor boys of the parish of Norton without expense to their parents;" but the condition of the legacy was the perpetuation of the donor's tomb. Mr. Holland gives no explanation of this somewhat unusual proviso; but it is worth recording nevertheless. Many years before his decease Chantrey attended at St. Martin's-in-the-Fields, with a friend, the funeral of Scott, who was shot in the duel with Chriestie. The graveyard was strewed with human bones, and the gravedigger was adding indiscriminately and irreverently to the heaps. Chantrey inquired of the sexton what eventually became of those last remains of mortality. The sexton replied with a smile, that when they grew too plentiful they were carted off in loads to the Thames. The friend described the effect of this answer upon the frame of Chantrey as painful in the extreme. His cheeks grew sickly white, and perspiration poured down them. At the moment he looked himself a corpse newly risen from the grave before him. "I will take care," he said with a shudder, "that they do not cart my bones to the Thames. They shall be undisturbed under my native sod." And, accordingly, there are five pounds per annum for 10 poor boys of the village of Norton, so long as they will remember industriously to pluck the weeds and to remove the nettles that deface the gravestones of Francis Chantrey, The sculptor subsequently paid a formal visit to Norton, and carefully selected the spot for his last resting-place. While looking for it he encountered the gravedigger, who approached him mattock on shoulder ; "I am looking out a place for a grave," said Chantrey, "but I don't mean you to dig it." "I hope I shall," replied the gravedigger quietly and civilly: and it is likely enough that he did, for within a year the renowned sculptor was deposited near the humbler family dust that had mingled with the earth before him.

1851.

ANCIENT EGYPT.

Most persons know that within the last half century great researches have been made by individual or national enterprise into the poetry and antiquities of Egypt by the enterprise of travellers and the diligence of archæologists, among whom England claims the names of Young, Wilkinson, and Vyse. Few perhaps know what has been the result of these researches. They lie scattered over a number of works in different languages, beyond the reach even of the ordinary student, much more of the general reader. Mr. Kenrick has undertaken the task of supplying a synopsis, and this task he appears to us to have accomplished excellently well.*

He commences with the land of Egypt. In the East great rivers are the parents of civilized nations. A great river which by its deposit forms a long valley and a broad delta of rich alluvial soil in the midst of deserts was the parent, the nourisher, and the god of the oldest civilized nation of the earth. The Nile is Egypt; the Egyptians were those who lived below the cataracts and drank the Nile. Above the cataracts they pushed their arms into Ethiopia, and left there the monuments of

* Ancient Egypt under the Pharaohs. By John Kenrick, M. A. In two volumes. B. Fellowes.

their dominion. To the west they were at once defended and confined by a desert impassable to armies, but which the oasis rendered passable to the caravan. On the north was an almost harborless sea. On the east was another desert, through which roads led to the ports of the Red Sea and the mines of Sinai. On the north-east the Arabian desert formed an imperfect barrier. It was traversed by the hosts of Sesostris and Sheshonk, of Nebuchadnezzar and Cambyses, and across its sands Egypt communicated commercially and politically, with the other seats of ancient civilization, which, broken by the recurring desert, formed an irregular chain from Philistia to China.

Of the singular productions of Egypt, the hippopotamus, the crocodile, the ibis, the papyrus, we need not speak. There were few beasts of chase, and the Egyptian conquerors did not begin like those of central Asia by being mighty hunters. It was a land of corn and of the vine, of fruit trees and all herbs. The nations sought its granaries in famine; the Israelites in the wilderness thirsted for the cooling vegetables of its gardens. Fish abounded in the Nile, waterfowl in the marshes. Nature yielded freely, but perhaps for that very reason the mind of man was less exercised and less active. And the unvarying landscape, the unchanging sky, the small number and unpoetic or even grotesque forms of the plants and animals, may partly account for the lack of imagination evinced by the most formal and most stationary of nations, scarcely excepting the Chinese.

Who and whence were the Egyptians? This question Mr. Kenrick has to ask, and, like others, to leave unanswered. This is the secret which the grave of the

Pharaohs will not yield. Physiology supplies no clue. The mummy cases, the paintings and sculptures, depict a race short, slight, with low foreheads, high cheek bones, long eyes, hair now crisp now curled, and a complexion which the conventionality of the painter's art makes to differ in men and women, but which probably was brown with a tinge of red, dark compared with that of the Syrian, black compared with that of the Greek. Thick lips are frequently seen, but they are supposed to indicate intermarriage with Ethiopians. From the negro the Egyptians were far removed, nor can they be connected with any other known race. If we turn to language, a surer guide perhaps than physiology, we are again completely baffled. The Coptic has been identified through many etymologies with the old Egyptian; and of the Coptic, though it became a dead language in the 12th century, much literature remains. It is an uncultivated and formal tongue, with monosyllabic roots and rude inflections, totally different from the neighboring languages of Syria and Arabia, totally opposite to the copious and polished Sanscrit. The last fact at once severs Egypt from India, and destroys every presumption of affinity that may arise from the presence in both countries of caste, of animal worship, and of a religion derivable from primitive adoration of the powers of nature. The hypothesis of an Ethiopian origin sprang from the notion, natural but untrue, that population would follow the course of the descending river. And no tradition among the Egyptians themselves told of a parent stock or of another land.

Respecting the mighty works of Egypt little mystery

remains. The great pyramids had been rifled by the Caliphs, if not by earlier hands, and no inscriptions have been found. But no doubt exists that they were the sepulchres of the Kings of Memphis. The Queens and the "princes of Noph" reposed in smaller pyramids beside the Kings. These mountains of wasted masonry belong to the earliest ages of the Pharaonic monarchy, before the time of the Sesostrian conquests, and therefore they bespeak the toil and suffering, not of captives, but of native slaves. Before them couches the Sphinx, hewn from the rock, to spare, as a Greek inscription says, each spot of cultivable land. His riddle—for it is a *male*—is read. He represents, perhaps portrays, the reigning king, and the thick lips may indicate Ethiopian blood. The lion's body represents the monarch's might—the human head his wisdom. The rock from which the figure is cut broke the view of the pyramids, and to convert it into the Sphynx was a stroke of Egyptian genius. Pyramids were, in the Pharaonic times, peculiar to Memphis. The countless tombs of Thebes are excavated in the rocky face of the Libyan hills. Those of the Theban Pharaohs stand apart, and we approach through a narrow gorge called the "Gate of Kings." The paintings, sculptures, and inscriptions on these tombs, literally the eternal *houses* of the dead, are the Pompeii of the Egyptian antiquary. At Thebes are the magnificent and temple-like palaces of the greatest of the Pharaohs, the halls of their assemblies and their counsels, the records of their wars and conquests. At Thebes, too, is the Memnon, a mutilated statue of Amnoph, which never was vocal except by trick or in imagination, and the Obelisks, whose form is sufficiently explained, without obscenity or mystery, by the fancy for monolithic monuments and the possession of large blocks of granite. The remains of the Labyrinth do not enable us to pronounce whether its 27 halls were a burial-place for kings or crocodiles, or a place of assembly for the provinces of Egypt.

Very various and very extravagant notions have been formed of the population of ancient Egypt. That it was dense may well be inferred from the length of time through which it multiplied in a limited space, and from that evident parsimony of land which drove tombs and monuments to the rocks, and cities to the edge of the desert. Calculations based on the number of cities and on the number of men of military age, have plausibly placed the sum at about 5,000,000.

Agriculture was the chief business of the Egyptians, and the chief business of agriculture consisted in distributing and detaining, by canals and dams, the precious waters of the Nile. The sheep and cattle were numerous. A grandee of Eilytheia possessed 122 cows and oxen, 300 rams, 1,200 goats, 1,500 swine. Lower Egypt contained the great pasture lands, and was the abode of the herdsmen—a lawless race, and, *therefore*, an abomination to their more civilized countrymen. The ass was the beast of burden. The horse was bred for the war-chariot—that great attribute of ancient power. The breed was small but fine, and peculiar to the country. They were kept in stables along the Nile, and hence they do not appear in the landscapes. Horticulture was extensively and elaborately practised, both for use and pleasure; and the Pharaohs, like Solomon, "made them gardens and orchards, planted trees in them of all kinds of fruit, and made them pools of water to water therewith the wood that bringeth forth trees."

When forced to serve on shipboard by the enterprise of their own monarchs or by their Persian conquerors, the Egyptians appear not to have made bad sailors. They fought well at Salamis. But their natural tendency was to shun the sea, which they regarded as the element of the Destroyer Typhon. Their navigation was on the Nile, which formed the highway of their commerce, the path of their processions and their pilgrimages, and their passage to the tomb. The river being thus the universal road, and being moreover without bridges, must have swarmed with boats of all descriptions—the heavy bari of the merchant, the light papyrus or earthenware skiff of the common people, and the sumptuous barge of Royalty, whose golden pavilion, masts, and rudder, fringed and embroidered sails, and sculptured prow, remind us of the galley of Cleopatra. The caravans of surrounding nations visited Egypt with their precious and fragrant merchandise to exchange for her corn and manufactures. But the Egyptian trader appears seldom to have visited other countries either by land or sea.

The army was a warrior caste. Its might consisted in its chariots. No mounted cavalry appear in any of the monuments. With this exception they had every kind of force, and every weapon known to ancient warfare. They used the long bow and drew the arrow, like the English archers, to the ear. Their armour was imperfect, and more often of quilting than of mail. They had regular divisions, with standards, and regular camps. Their sieges were unscientific, and their means of assault, scaling ladders, sapping hatchets and long pikes brought up to the walls under a sort of shed. Of their battles no definite notion can be formed. All is lost in the King, whose gigantic figure, drawn by gigantic horses, crushes, massacres, or grasps by the hair scores of his pigmy enemies, whose hands after the victory are laid in heaps before him, counted by attendant scribes. Thus it is that Rameses the Great and the other Pharaohs are seen warring against the Assyrian, and Chaldean against the Jew, the Edomite, the Ethiopian, and the "nine bows" of Libya, and assailing the "fenced cities" of strange races that have long passed away.

In the lower parts of civilization and mechanical arts, the Egyptians had attained high perfection. Their machinery and tools appear to have been defective, but the defect was supplied by skill of hand, traditional and acquired, as it is among the Chinese. They were cunning workmen in metals, in jewellery, in engravings, in enamel, in glass, in porcelain, and in pottery. Their fine linen and embroidery were famous. For their chariots Solomon gave 600 shekels of silver; and they fashioned into a hundred articles of luxury the ivory of Africa, the mahogany of India, and the cedar of Lebanon. As no specimens remain of their domestic architecture, it is supposed rather than ascertained that their houses were of a simple story with a terraced roof. The rooms of great men were, at least, richly and elegantly painted, and furnished with tables, chairs, and couches, which have supplied models for the upholstery of modern times.

Architecture is the most material of the arts. It was the art in which the Egyptians most excelled. They seem to have understood, in some degree, the grandeur which results from proportion and agreement, as well as that which results from size. The profuse and elaborate sculpture with which their temples are covered does not mar their majesty. Their heaviness is relieved by the glowing sun and the deep sky. But the impression produced must always have been that of cost and power rather than of art. Some changes of style are noticed. The golden age was that of the Pharaohs of the 19th dynasty, when the power and greatness of the nation were at the highest. More florid and less majestic forms mark the era of the Ptolemies. But in this respect, as in others, the Egyptians seem to have maintained their stationary character; and the remains of Meroe, which are now known to be among the latest, have been taken for the earliest of all the monuments.

In sculpture the summit of manual skill was reached. But religion, the mistress and tyrant of Egyptian art, prescribed for the images of the gods her unalterable and often hideous forms, and the rules of an hereditary craft, which fixed certain proportions for each part of the statue, and gave the execution of the several parts to several workmen, laid another chain on the genius of the artist. Painting seems not to have advanced beyond the barbarous excellence of brilliant colors. Drawing and design were monstrous, and the laws of perspective, and even of vision, unknown or disregarded. Of music, we learn from Plato that it was restricted to certain established tunes of approved moral tendency, and the wayward Athenian thought all restraint wholesome as he saw that some license was pernicious.

If we pass to science, we shall find no reason for supposing that the advances of modern times were anticipated by the mysterious wisdom of the Egyptians. Something they must have known of astronomy to practise astrology, to divide the ecliptic, and to effect the exact orientation of the Pyramids. Some knowledge of chemistry is implied in the manufacture of porcelain; some knowledge of physiology, pathology, pharmaceutics, and surgery, in their division of the medical art; something of geometry in their measurement of land; and something of mechanics in their enormous buildings and monuments. But their great engines were multitudes of labourers, aided by such natural expedients as the lever, the roller, and the inclined plane, which can scarcely be called machines. In other sciences there is evidence of long and careful observation, but nothing to prove an acquaintance with the *laws* of nature. Progress in the medical art was precluded by the necessity of adhering to the precepts of the sacred books. Science was monopolized by the priests; and it is said that by them the king was regularly sworn to retain the old and unintercalated year. The want of decimal notation, and the consequent clumsiness of the system of numeration, would go far to preclude the improvement of arithmetic, or any science into which calculation entered.

Literature the Egyptians appear to have had none, except of the monumental or sacred kind, including under the latter head the sacred books of science. But the art of writing was practised by them, or at least by the learned part of them, more extensively than by any contemporary nation. Mr. Kenrick gives us a full history of the interpretation of hieroglyphics, the key to which was first given by the parallel inscriptions in hieroglyphics and Greek found on the famous Rosetta stone, and metes to Young and Champollion their due share in that discovery, of which each uncandidly claims the whole. The hieroglyphics are now known to be of three kinds, all of which are generally mingled in the same inscription—the pictorial, the symbolical, and the phonetic. The pictorial hieroglyphic is the simple picture of the thing signified. Symbolical hieroglyphics are, among others, a crescent for a month, the maternal vulture for maternity, the filial vulpanser for son, the bee for a people obedient to their king, the bull for strength, the ostrich feather with its equal filaments for truth, the lotus for Upper and the papyrus for Lower Egypt. To these we may add the bird, which denotes a cycle of time (in Coptic *phanech*), and about which such wild fables were received by the credulity of Herodotus and by that of the Fathers. But the greater part of the hieroglyphics are phonetic like our alphabet, and are being slowly and precariously deciphered into the words of a language which is identified with the ancient form of Coptic.

The religion of the Egyptians must be gathered chiefly from the sculptures and paintings. The religious inscriptions and funeral papyri remain undeciphered. The account of Herodotus is rendered suspicious by his solicitude to force the Pantheon of Egypt into a conformity with that of Greece. The accounts of the later Greeks are tainted by their philosophising and mysticising spirit. That the Egyptian theology embodied no profound physical or metaphysical system is evident from the fact that it was not formed at once, but by gradual addition and development, and that it was to the last partly local. It appears to have been, like the other religions of the Pagan world—of Greece and Italy, of Phœnicia and India—a worship of the powers of nature represented by great natural objects, such as the sun and moon, or by forms bestial or human, which were selected as symbolical of their attributes. On this groundwork imagination wrought, as among the Greeks, though to a less extent and in a different way. We cannot tell how far the more reflective minds may have advanced towards the conception of a single God, either independent of or permeating the material world; but contact with the philosophic Greeks in the age of the Ptolemies can hardly have failed to lead to some speculations of this kind, and the accounts derived from Greek sources of Egyptian mysticism, though false of early, were no doubt, in part at least, true of later times. Amuna or Ammon appears to have been nominally the chief of the gods. His attributes are to some extent identified with those of the sun; but they are not easily distinguished from the attributes of several subordinate deities. His ram's head is still a mystery. Thoth was the god of intellect and learning. His representatives were the ape and the ibis; the former, it is supposed, because it approaches nearest in intellect to man; the latter, because its black and white feather resemble, or may be imagined to resemble, writing. The popular divinity was Osiris, the god at once of the Nile and the realms below. Typhon, the scorching wind of the desert which dries up the waters of the Nile, was the antagonist and murderer of Osiris; and at a more advanced stage of religious speculation the two may have represented the conflicting powers of Good and Evil. Sacrifices were offered for the ordinary purposes—to conciliate the favor of the gods, to requite their benefits, and to avert their wrath. Typhonian, that is, red-haired men, were immolated when they fell into the hands of the natives in honour of Osiris, whose name is concealed in that of the fabled Busiris. That the practice of offering human sacrifices is compatible with a high degree of civilization we know from the examples of Greece, of Rome, and Mexico. There were great gatherings in honour of the gods, in the nature of pilgrimages or holy fairs, which were celebrated with festivity, with noisy music, with illuminations, and with license. There were mysteries, which were not, in Egypt at least, initiations into any thing different from the popular religion; but merely representations—celebrated amidst nocturnal gloom—of the sufferings of Osiris. If strangers in Egypt underwent painful initiation, it was an initiation into the knowledge of the priests, and not into their mysteries. The Egyptians believed in the existence of the soul after death; they believed that it would be judged in Amenthe by Osiris and his forty-two assessors, before whom it was brought by Analis; they had an Elysium, surrounded by waters, where the Osirian—that is, the happy dead—ploughed, sowed, reaped, and thrashed, as on earth—a singular want of fancy. Retributive pains, by fire and steel, are also supposed to have been detected among the paintings. At the same time they held and taught to the Greeks the doctrine of metempsychosis. It is difficult to reconcile with either of these notions their belief that the spirit dwelt in the body so long as the body could be rescued from decay, and the reasons which they gave for bestowing such prodigality of labour on their sepulchres—that the tomb was man's eternal home. The darkness of uninterpreted hieroglyphics still rests to a great extent on the religious creed and practices of the Egyptians. But three things we think we can discern from the information which Mr. Kenrick has collected:—1. That the Egyptian religion was to all essential respects like the other religions of Paganism, and traceable to the same sources; and consequently that whatever may be Egypt's "place in universal history," she is not likely to assume an extraordinarily important place in the history of theology; or to affect, in any material respect, our views as to the origin of religion. 2. That no connection is to be traced between the religion of the Egyptians and the religion of the Hebrews. A more decided polytheism than that of Egypt cannot be imagined. So far from recognising any thing like the supremacy of a single Divine Being in their theological system, we can scarcely even trace any thing answering to that primacy of Jupiter which preserves at least a vestige of monotheism in the religion of the Greeks. The rite of circumcision, which is supposed to have been borrowed by one nation from the other, was not practised by the Egyptians as a religious ceremony, nor upon infants, nor universally. And it is remarkable that the belief in the conscious existence of the soul and a retributive state after death—a doctrine hardly to be lost when once imparted—seems to have been so prominent in the one faith while it was so much the reverse of prominent in the other. 3. That there was no connection between the mythology of Egypt and that of Greece. Subtract what is common to all polytheistic systems, and what is common to all systems of natural religions, and absolutely no similarity remains. On the one side are forms of human beauty, majesty, and passion, in which the original groundwork of nature-worship is as much as possible concealed by the working of a plastic imagination; on the other side are forms bestial or grotesque, featureless and passionless, exhibiting nature-worship in one of its lowest stages. But in every respect, in language, in physiognomy, in mind, in political tendencies, in manners, as well as in religion, the contrariety between the Egyptian and the Athenian is complete. There is nothing on the other side except the vain pretensions of the priests of Thebes, the credulity of Herodotus, and the wildest legends of the mythical age; and we are surprised that so strict an ethnologist as Mr. Kenrick should be inclined to admit even the general fact of an Egyptian colonization.

The most degrading part of the religion of the Egyptians was their animal worship, which they carried to a higher pitch than any other people, not excepting the Hindoos. Almost the whole animal and some part of the vegetable kingdom enjoyed either a national or a local sanctity. God, it was said, grew in the gardens. The most cogent reasons of policy and the terrible name of Rome failed to save from death the Roman who had killed a cat. Fancy had first assigned to each god his favorites or symbols among beasts or plants. Then the beasts and plants themselves were reverenced, and at last worshipped. Stately avenues of colossal statues, magnificent porticoes, and columned courts, ushered the awe-stricken devotee into the sacred presence of an ibis or an ape. The highest object of this superstition, the bull Apis, was regarded as an actual incarnation of Osiris. No rational account of such a system can be given. The serpent cannot have been respected for its utility. The ibis cannot have been honoured as the destroyer of the sacred serpent. Nothing divine can have been perceived in the beetle or the ape. The connection between the god and the beast was originally the offspring of a grotesque imagination, and priestcraft and the superstitious tendency of the people did the rest.

The political constitution of Egypt was based on caste. The privileged castes were those of the warriors and the priests, who, with the Pharaohs, held in fee all the land of Egypt. The Government was an hereditary monarchy. When election was necessary, the two privileged castes chose from among their own members; the people enjoyed only the right of acclamation. If the choice fell on a warrior, he was at once received into the order and initiated into the wisdom of the priests. Legislation was the prerogative of the King; but he was bound to rule and judge according to the law. He was much in the hands of the priests, who imposed strict rules upon his life, and by a daily homily made the duties and virtues of sovereignty familiar, perhaps too familiar, to the Royal ear. The priests, in fact, were the lords of Egypt. Exclusively possessed of science, and even of letters, numerous, wealthy, united in a single polity, a confined territory and an isolated people, unchecked by any literary, philosophical, or foreign influence, they must have exercised a dominion unrivalled by any priesthood in the history of the world. The result was a land of temples of deified apes and consecrated onions, a literature of religious inscriptions and funeral scrolls, a Government apparently mild and humane, an enduring polity and long internal peace, an intense and stubborn nationality, a civilization wonderful but low, which in every department, from the act of government to the art of writing, appears to have remained as nearly as possible at a fixed point for about 2,000 years. The mummy, as it is the characteristic product, is the fit emblem of ancient Egypt. Yet material happiness appears to have been enjoyed. From sports, from caricatures, from the fanciful decorations of their houses, from their use of music as a daily recreation, we should judge that the Egyptians were not a gloomy people; and that their social and political system aimed, though imperfectly, at a high standard, may be inferred from the reverence, however exaggerated, which was entertained for it by the Greeks.

THE END.

HISTORICAL AND BIOGRAPHICAL WORKS.

ARNOLD, (Dr.) Early History of Rome. 2 vols. 8vo. - - -$5 00
ARNOLD, (Dr.) History of the Later Roman Commonwealth. 8vo. - - - - - - - 2 50
ARNOLD, (Dr.) Lectures on Modern History, edited by Professor Reed. 12mo. - - - - 1 25
ARNOLD, (Dr.) Life and Correspondence, by the Rev. A. P. Stanley. 2d ed. 8vo. - - 2 00
BURNETT'S History of the Northwestern Territory. 8vo. - - 2 50
CARLYLE'S Life of Schiller. A new edition. 12mo. - - 75
COIT'S History of Puritanism. 12mo. - - - - - - 1 00
EVELYN'S Life of Mrs. Godolphin. edited by Bishop of Oxford. 12mo. - - - - 50
FROST (Professor) History of the United States Navy. Plates. 12mo. 1 00
FROST, (Professor) History of the United States Army. Plates. 12mo. - - - - - - 1 00
FROST, (Professor) History of the Indians of North America. Plates. 12mo. - - - - - - 1 00
FROST, (Professor) History of the Colonies of America. 12mo. Illustrated - - - - - 1 00
FROST, (Professor) Life of Gen. Zachary Taylor. 12mo. Illustrated. - - - - - - 1 25
GUIZOT'S History of Civilization in Europe, edited by Professor Henry. 12mo - - - 1 00
GUIZOT'S Complete History of Civilization, translated by Hazlett. 4 vols. - - - - 3 50
GUIZOT'S History of the English Revolution, 1640. 12mo. - 1 25
GAYARRE'S Romance of the History of Louisiana. 12mo. - - 1 00
HULL, (General) Military and Civil Life. 8vo. - - - - 2 00
KING, (Colonel) History of the Argentine Republic. 12mo. - 75
KOHLRAUSCH'S Complete History of Germany. 8vo. - - 1 50
MAHON'S (Lord) History of England, edited by Professor Reed. 2 vols., 8vo. - - - - 5 00
MICHELET'S History of France from the Earliest Period. 2 vols. 5 50
MICHELET'S History of the Roman Republic. 12mo. - - 90
MICHELET'S History of the People 12mo. - - - - 63
MICHELET'S Life of Martin Luther. 12mo. - - - - - $0 7[illegible]
NAPOLEON, Life of, from the French of Laurent De L'Ardeche. 2 vols. 8vo. 500 cuts - - 4 [illegible]
O'CALLAGHAN'S Early History of New York. 2 vols. 8vo. - 5 [illegible]
ROWAN'S History of the French Revolution. 18mo. 2 vols. in 1 6[illegible]
SEWELL'S Child's History of Rome. 18mo. - - - - - 5[illegible]
SOUTHEY'S Life of Oliver Cromwell. 18mo. - - - - - 3[illegible]
SPRAGUE'S History of the Florida War. Map and Plates. 8vo. 2 5[illegible]
STEVEN'S History of Georgia. vol. 1 - - - - - - 2 5[illegible]
TAYLOR'S Natural History of Society in the Barbarous and Civilized State. 2 vols. 12mo. - 2 25
TAYLOR'S Manual of Ancient and Modern History. Edited by Professor Henry. 8vo. - 2 5[illegible]
TAYLOR'S Ancient History—Separate - - - - - - - 1 25
TAYLOR'S Modern History—Separate - - - - - - 1 5[illegible]
Used as a Text-book in several Colleges.
TWISS. History of the Oregon Territory. 12mo. - - - 7[illegible]

LAW BOOKS.

ANTHON'S Law Student; or, Guides to the Study of the Law in its Principles.
HOLCOMBE'S Digest of the Decisions of the Supreme Court of the U. S., from its Commencement to the present time. Large 8vo., law sheep - - 6 0[illegible]
HOLCOMBE'S Supreme Court Leading Cases on Commercial Law. 8vo. law sheep 4 0[illegible]
HOLCOMBE'S Law of Debtor and Creditor in the United States and Canada. 8vo. - - - 3 5[illegible]
SMITH'S Compendium of Mercantile Law. With Large American Additions, by Holcombe and Gholson. 8vo., law sheep - 4
These volumes are highly commended by Justices Taney and Woodbury, Daniel Webster, Rufus Choate, and Chancellor Kent, &c.
WARREN'S Popular and Practical Introduction to Law Studies. With American additions, by Thomas W. Clerke. 8vo., law sheep - - - - - - 3 [illegible]

NEW ILLUSTRATED JUVENILES.

AUNT FANNY'S STORY BOOK. Illustrated. 16mo. - $ 50
THE CHILD'S PRESENT. Illustrated. 16mo. - - -
HOWITT'S PICTURE AND VERSE BOOK. Illustrated with 100 plates. 75 cts.; gilt - - 1 00
HOME FOR THE HOLIDAYS. Illustrated. 4to., 25 cts.; cloth 50
STORY OF JOAN OF ARC. By R. M. Evans. With 23 illustrations. 16mo. - - - 75
ROBINSON CRUSOE. Pictorial Edition. 300 plates. 8vo. - 1 50
THE CARAVAN; A COLLECTION OF TALES AND STORIES FROM THE GERMAN. Translated by G. P. Quackenboss. Illustrated by Orr. 16mo.
INNOCENCE OF CHILDHOOD. By Mrs. Colman. Illustrated 50
HOME RECREATIONS, comprising Travels and Adventures, &c. Colored Illustrations. 16mo. 87
FIRESIDE FAIRIES. A New Story Book. My Miss Susan Pindar. Finely Illustrated. 16mo.
STORY OF LITTLE JOHN. Trans. from the French. Illus. 62
LIVES AND ANECDOTES OF ILLUSTRIOUS MEN. 16mo. 75
UNCLE JOHN'S PANORAMIC PICTURE BOOKS. Six kinds, 25 cts. each; half-cloth 50
HOLIDAY HOUSE. Tales, by Catherine Sinclair. Illustrated 75
PUSS IN BOOTS. Finely illus. by O. Speckter. 50c.; ex. glt. - 75
TALES AND STORIES for Boys and Girls. By Mary Howitt 75
AMERICAN HISTORICAL TALES for Youth. 16mo. - 75

LIBRARY FOR MY YOUNG COUNTRYMEN.

ADVENTURES of Captain John Smith. By the Author of Uncle Philip - - - - - 38
ADVENTURES of Daniel Boon. By do. - - - - - - 38
DAWNINGS of Genius. By Anne Pratt - - - - - - 38
LIFE and Adventures of Henry Hudson. By the Author of Uncle Philip - - - - - - 38
LIFE and Adventures of Hernan Cortez. By do. - - - - 38
PHILIP RANDOLPH. A Tale of Virginia. By Mary Gertrude. 38
ROWAN'S History of the French Revolution. 2 vols. . . . 75
SOUTHEY'S Life of Cromwell 38

TALES FOR THE PEOPLE AND THEIR CHILDREN.

ALICE FRANKLIN. By Mary Howitt - - - - $ 38
LOVE AND MONEY. By do. - 38
HOPE ON, HOPE EVER! Do. 38
LITTLE COIN, MUCH CARE. By do. - - - - - - 38
MY OWN STORY. By do. - 38
MY UNCLE, THE CLOCKMAKER. By do. - - - - 38
NO SENSE LIKE COMMON SENSE. By do. - - - 38
SOWING AND REAPING. Do. 38
STRIVE AND THRIVE. By do. 38
THE TWO APPRENTICES. By do. - - - - - 38
WHICH IS THE WISER? Do. 38
WHO SHALL BE GREATEST? By do. - - - - - - 38
WORK AND WAGES. By do. 38
CROFTON BOYS, The. By Harriet Martineau - - - - 38
DANGERS OF DINING OUT By Mrs. Ellis - - - - 38
FIRST IMPRESSIONS. By do. 38
MINISTER'S FAMILY. By do. 38
SOMMERVILLE HALL. By do. 38
DOMESTIC TALES. By Hannah More. 2 vols. - - - 75
EARLY FRIENDSHIP. By Mrs. Copley . - - - - - 38
FARMER'S DAUGHTER, The By Mrs. Cameron - - -
LOOKING-GLASS FOR THE MIND. Many plates - - 45
MASTERMAN READY. By Capt. Marryat. 3 vols. - 1 2
PEASANT AND THE PRINCE. By H. Martineau - - - 38
POPLAR GROVE. By Mrs. Copley - - - - - - 38
SETTLERS IN CANADA. By Capt. Marryatt. 2 vols. - 75
TIRED OF HOUSEKEEPING. By T. S. Arthur - - - 38
TWIN SISTERS, The. By Mrs. Sandham - - - - - 38
YOUNG STUDENT. By Madame Guizot. 3 vols. - - 1 1

SECOND SERIES.

CHANCES AND CHANGES By Charles Burdett - - 38
NEVER TOO LATE. By do 38
GOLDMAKER'S VILLAGE. By H. Zschokke - - - - 38
OCEAN WORK, ANCIENT AND MODERN. By J. H. Wright - - - - 38
THE MISSION; or, Scenes in Africa. By Capt. Marryatt. 2 vols. 75
STORY OF A GENIUS - - 38

ILLUSTRATED STANDARD POETS.

HALLECK'S COMPLETE POETICAL WORKS. Beautifully illustrated with fine Steel Engravings and a Portrait. 1 vol. 8vo., finest paper, cloth extra gilt edges, $3; morocco extra, $5; morocco antique, $6.

YRON'S COMPLETE POETICAL WORKS. Illustrated with elegant Steel Engravings and Portrait. 1 vol. 8vo., fine paper, cloth, $4; cloth, gilt edges, $4 50 morocco extra, $6 50.

Cheaper edition, with Portrait and Vignette, $2 50.

OORE'S COMPLETE POETICAL WORKS. Illustrated with [illegible] Steel Engravings and Portrait. 1 vol. 8vo., fine paper, cloth, $4; cloth, gilt edges, $5; morocco extra, $7.

Cheaper edition, with Portrait and Vignette, $2 50.

SOUTHEY'S COMPLETE POETICAL WORKS. Illustrated with several beautiful Steel Engravings. 1 vol. 8vo., fine paper, cloth, $3 50; cloth, gilt edges, $4 50; morocco extra, $6 50.

SACRED POETS (The) of England and America, for Three Centuries. Edited by Rufus W. Griswold. Illustrated with Steel Engravings. 1 vol. 8vo., cloth $2 50; gilt edges, $3; morocco, $3 50; morocco extra, $4.

POEMS BY AMELIA. New and enlarged edition, beautifully illustrated with original designs, by Weir, and Portrait of the Author. 1 vol. 8vo., cloth extra, gilt edges, $3; morocco extra, $4; morocco antique, $5: 12mo., without Plates, $1 25; gilt edges, $1 50.

No expense has been spared in the mechanical execution of the above popular standard authors.

CABINET EDITIONS.

CAMPBELL'S COMPLETE POETICAL WORKS. Illustrated with Steel Engravings and a Portrait. 16mo., cloth, $1 50; gilt edges, $2 25; morocco extra, $3.

BUTLER'S HUDIBRAS, with Notes by Nash. Illustrated with Portraits. 16mo cloth, $1 50; gilt edges, $2 25; morocco extra, $3.

DANTE'S POEMS. Translated by Cary. Illustrated with a fine Portrait and 12 Engravings. 16mo., cloth, $1 50; gilt edges, $2 25; morocco extra, $3.

TASSO'S JERUSALEM DEL VERED. Transtated by Wiffen. Illustrated with a Portrait and Steel Engravings. 1 vol. 16mo. Uniform with "Dante." Cloth $1 50; gilt edges, $2 25; morocco, $3.

BYRON'S CHILDE HAROLD'S PILGRIMAGE. 16mo. Illustrated, cloth $1 25; gilt edges, $2; morocco extra, $2 50.

URNS' COMPLETE POETICAL WORKS, with Life, Glossary, &c. 16mo cloth, illustrated, $1 25; gilt edges, $2; morocco extra, $2 50.

OWPER'S COMPLETE POETICAL WORKS, with Life, &c. Morocco extra, 2 vols. in 1, $3; cloth, $1 50; gilt edges, $2 50.

MILTON'S COMPLETE POETICAL WORKS, with Life, &c. 16mo., cloth, illustrated, $1 25; gilt edges, $2; morocco extra, $2 50.

SCOTT'S POETICAL WORKS, with Life, &c. Cloth, 16mo., illustrated, $1 25; gilt edges, $2; morocco extra, $2 50.

HEMANS' COMPLETE POETICAL WORKS. Edited by her Sister. 2 vols., 16mo., with 10 Steel Plates, cloth, $2 50; gilt edges, $4; Turkey morocco, $5.

POPE'S POETICAL WORKS. Illustrated with 24 Steel Engravings 16mo cloth, $1 50; gilt edges, $2 25; morocco, $3.

NOVELS AND TALES.

CORBOULD'S History and Adventures of Margaret Catchpole. 8vo. 2 Plates 25 cts.
DON QUIXOTTE de la Mancha. Translated from the Spanish. Illustrated wit 18 Steel Engravings. 16mo, cloth. $1 50.
DUMAS' Marguerite de Valois. A Novel. 8vo. 25 cts.
ELLEN MIDDLETON. A Tale. By Lady Fullerton. 12mo. 75 cts.
FRIENDS AND FORTUNE. A Moral Tale. By Miss Dewey. 12mo. 75 ct
GOLDSMITH'S Vicar of Wakefield. Illustrated. 12mo. 75 cts.
RACE LESLIE. A Tale. 12mo. 75 cts.
RANTLEY MANOR. A Tale. By Lady Fullerton. 12mo. Paper, 50 cts cloth, 75 cts.
LADY ALICE; or, The New Una. 8vo. Paper, 38 cts.
LAMARTINE'S Les Confidences et Raphael. 8vo. $1.
LAMARTINE'S CONFIDENTIAL DISCLOSURES. 12mo. 50 cts.
LOVER'S (Samuel) Handy Andy. 8vo. Paper, 50 cts.
——— £ s. d. Treasure Trove. 8vo. Paper, 25 cts.
MACKINTOSH (M. J.) Two Lives, or, To Seem and To Be. 12mo Paper 50 cts.; cloth, 75 cts.
——— Aunt Kitty's Tales. 12mo. Paper, 50 cts.; cloth, 75 cts
——— Charms and Counter Charms. Paper, 75 cts. cloth, $1
MAXWELL'S Way-side and Border Sketches. 8vo. 25 cts.
——— Fortunes of Hector O'Halloran. 8vo. 50 cts.
MANZONI. The Betrothed Lovers. 2 vols. 12mo. $1 50
MAIDEN AUNT (The). By S. M. 12mo. 75 cts.
SEWELL (Miss). Amy Herbert. A Tale. 12mo. Paper, 50 cts.; cloth, 75 cts.
——— Gertrude. A Tale. 12mo. Paper, 50 cts.; cloth, 75 cts.
——— Laneton Parsonage. 3 vols. 12mo. Paper, $1 50; cloth $2 25.
——— Margaret Percival. 2 vols Paper, $1; cloth, $1 50.
——— Walter Lorimer, and other Tales. 12mo. 75 cts.
TAYLOR, (General) Anecdote Book, Letters, &c. 8vo. 25 cts.
ZSCHOKKE. Incidents of Social Life. 12mo. $1.

MINIATURE CLASSICAL LIBRARY.

Published in elegant form, with Frontispiece.

POETICAL LACON; or Aphorisms from the Poets. 38 cts
BOND'S Golden Maxims. 31 cts.
CLARKE'S Scripture Promises. Complete. 38 cts.
ELIZABETH; or the Exiles of Siberia. 31 cts.
GOLDSMITH'S Vicar of Wakefield. 38 cts.
——— Essays 38 cts.
GEMS from American Poets. 38 cts.
HANNAH MORE'S Private Devotions. 31 cts.
——— Practical Piety. 2 vols. 75 cts.
HEMANS' Domestic Affections. 31 cts
HOFFMAN'S Lays of the Hudson, &c. 38 cts.
JOHNSON'S History of Rasselas. 38 cts.
MANUAL of Matrimony. 31 cts.
MOORE'S Lallah Rookh. 38 cts.
——— Melodies. Complete. 38 cts.
PAUL and Virginia. 31 cts.
POLLOK'S Course of Time. 38 cts.
PURE Gold from the Rivers of Wisdom. 38 cts.
THOMSON'S Seasons. 38 cts.
TOKEN of the Heart.—Do. of Affection.—Do. of Remembrance.—Do. of Friendship.—Do. of Love; each, 31 cts.
USEFUL Letter Writer. 38 cts.
WILSON'S Sacra Privata. 31 cts.
Young's Night Thoughts 38 cts.

www.ingramcontent.com/pod-product-compliance
Lightning Source LLC
LaVergne TN
LVHW020237110826
845151LV00003B/952

* 9 7 8 1 4 2 5 5 2 9 7 9 6 *